How to File
For Divorce
in California

HOW TO FILE FOR DIVORCE IN CALIFORNIA

with forms

Second Edition

David Jon Lee
Edward A. Haman
Attorneys at Law

SPHINX® PUBLISHING
A Division of Sourcebooks, Inc.®
Naperville, IL • Clearwater, FL

Second Edition, 2000

Published by: **Sphinx® Publishing, A Division of Sourcebooks, Inc.®**

Naperville Office
P.O. Box 4410
Naperville, Illinois 60567-4410
630-961-3900
Fax: 630-961-2168

Clearwater Office
P.O. Box 25
Clearwater, Florida 33757
727-587-0999
Fax: 727-586-5088

Interior and Cover Design: Sourcebooks, Inc.®
Interior and Cover Production: Amy S. Hall, Sourcebooks, Inc.®

This publication is designed to provide accurate and authoritative information in regard to the subject matter covered. It is sold with the understanding that the publisher is not engaged in rendering legal, accounting, or other professional service. If legal advice or other expert assistance is required, the services of a competent professional person should be sought.

From a Declaration of Principles Jointly Adopted by a Committee of the American Bar Association and a Committee of Publishers and Associations

Library of Congress Cataloging-in-Publication Data
Lee, David Jon.
    How to file for divorce in California : with forms / David Jon Lee, Edward A. Haman.--
2nd ed.
        p.   cm.
    Includes index.
    ISBN 1-57248-126-9 (pbk.)
    1. Divorce--Law and legislation--California--Popular works. 2. Divorce--Law and
legislation--California--Forms. I. Haman, Edward A. II. Title.

KFC126.Z9 L44 2000
346.79401'66--dc21
                                                                    99-086140

CONTENTS

USING SELF-HELP LAW BOOKS. 1

INTRODUCTION. 5

CHAPTER 1: MARRIAGE "INS AND OUTS". 7
    Marriage
    Divorce
    Nullity (Annulment)
    Legal Separation
    Do You Really Want a Divorce?

CHAPTER 2: THE LEGAL SYSTEM. 17
    Theory vs. Reality
    Divorce Law and Procedure
    Legal Research

CHAPTER 3: LAWYERS 27
    Do You Want a Lawyer?
    Selecting a Lawyer
    Working with a Lawyer

CHAPTER 4: EVALUATING YOUR SITUATION 35
    Your Spouse
    Gathering Information
    Property and Debts
    Child Custody and Visitation
    Child Support
    Spousal Support (Alimony)
    Which Procedure to Use

CHAPTER 5: GENERAL PROCEDURES 63

Family Law Facilitator Act

An Introduction to Legal Forms

Filing with the Court Clerk

Notifying Your Spouse

Courtroom Manners

Negotiating

CHAPTER 6: SUMMARY DISSOLUTION PROCEDURE 81

Can You Use the Summary Dissolution Procedure?

Joint Petition for Summary Dissolution of Marriage

Request for Judgment, Judgment of Dissolution of Marriage,
     and Notice of Entry of Judgment

Notice of Revocation of Petition for Summary Dissolution

CHAPTER 7: UNCONTESTED DIVORCE PROCEDURE 89

Summons—Family Law

Petition

Declaration under Uniform Child Custody Jurisdiction Act (UCCJA)

Confidential Counseling Statement

Starting Your Divorce Proceeding

Preliminary Declaration of Disclosure

Schedule of Assets and Debts

Income and Expense Declaration

Serving Your Spouse

When Your Spouse Won't Cooperate

Final Declaration of Disclosure

Stipulation for Child Support

Marital Settlement Agreement (MSA)

Request to Enter Default

Declaration for Default or Uncontested Dissolution

Appearance, Stipulation, and Waivers

Military Service Considerations

Judgment

Wage and Earnings Assignment Order

Notice of Entry of Judgment

CHAPTER 8: CONTESTED DIVORCE PROCEDURE 135

Procedure Differences from Uncontested Divorce

Collecting Information

Property and Debts
Child Custody and Visitation
Child Support
Spousal Support (Alimony)

CHAPTER 9: THE COURT HEARING 145
Preparation
The Hearing
Public Assistance

CHAPTER 10: WHEN YOU CAN'T FIND YOUR SPOUSE 151
The Diligent Search
Preparing and Filing Court Papers
Publishing

CHAPTER 11: SPECIAL CIRCUMSTANCES 157
When You Can't Afford Court Costs
Protecting Yourself, Your Children, and Your Property
Temporary Support and Custody
Taxes
If Your Spouse Also Files for Divorce

APPENDIX A: CALIFORNIA STATUTES 169

APPENDIX B: FORMS 177

INDEX 289

Using Self-Help Law Books

Before using a self-help law book, you should realize the advantages and disadvantages of doing your own legal work and understand the challenges and diligence that this requires.

THE GROWING TREND

Rest assured that you won't be the first or only person handling your own legal matter. For example, in some states, more than seventy-five percent of the people in divorces and other cases represent themselves. Because of the high cost of legal services, this is a major trend and many courts are struggling to make it easier for people to represent themselves. However, some courts are not happy with people who do not use attorneys and refuse to help them in any way. For some, the attitude is, "Go to the law library and figure it out for yourself."

We write and publish self-help law books to give people an alternative to the often complicated and confusing legal books found in most law libraries. We have made the explanations of the law as simple and easy to understand as possible. Of course, unlike an attorney advising an individual client, we cannot cover every conceivable possibility.

COST/VALUE ANALYSIS

Whenever you shop for a product or service, you are faced with various levels of quality and price. In deciding what product or service to buy, you make a cost/value analysis on the basis of your willingness to pay and the quality you desire.

When buying a car, you decide whether you want transportation, comfort, status, or sex appeal. Accordingly, you decide among such choices as a Neon, a Lincoln, a Rolls Royce, or a Porsche. Before making a decision, you usually weigh the merits of each option against the cost.

When you get a headache, you can take a pain reliever (such as aspirin) or visit a medical specialist for a neurological examination. Given this choice, most people, of course, take a pain reliever, since it costs only pennies; whereas a medical examination costs hundreds of dollars and takes a lot of time. This is usually a logical choice because it is rare to need anything more than a pain reliever for a headache. But in some cases, a headache may indicate a brain tumor and failing to see a specialist right away can result in complications. Should everyone with a headache go to a specialist? Of course not, but people treating their own illnesses must realize that they are betting on the basis of their cost/value analysis of the situation. They are taking the most logical option.

The same cost/value analysis must be made when deciding to do one's own legal work. Many legal situations are very straight forward, requiring a simple form and no complicated analysis. Anyone with a little intelligence and a book of instructions can handle the matter without outside help.

But there is always the chance that complications are involved that only an attorney would notice. To simplify the law into a book like this, several legal cases often must be condensed into a single sentence or paragraph. Otherwise, the book would be several hundred pages long and too complicated for most people. However, this simplification necessarily leaves out many details and nuances that would apply to special or unusual situations. Also, there are many ways to interpret most legal questions. Your case may come before a judge who disagrees with the analysis of our authors.

Therefore, in deciding to use a self-help law book and to do your own legal work, you must realize that you are making a cost/value analysis. You have decided that the money you will save in doing it yourself outweighs the chance that your case will not turn out to your satisfaction. Most people handling their own simple legal matters never have a problem, but occasionally people find that it ended up costing them more to have an attorney straighten out the situation than it would have if they had hired an attorney in the beginning. Keep this in mind while handling your case, and be sure to consult an attorney if you feel you might need further guidance.

LOCAL RULES   The next thing to remember is that a book which covers the law for the entire nation, or even for an entire state, cannot possibly include every procedural difference of every jurisdiction. Whenever possible, we provide the exact form needed; however, in some areas, each county, or even each judge, may require unique forms and procedures. In our state books, our forms usually cover the majority of counties in the state, or provide examples of the type of form which will be required. In our national books, our forms are sometimes even more general in nature but are designed to give a good idea of the type of form that will be needed in most locations. Nonetheless, keep in mind that your state, county, or judge may have a requirement, or use a form, that is not included in this book.

CHANGES IN THE LAW   You should not necessarily expect to be able to get all of the information and resources you need solely from within the pages of this book. This book will serve as your guide, giving you specific information whenever possible and helping you to find out what else you will need to know. This is just like if you decided to build your own backyard deck. You might purchase a book on how to build decks. However, such a book would not include the building codes and permit requirements of every city, town, county, and township in the nation; nor would it include the lumber, nails, saws, hammers, and other materials and tools you would need to actually build the deck. You would use the book as your guide, and then do some work and research involving such matters as whether you need a permit of some kind, what type and grade of wood are available in your area, whether to use hand tools or power tools, and how to use those tools.

Before using the forms in a book like this, you should check with your court clerk to see if there are any local rules of which you should be aware, or local forms you will need to use. Often, such forms will require the same information as the forms in the book but are merely laid out differently or use slightly different language. They will sometimes require additional information.

Besides being subject to local rules and practices, the law is subject to change at any time. The courts and the legislatures of all fifty states are constantly revising the laws. It is possible that while you are reading this book, some aspect of the law is being changed.

In most cases, the change will be of minimal significance. A form will be redesigned, additional information will be required, or a waiting period will be extended. As a result, you might need to revise a form, file an extra form, or wait out a longer time period; these types of changes will not usually affect the outcome of your case. On the other hand, sometimes a major part of the law is changed, the entire law in a particular area is rewritten, or a case that was the basis of a central legal point is overruled. In such instances, your entire ability to pursue your case may be impaired.

To help you with local requirements and changes in the law, be sure to read the section in chapter 2 on "Legal Research."

Again, you should weigh the value of your case against the cost of an attorney and make a decision as to what you believe is in your best interest.

INTRODUCTION

Going through a divorce is probably one of the most common, and most traumatic, encounters with the legal system. At a time when you are least likely to have extra funds, paying a divorce lawyer can be one of the most expensive bills to pay. In a contested divorce case, it is not uncommon for the parties to run up legal bills of over $10,000. Horror stories abound of lawyers charging substantial fees with little progress to show for it. This book will enable those of you without high-risk issues to obtain a divorce without hiring a lawyer. Even if you do hire a lawyer, this book will help you to work with him or her more effectively, which can also reduce the legal fee.

This is not a law school course, but a practical guide to get you through the system as easily as possible. Legal jargon has been nearly eliminated. For ease of understanding, this book uses the term *spouse* to refer to your husband or wife (whichever applies), and the terms *child* and *children* are used interchangeably.

Please keep in mind that different judges, and courts in different counties, may have their own particular (if not peculiar) procedures, forms, and ways of doing things. The court clerk's office can often tell you if it has any special forms or requirements, but court clerks will not give you legal advice.

The first two chapters of this book will give you an overview of the law and the legal system. Chapter 3 will help you decide if you want an attorney. Chapter 4 will help you evaluate your situation and give you an idea of what to expect if you decide to go through with a divorce. The remaining chapters will show you what forms you need, how to fill out the forms, and what procedures to follow. You will also find two appendices in the back of the book. Appendix A contains selected portions of the California law and court rules dealing with property division, alimony, and child support. Although these provisions are discussed in the book, it is sometimes helpful to read the law exactly as it is written.

Appendix B contains the forms you will complete. You will not need to use all of the forms. This book will tell you which forms you need, depending upon your situation. Most of the forms in appendix B are California Judicial Council forms, which are found in the Family Code and which must be used according to the local rules of almost all courts. The California Judicial Council forms are updated periodically, and courts will not accept the old version of a form. Therefore, you should check with the court clerk's office to be sure you use the most current version of a form.

Be sure to read "An Introduction to Legal Forms" in chapter 5 before you use any of the forms in this book.

Marriage "Ins and Outs"

Several years (or maybe only months) ago you made a decision to get married. This chapter will discuss, in a general way, what you got yourself into, how to get out, and whether you really want to do so.

Marriage

Marriage is frequently referred to as a contract. It is a legal contract, and for many it is also a religious contract. This book will deal only with the legal aspects. The wedding ceremony involves the bride and groom reciting certain vows, which are actually mutual promises about how they will treat each other. There are legal papers signed, such as a marriage license and a marriage certificate. These formalities create certain rights and obligations for the husband and wife. Although the focus at the ceremony is one the emotional aspects of the relationship, the legal reality is that financial and property rights are being created. It is these financial and property rights and obligations that cannot be altered without a legal proceeding.

Marriage gives each party certain rights in property, and it creates certain obligations of support for the spouse and any children they have together (or adopt). Unfortunately, most people don't fully realize that these rights and obligations are being created until it comes time for a divorce. California does not recognize either common law marriage or same sex marriage.

DIVORCE

A divorce is the most common method of terminating or breaking the marriage contract. In California, a divorce is officially called a *dissolution of marriage*. The laws, court rules, and legal papers all use this official term. In this book, the terms *divorce* and *dissolution of marriage* are used interchangeably and have the same meaning. In a divorce, the court declares the marriage contract broken, divides the parties' property and debts, decides if either party should receive support, and determines the custody, support, and visitation with respect to any children the parties may have. Traditionally, a divorce could only be granted under certain specific circumstances, such as for *adultery* or *mental cruelty*. Today, a divorce is granted simply because one or both of the parties want one. The wording used is that "irreconcilable differences" have arisen in the marriage, and that such irreconcilable differences are "irremediable."

Another ground for divorce is the *incurable insanity* of a spouse, but it is difficult to figure out why anyone would use this ground even if the spouse is incurably insane, as it's much easier to use the ground that the marriage differences are irreconcilable and irremediable.

NULLITY (ANNULMENT)

In California, the legal procedure for an annulment is now called a *nullity* proceeding. The basic difference between divorce and nullity is that while a divorce recognizes the marriage as once valid but now broken, a nullity recognizes the marriage not as "broken" but as invalid. You can consider a divorce like an expired passport and a nullity like an invalid passport. Simply put, when you get a divorce you say, "My marriage didn't work." When you get a nullity you say, "My marriage wasn't valid."

A divorce is easier to get than a nullity. A divorce is yours for the asking; that's why it's called *no fault* divorce. You just put an "x" in the appropriate box on the Petition (form 3) and you'll get your divorce. For a nullity, you must prove one or more of the following specified grounds with evidence:

1. One of the parties was too young to get married. In California, both parties must be at least eighteen years old to get married (there is an exception where the under-age person has parental consent, is capable of consenting to and consummating marriage, and has a court order granting permission to marry).

2. One of the parties is guilty of fraud. For example, where one party just got married in order to have the right to inherit from the other, with no intention of ever living together as husband and wife.

3. One party was under duress when he or she got married. *Duress* means that the person was threatened, or was under some kind of pressure, so that he or she did not get married voluntarily.

4. One party didn't have the mental capacity to get married. This means the person was suffering from mental illness or disability (such as being severely retarded), to such an extent that the person didn't understand he or she was getting married; or possibly didn't even understand the concept of marriage.

5. One party was already married to another person. This might occur if one party married, mistakenly believing the divorce from his or her previous spouse was final.

6. The marriage is incestuous. California law prohibits marriage between certain family members, such as brother and sister, aunt and nephew, or uncle and niece.

If your spouse desires, there are several arguments he or she could make to further complicate the case. This area of the law is not as well defined as divorce. The nullity procedure can be complicated, may require expert testimony, and should not be attempted without consulting a lawyer.

LEGAL SEPARATION

California permits a *legal separation*. This procedure is not available in all states, and is used to divide the property and provide for child custody and support in cases where the husband and wife live separately, but remain married. This is usually used to break the financial rights and obligations of a couple whose religion does not permit divorce. It may also be of advantage where a divorce would cause one of the parties to lose social security, veteran's, or other benefits; or cause a spouse with a serious illness or disability to lose medical insurance.

Some states refer to this procedure as *divorce from bed and board*. It is an old procedure that is gradually fading. The term *legal separation* is used in two contexts in California: (1) When a spouse physically separates (e.g., leaves the house) with the intent to obtain a divorce, the parties are said to be legally separated; and (2) When a spouse obtains a formal legal separation in court. In both instances, the sweep of the community property laws stop and the assets and debts obtained by a spouse after such legal separation are that spouse's separate assets and debts. A spouse does not have to leave the house to be legally separated; the decision to divorce without the intent to reconcile is what is important. When a spouse obtains a court legal separation, the grounds are the same as for a dissolution of marriage. So unless you are seeking a legal separation for one of the specific reasons stated above, there is usually little reason to get a legal separation instead of a dissolution of marriage.

See an attorney if you believe you might need a legal separation instead of a divorce.

DO YOU REALLY WANT A DIVORCE?

Before beginning a divorce, you should think about its effects on your life. This section discusses these effects and offers alternatives if you want to try to save your relationship. Even if you feel absolutely sure that you want a divorce, you should still read this section so that you are prepared for what may follow.

DIVORCE—
THE LEGAL
PROCEEDINGS

Divorce is the breaking of your matrimonial bonds—the termination of your marriage contract and partnership. The stress created is that of going through a court system and having to deal with your spouse as you go through it. Divorce can be confrontational and emotionally explosive. There are generally five matters to be resolved through divorce:

1. The divorce of two people: Basically, this gives each the legal right to marry someone else

2. The division of their property (and responsibility for debts)

3. The care and custody of their children

4. Spousal support

5. Child support

Although it is possible for divorce to be granted after six months from the time one spouse serves the other spouse with the initial summons and petition, the legalities may continue for years, caused by emotional battles over the children or financial battles over accounts and family businesses.

SOCIAL AND
EMOTIONAL
DIVORCE

Divorce has a tremendous impact on your social and emotional lives that will continue long after the divorce. These impacts include:

Lack of companionship. Even if your marriage is one of the most miserable, you may still notice at least a little emptiness or loneliness after the divorce. It may not be that you miss your spouse in particular, but just miss another person being around.

Grief. Divorce may be viewed as the death of a marriage, or maybe the funeral ceremony for the death of a marriage. And like the death of anyone you've been close to, you will feel a sense of loss. This can take you through all of the normal feelings associated with grief. You'll get angry and frustrated over the years you've "wasted." You'll feel guilty because you "failed to make the marriage work." You'll find yourself saying, "I can't believe this is happening to me." And, for months or even years, you'll spend a lot of time thinking about your marriage. It can be extremely difficult to put it all behind you and get on with your life.

The single's scene: dating. You may find that you are dropped from friends' guest lists as your current friends, who are probably all married, no longer find that you as a single person fit in with their circle. If you want to avoid solitary evenings before the TV, you'll find yourself trying to get back into the "single's scene." This can be very difficult, especially if you have custody of the kids.

FINANCIAL
DIVORCE

Many married couples are just able to make ends meet. After getting divorced, there are suddenly two rent payments, two electric bills, etc. For the spouse without custody, there is also child support to be paid. For at least one spouse, and usually for both, money becomes even tighter than it was before the divorce. Also, once you've divided your property, each of you may need to replace the items the other person got to keep.

CHILDREN AND
DIVORCE

The effect upon your children, and your relationship with them, can often be the most painful and long-lasting aspect of divorce. Your relationship with your children may become strained as they work through their feelings of blame, guilt, disappointment, and anger. This strain may continue for years. You and your children may even need professional counseling. Also, as long as child support and visitation are involved, you will be forced to have some contact with your ex-spouse.

ALTERNATIVES
TO DIVORCE

By the time you've purchased this book, and read this far, you may have already decided that you want a divorce. However, if what you've just read and thought about has made you want to make a last effort to save your marriage, there are a few things you can try. These are only very basic suggestions. Details and other suggestions can be offered by professional marriage counselors.

Talk to your spouse. Choose the right time (not when your spouse is trying to unwind after a day at work, or is trying to quiet a screaming baby) to talk about your problems. Try to establish a few ground rules for the discussion, such as:

☛ Talk about how you feel, instead of making accusations that may start an argument.

☛ Each person listens while the other speaks (no interrupting).

☛ Each person must say something that he or she likes about the other and about the relationship.

As you talk, you may want to discuss such things as where you'd like your relationship to go, how it has changed since you got married, and what can be done to bring you closer together.

Change your thinking. Many people get divorced because they won't change something about their outlook or their life-style. Then, once they get divorced, they find they've made that same change they resisted for so long. For example, George and Wendy were unhappy in their marriage. They didn't seem to share the same life-style. George felt overburdened with responsibility and bored. He wanted Wendy to be more independent and outgoing, to meet new people, to handle the household budget, and to go out with him more often. But Wendy was more shy and reserved, wasn't confident in her ability to find a job and succeed in the "business world," and preferred to stay at home. Wendy wanted George to give up some of his frequent nights "out with the guys," to help with the cooking and laundry, to stop leaving messes for her to clean up, and to stop bothering her about going out all the time. But neither would try change, and eventually all of the "little things" built up into a divorce.

After the divorce, Wendy was forced to get a job to support herself. Now she's made friends at work, she goes out with them two or three nights a week, she's successful and happy at her job, and she's quite competent at managing her own budget. George now has his own apartment, and has to cook his own meals (something he finds he enjoys), and do his own laundry. He's also found it necessary to clean up his own messes and keep the place neat, especially if he's going to entertain guests. George has even thought about inviting Wendy over for dinner and a quiet evening at his place. Wendy has been thinking about inviting George out for a drink after work with her friends.

Both George and Wendy have changed in exactly the way the other had wanted. It's just too bad they didn't make these changes before they got divorced! If you think some change may help, give it a try. You can always go back to a divorce if things don't work.

Counseling. Counseling is not the same as giving advice. A counselor should not be telling you what to do. A counselor's job is to assist you in figuring out what you really want to do. A counselor's job is mostly to ask questions that will get you thinking. Actually, just talking things out with your spouse is a form of self-counseling. The only problem is that it's difficult to remain objective and non-judgmental. You both need to be able to calmly analyze what the problems are and discuss possible solutions.

Very few couples seem to be able to do this successfully, which is why there are professional marriage counselors. As with doctors and lawyers, good marriage counselors are best discovered by word of mouth. You may have friends who can direct you to someone who helped them. You can also check with your family doctor or your clergyman for a referral, or even check the telephone yellow pages under "Marriage and Family Counselors" or a similar category. You can see a counselor either alone or with your spouse. It may be a good idea for you to see a counselor even if you are going through with the divorce.

Another form of individual counseling is talking to a close friend. Just remember the difference between counseling and advice giving! Don't let your friend tell you what you should do.

Trial separation. Before going to the time, expense, and trouble of getting a divorce, you and your spouse may want to try just getting away from each other for awhile. This can be as simple as taking separate vacations, or as complex as actually separating into separate households for an indefinite period of time. This may give each of you a chance to think about how you'll like living alone, how important or trivial your problems are, and how you really feel about each other.

IMMIGRATION
STATUS

If you are not a citizen of the United States, and think that your immigration status in the United States could be jeopardized by a divorce, you should consult an immigration attorney before filing any court papers.

THE LEGAL SYSTEM 2

This chapter will give you a general introduction to the legal system. There are things you need to know in order to obtain a divorce (or help your lawyer get the job done) and to get through the legal system with minimum stress. These are some of the realities of our system. If you don't learn to accept these realities, you will experience much stress and frustration.

THEORY VS. REALITY

Our legal system is a system of rules. There are basically three types of rules:

1. *Rules of Law:* These provide the basic substance of the law, such as a law telling a judge how to go about dividing your property.

2. *Rules of Procedure:* These tell how matters are to be handled in the courts, such as requiring court papers to be in a certain form, delivered to the other party in a certain manner, or filed within a certain time.

3. *Rules of Evidence:* These require facts to be proven in a certain way.

The theory is that these rules allow each side to present evidence most favorable to that side, and an independent person or persons (the judge or jury) will be able to figure out the true facts (i.e., which evidence is more reliable). Then certain legal principles will be applied to those facts, which will give a fair resolution of the dispute between the parties. These legal principles are supposed to be relatively unchanging so that we can all know what will happen in any given situation and can plan our lives accordingly. This will provide order and predictability to our society. Any change in the legal principles is supposed to occur slowly, so that the expected behavior in our society is not confused day to day.

THE SYSTEM IS NOT PERFECT

Contrary to how it may seem, legal rules are not made just to complicate things and confuse everyone. They are attempts to make the system fair and just. They have been developed over hundreds of years, and in most cases, they do make sense. Unfortunately, our efforts to find fairness and justice have resulted in complex rules. The legal system affects our lives in important ways, and it is not a game. However, it can be compared to a game in some ways. The rules are designed to apply to all people and in all cases. Sometimes the rules don't seem to give a fair result in a certain situation, but the rules are still followed. Just as a referee can make a bad call, so can a judge. There are also cases where one side wins by cheating.

THE SYSTEM IS OFTEN SLOW

Even lawyers get frustrated at how long it can take to get a case completed (especially if they don't get paid until it's done). Whatever your situation, things will take longer than you expect. Patience is required to get through the system with minimum stress. Don't let your impatience or frustration show. No matter what happens, keep calm and be courteous.

NO TWO CASES ARE ALIKE

Just because your friend's case went a certain way doesn't mean that yours will have the same result. The judge can make a difference, and more often than not, the circumstances will make a difference. Just because your co-worker makes the same income as you and has the same number of children, you can't assume you will be ordered to pay the same amount of child support. There are usually other circumstances your co-worker doesn't tell you or understand.

HALF OF THE
PEOPLE "LOSE"

Remember, there are two sides to every legal issue, and there is usually only one winner. Don't expect to have every detail go your way, especially if you let the judge decide.

DIVORCE LAW AND PROCEDURE

This section will give you a general overview of the law and procedures involved in getting a divorce. To most people, including lawyers, the law appears complicated and confusing. Fortunately, many areas of the law can be broken down into steps. Divorce is one of those areas.

THE PLAYERS

The law and the legal system are often compared to games, and just like with games, it is important to know the players:

The Office of the Family Law Facilitator. This is an office created by the California Legislature to help people who are not represented by a lawyer in various family law matters. Check with your superior court clerk to find out if an Office of the Family Law Facilitator has been implemented in your county. If so, be sure to contact the Office before you prepare or file any forms. For more information, see the section at the beginning of chapter 5 entitled "Family Law Facilitator Act."

The judge. Getting the divorce itself, what lawyers call *status*, is usually automatic; but how your property will be divided, which of you will get custody of the children, and how much the other will pay for child support and spousal support is the province of the judge and a mathematical calculation usually performed with a computer program. The judge is the last person you want to make angry with you. In general, judges have large caseloads and like it best when your case can be concluded quickly and without hassle. This means that the more you and your spouse agree upon, and the more complete your paperwork, the better the judge will like it. Most likely, your only direct contact with the judge will be at the final hearing, which may last five minutes if you and your spouse can agree on all issues. And, if you and your spouse can agree on all issues, neither of you may have to appear in court at all. You could attempt to file all the correct papers, including the proposed Judgment, with the court clerk for the judge to review and sign. However, if something is lacking on your forms, they will be kicked back by either the clerk or the judge, and you could be swimming in forms for some time.

The judge's clerk. The judge has a clerk who sits at the side of the judge's bench. This clerk prepares the *minute order* (this is a summary of what occurred) of the hearing. When you appear for a hearing always check in with the clerk (or sometimes the bailiff), who has a desk usually just behind the railing in the courtroom. This clerk will not have time to help you with your papers if they are not in order. The clerk is there to help the judge, not you. Above all, be courteous. He or she has the judge's ear.

The court clerk. The court clerk handles the files for all of the judges. The clerk's office is the central place where all of the court files are kept. The clerk files your court papers and keeps the official records of your divorce. Most people who work in the clerk's office are friendly and helpful. While they can't give you legal advice (such as telling you what to say in your court papers), they can help explain the system and the procedures (such as telling you what type of papers must be filed). The clerk has the power to accept or reject your papers, so you don't want to anger the clerk. If the clerk tells you to change something in your papers, just change it. Don't argue or complain.

Lawyers. Lawyers serve as guides through the legal system. They try to guide their own clients and be advocates for them. Try to be polite in dealing with your spouse's lawyer (if he or she has one). You won't get anywhere by being antagonistic. Generally, the lawyer is just doing his or her job to get the best situation for the client. If you find you can't deal with your spouse's attorney, get a lawyer also. Chapter 3 will provide more information to help you decide if you need a lawyer.

This book. This book will serve as your map through the legal system. If you start getting lost, or the dangers seem to be getting worse, you better hire a lawyer to jump to your aid.

THE LAW   The law of divorce, as well as any other area of law, comes from two sources: (1) California statutes, which are laws passed by the California Legislature; and (2) past decisions of the California appeal courts. A portion of the California statutes, relating to property division, spousal support, and child support, can be found in appendix A of this book.

> ***Residency requirement:*** One basic law you need to be aware of is that either you or your spouse must have lived in California for at least six months, and in the county where the divorce case is being filed for at least three months, immediately before filing your Petition with the court. (Note: If you don't meet these residency requirements and need to file immediately, an attorney may be able to guide you around this obstacle.)

The other source of law, the past decisions of the California appeal courts, are more difficult to locate and follow. However, if you wish to learn more about how to find these court decisions, see the section on "Legal Research" later in this chapter.

You will need to show the following in a divorce:

1. That your marriage has differences which are "irreconcilable and irremediable." (This is done simply by stating so, which means that your marriage relationship is broken and can't be saved.)

2. How your property should be divided between you and your spouse.

3. If spousal support should be awarded, and in what amount.

4. How custody of your children is divided and how they should be supported.

THE PROCEDURE   The procedural requirements come from the California statutes, the California Rules of Court, and the local rules of court. The basic uncontested divorce process may be viewed as a five-step process:

1. File court papers asking the judge to grant a divorce (which includes dividing your property and deciding how the children will be taken care of, as well as child and spousal support).

2. Notify your spouse that you are filing for divorce.

3. File papers explaining your financial situation, and upon what you and your spouse have agreed.

4. Obtain a hearing date.

5. Attend a hearing before the judge, and have the judge sign a judgment to finalize the divorce.

There is a Summary Dissolution procedure which some people can use that allows you to skip some of these steps. (See chapter 6.) Now we'll look at these steps in a little more detail, and later chapters will tell you how to carry out these steps.

Preparing and filing a Petition. A Petition (form 3 or form 23) is simply a written request for the judge to grant you a divorce and divide your property. Petition forms are provided in appendix B of this book, and full instructions are provided in later chapters. Once the Petition is completed, it is taken to the court clerk to be filed.

Notifying your spouse. After you've prepared the Petition, you need to officially notify your spouse. Even though your spouse may already know that you are filing for divorce, you still need to have him or her officially notified. This is done by having a copy of your Petition delivered to your spouse. This must be done in a certain way, which will be explained in detail later. (This step is eliminated in the Summary Dissolution procedure.)

Obtaining a hearing date. Once all of your paperwork has been filed, you need to set a date for a hearing for the granting of a divorce. This is done by filing a request for an uncontested or a contested hearing with the court clerk.

The hearing. Finally, you go to the hearing. The judge will review the papers you have submitted and any additional information you have, and will make a decision about whether to grant the divorce, how your property should be divided, whether spousal support is payable, how custody of your children will be divided, and how the children are to be supported. If you and your spouse agree on these matters, the judge may simply approve your agreement if he or she finds the agreement is in the best interests of the children.

CONCILIATION

If you live in a county with a Conciliation Court and have any disagreements about child custody or visitation, the judge will order you and your spouse to participate in a mediation process called *conciliation*. Therefore, in order to save time, if you have such disagreements, call the court conciliation services immediately for an appointment. You will not be allowed to present your case to the judge before the court mediator speaks with you about the children. Often, the mediator can resolve the dispute by dispelling any misinformation that you or your spouse may have regarding your children.

LOCAL VARIATIONS AND RULES

Unfortunately, each county superior court is like a little fiefdom, and each has its own multitude of policies called *local court rules*. Additionally, be aware that an individual judge may have particular policies for his or her courtroom, the court rules are not always followed, and the rules can change frequently. This fluidity is caused by the huge caseload of the Family Law courts, not to mention the state legislature which is constantly tinkering with family law. The lesson here is that, to get your divorce through the system with minimum hassle, find out the local policy on major matters.

LEGAL RESEARCH

This book has been designed so that you don't need to do research. However, if you need or want to find out more about divorce law in California, this section will give you some guidance.

CALIFORNIA CODES

The main source of California divorce law is the portion of the California statutes called the *Family Code*. This is a set of laws passed by the California Legislature. A set can usually be found at the public library, although be sure they have the most recent set. The *Family Code* is also available on the Internet and at the law libraries in *West's Annotated California Codes* or *Deerings California Annotated Codes*.

These are volumes that contain the California statutes, followed by summaries (or *annotations*) of court cases that discuss each section of the statutes. Both of these sets contain all of the California statutes—not just those relating to divorce (e.g., *Probate Code* and *Criminal Code*). They are divided into various subjects, so look for the volumes marked *Family Code*.

CASE LAW

In addition to the laws passed by the legislature, law is also made by the decisions of the appeal courts. This *case law* will be found at a law library. Each county has a law library connected with the court, so ask the court clerk where the law library is located. Also, law schools have libraries which may be open to the public. Don't be afraid to ask the librarian for assistance. They cannot give you legal advice, but they can tell you where the books are located. Case law may be found in the annotations in *West's Annotated California Codes* or *Deerings California Annotated Codes*, referred to above, and places listed below:

CALIFORNIA DIGEST

West's California Digest, 2d gives short summaries of cases, and the place where you can find the court's full written opinion. The information in the digest is arranged alphabetically by subject.

CASE REPORTERS

Case reporters are books containing written opinions of appellate courts on cases that have been appealed to them. California has two versions of appellate cases: the official version published by statutory authority, and the unofficial version published by West Publishing as part of its National Reporter System. The case citations in both are similar. A case in the official reports will be referred to as, for example, *Smith v. Jones*, 19 C.A.4th 198 (1988). This tells you that the case titled *Smith v. Jones* may be found in volume 19 of the set of books called *California Appellate, Fourth Series*, on page 198. The number in parentheses (1988) is the year in which the case was decided. The same case in the unofficial reports would be referred to as, for example, *Smith v. Jones*, 48 CR 483 (1988), which tells you the case titled *Smith v. Jones* may be found in volume 48 of the set of books called *California Reports*, on page 483.

CALIFORNIA
JURISPRUDENCE

California Jurisprudence (*Cal. Jur.*) is a legal encyclopedia. You simply look up the subject you want ("Dissolution of Marriage"), in alphabetical order, and it gives you a summary of the law on that subject. It will also refer to specific court cases.

CALIFORNIA
RULES OF
COURT

The *California Rules of Court* are the rules which are applied in the various courts in California, and they also contain approved forms. These rules mainly deal with forms and procedures. You would primarily be concerned with the "Family Law Rules" beginning with Rule 1200.

OTHER
SOURCES

Other sources at the law library include:

☞ *California Practice Guide, Family Law,* published by the Rutter Group, a West Group affiliate.

☞ *California Family Law Practice and Procedure, 2d ed.,* published by Matthew Bender Company.

☞ *Practice Under the California Family Code,* published by the California Continuing Education of the Bar.

LAWYERS 3

A primary question you have is probably: "Do I need an attorney?" The answer will depend upon many factors, such as how comfortable you feel handling the matter yourself, whether your situation is complicated, how much opposition you get from your spouse, and whether your spouse has an attorney. There are no court-appointed lawyers for spouses in divorce cases, so if you want an attorney you will have to hire one, unless you qualify for legal aid.

Legal help is also available under the relatively new Family Law Facilitator Act. This act created an Office of the Family Law Facilitator to assist people who do not have a lawyer in various family law matters. For more information about this, see the section at the beginning of chapter 5 entitled "Family Law Facilitator Act."

You should get an attorney if your spouse is in the military and is unwilling either to respond to the Petition or to use the simplified divorce procedure described in chapter 6.

Rather than asking if you *need* a lawyer, a more appropriate question is: "Do I *want* a lawyer?" The next section discusses some of the "pros" and "cons" of hiring a lawyer, and some things you may want to consider in making this decision.

Do You Want a Lawyer?

One of the first questions you want to consider, and most likely one of the reasons you are reading this book, is: How much will an attorney cost? Attorneys come in all ages, shapes, sizes, sexes, racial and ethnic groups—and price ranges. For a very rough estimate, you can expect an attorney to charge from $300 to $2,000 for an uncontested divorce, and $1,500 and up for a contested divorce. Lawyers usually charge an hourly rate for contested divorces, ranging from about $75 to $300 per hour. Most new (and less expensive) attorneys are capable of handling a simple divorce, but if your situation became complicated, you would probably prefer an experienced lawyer. As a general rule, your legal bill will be more than what you thought it would cost at the beginning.

ADVANTAGES TO HIRING A LAWYER

The following are some of the advantages to hiring a lawyer:

☞ Judges and other attorneys will take you more seriously. Most judges prefer both parties to have attorneys. They feel this helps the case move in a more orderly fashion because both sides will know the procedures and relevant issues. Persons representing themselves often waste time on matters that have no bearing on the case.

☞ A lawyer will serve as a "buffer" between you and your spouse. This can lead to a quicker passage through the system by reducing emotions that confuse the issues.

☞ You can let your lawyer worry about the details. By having an attorney you need only become generally familiar with the contents of this book, as it will be your attorney's job to file the proper papers in the correct form and to deal with the court clerks, the judge, the process server, your spouse, and your spouse's attorney.

☞ Lawyers provide professional assistance with problems. In the event your case is complicated or suddenly becomes complicated, it is an advantage to have an attorney who is familiar with your case. It can also be comforting to have a lawyer to turn to for advice and to answer your questions.

ADVANTAGES TO
REPRESENTING
YOURSELF

The following are some advantages to representing yourself:

☛ You save the cost of a lawyer.

☛ Sometimes judges permit the unrepresented person a certain amount of leeway with the procedure.

☛ The procedure may be faster. Two of the most frequent complaints about lawyers received by the bar association involve delay in completing the case and failure to return phone calls. Most lawyers have a heavy caseload, which sometimes results in cases being neglected for periods of time. If you are following the progress of your own case, you'll be able to push it along the system diligently.

☛ Selecting an attorney is not easy. As the next section shows, it is difficult to know whether you are selecting an attorney that will make you happy.

MIDDLE
GROUND

You may want to look for an attorney who will be willing to accept an hourly fee to answer your questions and give you help as you need it. This way, you will save some legal costs but still get some professional assistance.

SELECTING A LAWYER

Selecting a lawyer is a two-step process. First, you need to decide with which attorney to make an appointment, then you need to decide if you want to hire that attorney.

FINDING A
LAWYER

The following are some suggestions to help you locate lawyers:

☛ Ask a friend. A common, and frequently the best, way to find a lawyer is to ask someone you know. This is especially helpful if the lawyer represented your friend in a divorce, or other family law matter.

☛ Lawyer Referral Service. You can find a referral service by looking in the yellow pages phone directory under "Attorney Referral Services" or "Attorneys." This is a service, usually operated by a bar association, designed to match a client with an attorney handling cases in the area of law the client needs. The referral service does not guarantee the quality of work, nor the level of experience or ability of the attorney. Finding a lawyer this way will at least connect you with one who is interested in divorce and family law matters and probably has some experience in this area.

☛ Yellow pages. Check under the heading for "Attorneys-Divorce" in the yellow pages phone directory. Many of the lawyers and law firms place display ads here indicating their experience and educational backgrounds. Look for firms or lawyers which indicate they practice in areas such as "divorce," "family law," or "domestic relations."

☛ Ask another lawyer. If you have used the services of an attorney in the past for some other matter (for example, a real estate closing, traffic ticket, or a will), you may want to call and ask if he or she could refer you to an attorney whose ability in the area of family law is respected.

EVALUATING A LAWYER

From your search, select three to five lawyers worthy of further consideration. Your first step will be to call each attorney's office, explain that you are interested in seeking a divorce, and ask the following questions:

☛ Does the attorney (or firm) handle divorces?

☛ How much will it cost? (Don't expect to get a definite answer, but they may be able to give you a range or an hourly rate. You will probably need to talk to the lawyer for anything more detailed.)

☛ How soon can you get an appointment?

If you like the answers you get, ask if you can speak to the attorney. Some offices will permit this, but others will require you to make an appointment. Make the appointment if that is what is required, but be sure to ask first what this appointment will cost (some attorneys will not charge for the first appointment, others will charge a nominal fee such as $20, and others will start the meter running at their regular hourly rate the moment you step into their office). Once you get in contact with the attorney (either on the phone or at the appointment), ask the following questions:

☛ How much will it cost? You probably won't get an exact amount, but you may get a range, based on an hourly rate and what variables can add to the time required.

☛ How will the fee be paid?

☛ How long has the attorney been in practice?

☛ How long has the attorney been in practice in California?

☛ What percentage of the attorney's cases involve divorce cases or other family law matters? (Don't expect an exact answer, but you should get a rough estimate that is at least twenty percent.)

☛ How long will it take? (Don't expect an exact answer, but the attorney should be able to give you an average range and discuss things which may make a difference.)

If you get acceptable answers to these questions, it's time to ask yourself the following questions about the lawyer:

☛ Do you feel comfortable talking to the lawyer?

☛ Is the lawyer friendly toward you? You probably don't want a lawyer who is arrogant with you, talks down to you, or is intimidating toward you (although some of these behaviors may be acceptable when directed toward your spouse or your spouse's lawyer).

☛ Does the lawyer seem confident?

☛ Does the lawyer seem to be straight-forward with you and able to explain things so that you understand?

If you get satisfactory answers to all of these questions, you probably have a lawyer with whom you will be able to work. Most clients are happiest if they feel comfortable with their attorney.

Working with a Lawyer

In general, you and your attorney will work best with each other if you both keep an open, honest, and friendly attitude. You should also consider the following suggestions.

ASK QUESTIONS

If you want to know something or if you don't understand something, ask your attorney. If you don't understand the answer, say so, and ask him or her to explain it again. There are many points of law that many lawyers don't fully understand, so you shouldn't be embarrassed to ask questions. Many people who say they had a bad experience with a lawyer either didn't ask enough questions, or had a lawyer who wouldn't take the time to explain things to them. If your lawyer isn't taking the time to explain what he's doing, it may be time to look for a new lawyer.

BE THOROUGH

Give your lawyer complete information. Anything you tell your attorney is confidential. An attorney can lose his license to practice if he reveals information without your permission. So don't hold back. Tell your lawyer everything, even if it doesn't seem important to you. There are many things which seem unimportant to a non-attorney, but can change the outcome of a case. Also, don't hold something back because you are afraid it will hurt your case. It will definitely hurt your case if your lawyer doesn't find out about it until he hears it in court from your spouse's attorney! But if he knows in advance, he can plan to eliminate or reduce damage to your case.

ACCEPT REALITY

Listen to what your lawyer tells you about the law and the system. It's not your lawyer's fault that the law or the legal system doesn't work the way you think it should. For example, if your lawyer tells you that the judge can't hear your case for two months, don't demand that a hearing be set tomorrow. By refusing to accept reality, you are setting yourself up for disappointment.

PATIENCE

Be patient. This applies to being patient with the system (which is often slow as we discussed earlier), as well as with your attorney. Don't expect your lawyer to return your phone call within an hour. He or she may not be able to return it the same day either. Most lawyers are very busy and over-worked. It is rare that an attorney can maintain a full caseload and still make each client feel like the attorney's only client.

THE SECRETARY

Talk to the secretary. Your lawyer's secretary can be a valuable source of information. The secretary will often be able to answer your questions, and you won't get a bill for the his or her time.

DEALING WITH YOUR SPOUSE

Let your attorney deal with your spouse. It is your lawyer's job to communicate with your spouse or with your spouse's lawyer. Many lawyers have had clients lose or damage their cases when the client decides to say or do something on his own.

PROMPTNESS

Be on time. This applies to appointments with your lawyer and to court hearings.

KEEP YOUR CASE MOVING

Whenever you talk to your lawyer ask the following questions:

☛ What is the next step?

☛ When do you expect it to be done?

☛ When should I talk to you next?

If you don't hear from the lawyer when you expect, call him the following day. Don't remind him that he didn't call—just ask how things are going.

COMMUNICATE WITH YOUR LAWYER

Have a clear understanding with your lawyer. Make sure you and your lawyer both understand what is expected. Your lawyer must provide a written fee agreement if the matter is anticipated to incur $1,000 or more in fees. This agreement must spell out the flat fee agreement or the hourly rate, when payments are to be made, in what detail and how often the attorney will provide you with statements, among other requirements. Many attorneys will ask for initial deposits of from $500 to $5,000 or more, depending upon the complexity of the case, plus court filing fees, process server fees, and other anticipated costs for obtaining financial or personal information. Be wary if your attorney calls you or sends you a statement asking for more money before the initial papers are prepared or filed, or if you notice that most of the deposit is used before the initial papers are filed. Although courts favor settlements, numerous phone calls and letter writing by your attorney discussing possible settlement with your spouse or your spouse's attorney may not necessarily be the best use of your limited funds.

> Always demand that your attorney send you copies of all court documents and correspondence.

FIRING YOUR LAWYER

If you can no longer work with your lawyer, it is time to either go it alone or get a new attorney. You will need to send your lawyer a letter stating that you no longer desire his or her services and are discharging him or her from your case. Also state that you will be coming by the office the following day to pick up your file. The attorney does not have to give you his or her own notes but must give you the essential contents of your file (such as copies of papers already filed or prepared, and any documents that you provided). If he or she refuses to give your file to you, for any reason, contact the California State Bar about filing a complaint, or *grievance*, against the lawyer. Of course, you will need to settle any remaining fees charged for work that has already been done by the lawyer.

EVALUATING YOUR SITUATION 4

You should carefully consider the following matters before you file for divorce.

YOUR SPOUSE

First, you need to evaluate your situation with respect to your spouse. Have you both already agreed to get a divorce? If not, what kind of reaction do you expect from him or her? Your expected reaction can determine how you proceed. If your spouse reacts in a rational manner, you can probably use the uncontested procedure. If you expect an emotional and possibly violent reaction, then you will need to take steps to protect yourself, your children, and your property, and can expect to use the contested procedure. (Also, be sure to read chapter 11 on how to protect yourself.)

Unless you and your spouse have already decided to get a divorce, you may not want your spouse to know you are thinking about divorce. This is a defense tactic, although it may not seem that way at first. If your spouse thinks you are planning a divorce, he or she may do things to prevent you from getting a fair result. These things include withdrawing money from bank accounts, hiding information about income, and hiding assets. Collect all of the information you will need beforehand, and be prepared to protect yourself from violence, if necessary.

> **Caution:** Tactics such as withdrawing money from bank accounts and hiding assets are potentially dangerous. If you try any of these things you risk looking like the "bad guy" before the judge. This can result in anything from having disputed matters resolved in your spouse's favor, to being ordered to produce the assets (or be jailed for contempt of court).

Theoretically, the system would prefer you to keep evidence of the assets (such as photographs, sales receipts, or bank statements) to present to the judge if your spouse hides them. Then your spouse will be the bad guy. However, once your spouse has taken assets and hidden them, or sold them and spent the money, even a contempt order may not get the money or assets back. If you determine that you need to get the assets in order to keep your spouse from hiding or disposing of them, be sure you keep them in a safe place and disclose them on your Schedule of Assets and Debts (form 8). Do not dispose of them. If your spouse claims you took them, you can explain to the judge why you were afraid that your spouse would dispose of them and that you merely got them out of his or her reach.

Gathering Information

It is important that you collect all of the pertinent financial information. This information should include originals or copies of the following:

☐ Your most recent income tax return (and your spouse's if you filed separately) and the past two years' returns.

☐ The most recent W-2 tax forms for yourself and your spouse.

☐ Any other income reporting papers (such as interest, stock dividends, etc.).

□ Your spouse's three most recent paystubs, hopefully showing year-to-date earnings (otherwise, try to get copies of all paystubs since the beginning of the year).

□ Deeds to all real estate; and titles to cars, boats, or other vehicles.

□ Your and your spouse's will.

□ Life insurance policies.

□ Stocks, bonds, or other investment papers.

□ Pension or retirement fund papers and statements.

□ Health insurance card and papers.

□ Bank account or credit union statements.

□ Your spouse's social security number and driver's license number.

□ Names, addresses, and phone numbers of your spouse's employer, close friends, and family members.

□ Credit card statements, mortgage documents, and other credit and debt papers.

□ A list of vehicles, furniture, appliances, tools, etc., owned by you and your spouse. (See the next section in this chapter on "Property and Debts" for forms and a detailed discussion of what to include.)

□ Copies of bills or receipts for recurring, regular expenses, such as electric, gas or other utilities, car insurance, etc.

□ Copies of bills, receipts, insurance forms, or medical records for unusual medical expenses (including those for recurring or continuous medical conditions) for yourself, your spouse, or your children.

□ Any other papers showing what you and your spouse earn, own, or owe.

Make copies of these papers and secure them. Try to make copies of new papers as they come in, especially as you get close to filing court papers, and as you get close to a court hearing.

PROPERTY AND DEBTS

PROPERTY

This section is designed to help you get a rough idea of where things stand regarding the division of your property and to prepare you for completing the court papers you will need to file. The following sections will deal with your debts, child support, custody, and visitation. If you are still not sure whether you want a divorce, these sections may help you to decide.

This section assists you in completing the Schedule of Assets and Debts (form 8). Chapter 7 will discuss how this form fits into the overall scheme. Form 8, which is not used if you qualify for the summary dissolution procedure, provides a list of, and key information about, all of your property and debts. First, you need to understand how property is divided. Trying to determine how to divide assets and debts can be difficult. Under California law, assets and debts are separated into two categories: *community property* (meaning it is half yours and half your spouse's) and *separate property* (meaning it is yours or your spouse's alone).

> **Quasi-Community Property.** There is a subcategory under community property called *quasi-community property*, which is all property acquired by a spouse while living outside of California that would have been community property if the spouse had been living in California at the time. Out-of-state property acquired by a spouse at the time the spouse lives in California is not quasi-community property but rather it is community property.

In making the distinction between community and separate property, the following rules apply:

☞ If the asset or debt was acquired after the date you were married, it is presumed to be a community asset or debt. It is up to you or your spouse to prove otherwise.

☞ A separate asset or debt is one that was acquired before the date of your marriage or acquired by gift or inheritance at any time. Income from separate property is also separate property (for example, rent you receive from an investment property you had before you got married). If you exchange one of these assets or debts after your marriage, it is still separate. (For example: You had a $6,000 car before you got married. After the marriage, you traded it for a different $6,000 car. The new car is still separate property.) Also, property acquired after the date of separation, even though you're not yet divorced, is separate property.

☛ You and your spouse may sign a written agreement that certain assets and debts are to be considered community or separate.

> *Caution:* Be careful on this one. It looks simple but it isn't. In order for spouses to validly transfer any property between themselves (called *transmutation*), at least as to transfers as of January 1, 1985, the transfer must:
>
> 1. Be in writing.
>
> 2. Have the signed intelligent consent of the spouse giving up the property interest.
>
> 3. Specifically describe the property interest involved.
>
> 4. Specifically describe the consenting spouse's interest in the property.
>
> If the property was transferred orally, or in a writing that does not meet the above requirements, the transfer may or may not be valid, depending upon the proof.

☛ Community assets and debts are those which were acquired during your marriage, even if they were acquired by you or your spouse individually. This also includes the increase in value of a community asset during the marriage due to the use of community funds to pay for or improve the property or through appreciation. All rights accrued during the marriage in pension, retirement, profit-sharing, insurance, and similar plans are community assets. It is also possible for one spouse to make a gift of separate property to the other spouse, such as by commingling separate property with community property, thereby making it all community property.

☛ Real estate held jointly in both names is considered community property, and the spouse claiming otherwise must prove it.

☛ The value of any asset, community or separate, is determined as of the trial date, or as near to it as possible.

☛ Joint tenancy property of any kind is considered community property for divorce purposes.

Even though property may be categorized as separate or community under the above rules, oftentimes one spouse is entitled to reimbursement. This discussion about reimbursement and tracing is meant only to alert you to issues, not to guide you through them. The variations and complexities regarding these subjects are beyond the scope of this book. If you or your spouse contributed substantial funds from separate property to a community property asset, or if the community contributed substantial property to spouse's separate property, see a lawyer.

Generally tracing and reimbursement weave themselves in and around community and separate property. Tracing is just what you think it is— following the funds to their source, for example, tracing an expenditure from the community property bank account to a new roof on your spouse's separate property condo. Reimbursement is the return of funds advanced from community property for the benefit of a spouse's separate property, or the return of funds advanced from a spouse's separate property for the benefit of the community. Reimbursement can apply to transfers during marriage or during the separation period.

Another example: you and your spouse buy a house as community property. From a separate property bank account you had before marriage, you pay the mortgage payments. If you can trace the mortgage payments back to your separate account, and assuming you didn't agree in writing that the payments were gifts to the community, you'd be entitled to reimbursement of the mortgage payment principal, but not the interest, maintenance, insurance, or tax.

Some of the complexities:

1. You think the marriage is solid, so you transfer your separate property condo you had before marriage into joint tenancy with your spouse.

2. Same as 1 above, but you transfer into tenants in common with your spouse.

3. You and your spouse buy a home during marriage and you contribute a fifteen percent down payment from separate funds, and the mortgage payments are made thereafter from community property.

4. You and your partner buy a home as tenants in common before you marry your partner and then after marriage change title to joint tenants.

5. The homes in all the examples above experienced large appreciation during the marriage.

6. You live in your spouse's separate property home and then after children arrive, you and your spouse buy a larger home while keeping the first home.

7. You and your spouse refinance your spouse's separate property rental condo during marriage using your credit and using a portion of the refinance funds as a down payment on another home which you and your spouse acquire as community property.

How much is reimbursable? Exactly what is reimbursable? For what period of time should there be reimbursement? Has the property unwittingly been converted to community property? Was a gift intended? Should fair rental value be considered during the time you were living in your spouse's house?

The law was made somewhat more clear with the rule that as of January 1, 1994, a party "shall" be reimbursed for any contribution to community property from separate property unless the party has waived such right in writing. A companion section provides for the reimbursement to the community for expenses of education or training of one spouse, provided it results in added value to the community. For example, if the wife worked to put her husband through medical school, and the husband looks to greener marital pastures after becoming a successful doctor, the wife is going to be reimbursed in part for her efforts to put her husband through school.

The Schedule of Assets and Debts (form 8) and the instructions that follow, call for a specific listing of property and debt. The Petition (form 3) calls for only a general listing. You will notice that form 8 is divided into five columns, designated as follows:

Column 1)   "Assets—Description." This is the listing of all your property. Note that certain attachments are required, such as copies of deeds, account numbers, etc.

Column 2)   "Sep Prop." This refers to whether you consider the property in Column 1 separate or community. If you consider it separate, place either an "H" for "husband" or a "W" for "wife" in this column.

Column 3)   "Date Acquired." This is self-explanatory and requires at least a month and year date.

Column 4)   "Current Gross Fair Market Value." This refers to for what price you could sell the item.

Column 5)   "Amount of Money Owed or Encumbrance." This refers to the debt owed on the property, or any encumbrance like a mortgage or deed of trust. Attach to the form the latest statement showing such debt.

Use items 1 through 16 in Column 1 to list all of your property.

> ***What not to list.*** You will not need to list your clothing and other personal effects. Pots and pans, dishes and cooking utensils ordinarily do not need to be listed.

The following guidelines for each of the listed categories may help:

1. Real Estate. List each piece of property in which you have any interest. The description includes a street address for the property, as well as the legal description found on the deed. You might also use the county assessor's parcel number. Real estate (or any other property) may be in both of your names, in your spouse's name alone, or in your name alone. The only way to know for sure is to look at the deed to the property. (If you can't find your deed, ask a local realtor to get you a copy.) The owners of property are usually referred to on the deed as the *grantees*. In assigning a value to the property, consider the market value, which is the amount you could probably get for the property. This might be what similar houses in your neighborhood have sold for recently.

In dividing real estate and other appreciated assets, check out any potential tax consequences. If there are children, you may want one spouse to continue living in the home and defer the division of the equity (the difference between the fair market value and the debt) until the children reach a certain age. At that time, the house could be sold with the profit divided. In the meantime, the spouse living in the home with the children would pay the maintenance, mortgage, tax, and insurance, but capital improvements, such as a new roof, would be shared. Of course, you could exchange the equity in the home for the equity in another asset of approximately the same value. Whatever is best for the children is the rule here. Again, if there's substantial equity, consult with an attorney for this issue. In transferring real estate, unless one spouse knows about deeds, get a professional's help to make sure the deed is prepared properly.

2. Household Furniture, Furnishings, Appliances. List all furniture generally. You should include the type of piece (such as sofa, coffee table, etc.). Just estimate a value, unless you know what it's worth. Other than antiques, use garage sale prices. This category also includes such things as refrigerators, lawn mowers, and power tools. Again, estimate a value, unless you are familiar enough with them to simply know what they are worth. More importantly, try to dispose of this issue informally with your spouse. The judge will not be happy using his time to decide who should get the arm chair.

3. Jewelry, Antiques, Art, Coin Collections, etc. You don't need to list inexpensive "costume" jewelry. And you can plan on keeping your own personal watches, rings, etc. However, if you own an expensive piece you should include it in your list, along with an estimated value. Be sure to include silverware, original art, gold, coin collections, etc. Describe it so it can be identified.

4. Vehicles, boats, trailers. This includes cars, trucks, motor homes, recreational vehicles (RVs), motorcycles, boats, trailers, airplanes, and any other means of transportation for which the state requires a title and registration. Your description should include the following (which can usually be found on the title or on the vehicle itself):

☞ Year. The year the vehicle was made.

☞ Make: The name of the manufacturer, such as "Ford," "Honda," "Chris Craft," etc.

☞ Model: The model may be a name, a number, a series of letters, or a combination of these. For example, you know it's a Ford; but is it a Mustang, an LTD, or an Aerostar?

☞ Serial Number: This is most likely found on the vehicle, as well as on the title or registration.

Make a copy of the title or registration. Regarding a value, you can go to the public library and ask to look at the *blue book* for cars, trucks, etc. A blue book (which may actually be yellow, black, or any other color) gives the average values for used vehicles. Your librarian can help you find what you need. Another source is the classified advertising section of a newspaper to see how similar vehicles are priced. You might also try calling a dealer to see if he can give you a rough idea of the value. Be sure you take into consideration the condition of the vehicle.

5. Savings Accounts. List all accounts in which you have any interest. State the name on the account, the account number, and the bank and branch. Attach a copy of the latest statement if you have it.

6. Checking Accounts. List these the same as savings accounts.

7. Credit Union, Other Deposit Accounts. List these the same as savings and checking accounts.

8. Cash. This refers to cash you have available, not to money you have in accounts.

9. Tax Refund. Any expected tax refund or unspent tax refund should be listed here.

10. Life Insurance with Cash Surrender or Loan Value. This is any life insurance policy which you may cash in or borrow against, and therefore has value. Attach a copy of the declaration page for each policy. If you can't find a cash surrender value or declaration page in your papers, call the insurance company or agent and ask.

11. Stocks, Bonds, Secured Notes, and Mutual Funds. All stocks, bonds, or other "paper investments" should be listed. Write down the number of shares and the name of the company or other organization which issued them. Also, copy any notation such as "common" or "preferred" stock or shares. This information can be obtained from the stock certificate itself, or from a statement from the stock broker. Make a copy of the certificate or the statement.

12. Retirement and Pensions. The division of pensions, and military and retirement benefits can be complicated. Whenever these types of benefits are involved and you can't agree on how to divide them, you will need to consult an attorney or an actuary to determine the value of the benefits and how they should be divided. Unless you both agree to keep your own retirement benefit, or agree to cash out the benefits, you will need a QDRO (Qualified Domestic Relations Order) and an attorney. QDROs are beyond the scope of this book.

A general overview of this area will be helpful. The first principle is that separate property and community property interests in the asset should be determined, unless all the benefits were accrued during the time of marriage and before separation. The community property portion is half yours and half your spouse's, regardless of which spouse was the employee, and is that portion earned during marriage and before separation. This method of calculation in terms of time, however, is not applied if the benefit is not substantially related to the time of the employee's service. Some pension plans need actuarial evaluation. The value of other benefits such as IRAs, 401(k)s and 403(b)s, deferred compensation, profit sharing, SEPs, and Keogh plans (listed in the next section) might be on the latest statement, but again, if the amount is substantial, consult with an attorney to be safe. This asset may be the largest in the marriage. The plan will often have a death benefit payable to the survivor spouse and offer options regarding the benefit.

The two main methods of distributing these assets are in kind or cash out. A distribution *in kind* means that you and your spouse are each awarded one-half the community interest. A *cash out* means that the asset is exchanged for another asset of approximately equal worth. For example, if the house equity is about the same value as the actuarial value of the pension, one spouse would get the full house equity and the other the full pension. As you can surmise, the cash out method makes sense where one spouse would not realize any benefit for many years, where the valuation would be complex, or where the marriage is of short duration.

But if the amount is significant and the marriage is of long duration, the in kind division may be appropriate; if so, the in kind division is made a subject of a separate judgment which binds the pension plan. This separate judgment is called a QDRO, as mentioned on page 45.

A military pension is also treated as community property subject to division. Some restrictions apply, such as the portion subject to division can only be the disposable retired pay, which is the net monthly amount payable after certain required deductions, including any portion which is for disability. Some other restrictions are that the marriage must have a duration of at least ten years and that only active duty time is included.

Note that social security is not community property. However, a spouse's right to social security benefits arising from the working spouse's social security accrual is not affected by the divorce, provided the marriage lasted at least ten years.

13. Profit-Sharing, Annuities, IRAs, Deferred Compensation. Attach a copy of the latest statement. If you don't have it, you will need to contact the company or financial institution involved. You may need an actuary to determine the present community value.

14. Accounts Receivable and Unsecured Notes. Attach copies if you have them. This category mostly refers to businesses; however, if you have loaned money to anyone, you need to show this with details.

15. Partnerships and Other Business Interests. If you or your spouse are in business, whether the form of the business be a partnership, corporation, limited liability company, or sole proprietorship, you will probably need a CPA's help to determine the community value. This is a complicated area of the law and beyond the scope of this book.

16. Other Assets. This is simply a general reference to anything of significant value that doesn't fit in one of the categories already discussed. Examples might be a portable spa, an above-ground swimming pool, golf clubs, guns, pool tables, camping or fishing equipment, or farm animals or machinery.

17. Total Assets from Continuation Sheet. If there is not enough space to list all of your items of property in any category, you will need to use other sheets of paper. Here you will indicate the total of your assets from any such continuation sheet.

18. Total Assets. Add all of your figures in the market value and money owed columns, and write in the total here.

DEBTS   Items 19 through 24 of form 8 are for listing your debts. Included is a column to check if the debt is a separate debt. State the total amount that is owed, and fill in the date the debt was incurred. The following guidelines may be of some help in completing this section of form 8:

19. Student Loans. State the name and address of the institution to whom the loan is owed and the loan number.

20. Taxes. State the type of tax owed (e.g., "federal income tax," "state personal property tax," or "county property tax.") and the tax year.

21. Support Arrearages. If you or your spouse are behind on money ordered to be paid to a previous spouse for spousal or child support, list such amounts here, as well as providing a copy of the support order.

22. Loans—Unsecured. List all *unsecured* debts, except credit card debt which is listed separately as the next item. Unsecured debt is where the lender has no legal interest in any of your property to safeguard the loan. An example would be a *signature loan*, where a bank loans you the money on the strength of your signature only. A *secured* debt is one where the lender takes back an interest in your property, such as where the lender can foreclose on your home or repossess your car if you don't make your payments.

23. Credit Cards. List all of your credit card debts with copies of the latest statement.

24. Other Debts. List here any other debt of yours or your spouse that is not listed elsewhere on this form.

DIVIDING PROPERTY AND DEBTS   Once you have completed form 8, make a copy of it, then go back through it and try to determine who should end up with each item. The ideal situation is for both you and your spouse to go through the list together and divide things fairly. However, if this is not possible, you will need to offer a reasonable settlement to the judge. On a copy of this list, consider each item and make a check-mark to designate whether that item should go to the husband or wife. You may make the following assumptions:

☞ Your separate property will go to you.

☞ Your spouse's separate property will go to your spouse.

☞ You should get the items that only you use.

☞ Your spouse should get the items only used by your spouse.

☞ The remaining items should be divided, evening out the total value of all the community property, and taking into consideration who would really want that item.

To equally divide your property (we're only talking about community property here), you first need to know the total value of your property. Do not count the value of the separate property items. Add all the remaining community property amounts to get an approximate value of all community property.

When it comes time for the hearing, you and your spouse may be arguing over some or all of the items on your list. This is when you'll be glad that you made copies of the documents relating to the property on your list. Arguments over the value of property may need to be resolved by hiring appraisers to set a value; however, you'll have to pay the appraiser a fee. Dividing your property will be discussed further in later chapters.

Debts were listed on page 4 of form 8. Although there are cases where, for example, the wife gets a car but the husband is ordered to make the payments, generally whoever gets the property also gets the debt owed on that property. This seems to be a fair arrangement in most cases.

As with separate property, there is also separate debt. This is any debt incurred before you were married. You will be responsible for your separate debts, and your spouse will be responsible for his or hers.

Warning: If you and your spouse are jointly responsible for a debt, you are not relieved of your obligation to pay just because your spouse agrees to pay (or is ordered to pay) the debt in the divorce proceeding. If your spouse doesn't pay, the creditor can still come after you for payment. You would then need to take your spouse to court to get him or her to reimburse you.

CHILD CUSTODY AND VISITATION

As with everything else in divorce, things are ideal when both parties can agree on the question of custody of the children. Generally, the judge will accept any agreement you reach, provided it doesn't appear your agreement will cause harm to your children. With respect to child custody, the California Family Code, Section 3020, makes the following significant statement:

> The Legislature finds and declares that it is the public policy of this state to assure minor children frequent and continuing contact with both parents after the parents have separated or dissolved their marriage, and to encourage parents to share the rights and responsibilities of child rearing in order to effect this policy, except where the contact would not be in the best interest of the child...

California statutory and case law state there is no preference or presumption as to custody, and that the paramount rule is the best interests of the child. Most custody plans have *joint legal custody* to both parents and *primary physical custody* to one parent, where *legal* custody refers to parenting decisions involving schooling, medical care, religion, and the like, and *physical* custody refers to the child's primary residence with one parent and visitation rights to the other parent. An exceptional situation must exist to have *sole legal custody*.

Becoming more popular so that neither parent feels like he or she is a "visitor" to the child is both joint legal custody and joint physical custody, even where the physical custody is not equal periods of time.

If you and your spouse cannot agree on these matters, you will be ordered to see a court mediator if you are in one of the counties that have *Conciliation* departments. Only then will the judge hear your custody or visitation dispute. The judge cannot possibly know your child as well as you and your spouse, so doesn't it make sense for you to work this out yourselves? Otherwise, you are leaving the decision to a stranger.

If the judge must decide the question, he is required by law to have the health, safety, and welfare of the child as the primary concern. Other factors are:

☞ any abuse allegations;

☞ which parent is most likely to allow the other to visit with the child and to develop and maintain a close and continuing parent-child relationship;

☞ the love, affection and other emotional ties existing between the child and each parent;

☞ the ability and willingness of each parent to provide the child with food, clothing, medical care, and other material needs;

☞ the length of time the child has lived with either parent in a stable environment;

☞ the permanence, as a family unit, of the proposed custodial home; (This relates to where one of the parties will be getting remarried immediately after the divorce or, more often, to change of custody petitions at a later date.)

☞ the moral fitness of each parent;

☞ the mental and physical health of each parent;

☞ the home, school, and community record of the child;

☞ the preference of the child, providing the child is of sufficient intelligence and understanding; and

☞ any other fact the judge decides is relevant.

There are too many factors and individual circumstances to predict the outcome of a custody battle. The exception is where one parent is clearly unfit *and* the other can prove it. Drug abuse is the most common charge, but unless there has been an arrest and conviction, it is difficult to prove to a judge. In general, don't charge your spouse with being unfit unless you can prove it. Judges are not impressed with unfounded allegations, which can do your cause more harm than good.

If your children are older, consider their preference. Your fairness and respect for their wishes may benefit you in the long run. Just be sure that you keep in close contact with them and visit them often.

Custody battles and visitation skirmishes are always lose/lose/lose situations—for mother, father, and children, unless an obvious problem is present, for example physical abuse or drug abuse. Judges have a distaste for the revengeful mothers and whining fathers (or vice versa) who verbally spit at each other in the front of them. As soon as one dispute is resolved, there's sure to be another tomorrow, or next week, or next month. An immature father or mother will doom any parenting plan.

Nevertheless, a parenting plan must be included in every judgment or Marital Settlement Agreement (MSA). A parenting plan can be as simple as "joint legal and physical custody with reasonable visitation by one spouse when the child is with the other spouse." Unfortunately, such a plan has high risk for problems, especially in the first few traumatic years after the divorce, because it doesn't provide specific guidelines.

The child's age, maturity, and extracurricular activities, distance between the parents' homes, school location, and many other concerns must considered.

Remember that legal custody will always be joint unless there are exceptional circumstances. You may want to designate primary physical custody with one parent and give the other parent visitation for designated periods. You may want the children to live alternately with each parent for certain periods of time. You may want to spell out the visitation days and times, including provisions for Christmas, Easter, and summer vacations, mid-week and weekend visitations, and include at the end a provision that visitation shall be reasonable, but in the event of disagreement, the above schedule shall become effective. That way you've got a fall-back position if your spouse starts taking advantage.

Ultimately any parenting plan is up to you and your spouse, and no matter what parenting plan you devise, you can count on a monkey wrench being thrown in it by guess who? That's right—your child, who is completely oblivious to your schedule and your emotional problems. Some sample parenting plans are included in the Marital Settlement Agreement (MSA) (form 17).

A word should be said about grandparent visitation. The Family Code has two major provisions in this area. The first is where a parent joins the grandparent in the divorce action, and the second is where the grandparent separately petitions the court in the divorce proceeding. In the first instance, the court has the discretion to grant visitation to the grandparent if it is in the child's best interest. This is obviously a very broad standard. Where the grandparent petitions the court, a preexisting relationship with the child is required, and parental visitation will not be disrupted for the sake of grandparent visitation.

CHILD SUPPORT

GENERAL PRINCIPLES

Because child support stems from the child's right to support from parents, parents cannot waive this obligation between themselves, nor can they avoid it through voluntary unemployment or by voluntarily reducing income. If the judge thinks the paying parent has voluntarily reduced his or her income, the support amount will be based on ability to earn, not actual earnings.

For example, if at around the time of the dissolution, the paying parent was making $20 per hour and then voluntarily takes a position that only pays $10 per hour. Other circumstances being equal, the support amount can be based on $20 per hour earnings.

Child support continues until the child reaches majority (eighteen years); and it can continue until the child completes the twelfth grade or reaches nineteen years (whichever occurs first), provided the child is unmarried, not self-supporting, and in high school full time.

Because child support is a continuing obligation, either party at any time can ask the court to increase or decrease the amount based on changed circumstances, which is usually a change in income of one or both parties.

Sometimes parents have arguments regarding visitation. This is a separate issue from support, and the support check is still due. Many of these problems, however, have been solved by the Wage and Earnings Assignment Order (form 21) which is now automatic, subject to some exceptions. This is an order (signed by the judge) that is sent to the paying parent's employer, ordering the employer to take the support amount directly from the paycheck of its employee and send it to the recipient spouse. Problems in receiving support are beyond the scope of this book, and you should contact either the District Attorney in your county or an attorney.

DETERMINING
CHILD SUPPORT

The amount of child support is established by a statewide uniform guideline found the Family Code, Sections 4000 to 4253. The guideline is really mandatory—a specific amount that must be ordered unless the judge puts on the record the reasons for the variance. The amount is primarily the result of two factors: the income of each parent and the custody time each has with the child. Reasons for varying from the guideline would include delaying the sale of the family residence for the benefit of the children or an extraordinary financial hardship.

The principles on which the guidelines are based are found in Family Code section 4053 and include, among others, the following:

1. A parent's primary obligation is support of his or her minor children according to the parent's circumstances and station in life.

2. Both parents are mutually responsible for support.

3. Each parent's actual income and level of responsibility.

4. Each parent's ability to pay support.

5. The state's top priority is the interests of children.

6. Children should share in the standard of living of both parents.

7. The children's financial needs should be met through private financial resources as much as possible.

If you and your spouse can agree on the amount of support, the judge will probably go along with it as long as the child's provisions are adequate. Even so, your proposed Judgment (form 18) must have language that:

1. The parents are fully informed of their rights regarding child support.

2. The agreement was made freely without duress, coercion, or threat.

3. The agreement is in the best interests of the child and the amount will adequately meet the needs of the child.

Child support also includes mandatory additional amounts for child care, to enable the custodial or part-custodial parent to work, as well as health insurance for the child. These amounts are the actual amounts spent and are usually shared equally between the parents regardless of their incomes unless the income spread is enormous.

CALCULATING
CHILD SUPPORT

The amount of child support is calculated by a formula set forth in Family Code Section 4055. However, because of the formula's relative complexity, most (if not all) judges and attorneys use a computer program. Two popular programs are *Dissomaster* and *SupporTax*. An easy way to find out how much child support you will have to pay, or receive, is to call a family law attorney and ask the fee to determine child support if you supply the custody time and the pay stubs of you and your spouse. You can also ask the judge to assess the guideline amount at your hearing. Although the courts have a computer program, most judges prefer to have a computer printout presented to them initially, even though they will still calculate the amount on their own.

It is not recommended that you try to figure the amount by means of the formula. However, if you decide to do so anyway, Family Code Section 4055 and the following example tell you how to do it. That section is reprinted in appendix A. Some of the terms in the formula need clarification.

☞ *Gross income.* Your overall income from all sources before any deductions. It includes your wages or salary before any deductions, and other forms of income such as rent checks, commissions, royalties, interest, pensions, bonuses, overtime, workers' compensation benefits, spousal support from another marriage, and the like. Remember that child support you receive from a previous marriage is not income, but spousal support is. If you or your spouse are self-employed, gross income is total receipts less expenses of the business, such as inventory, salaries, supplies, etc.

☞ *Net income.* This is gross income less federal and state taxes, state disability insurance, mandatory deductions such as union dues, and in some cases, retirement contributions, and child and spousal support being paid to a former spouse by court order. An extraordinary, unavoidable expense may also be deducted from gross income if you can convince the judge.

☞ *Annual net disposable income.* This is explained in Family Code Section 4059, which is reprinted in appendix A. Generally, it is the money left over after mandatory payroll deductions.

Here's how the formula works. Suppose we have a husband and wife with a total net disposable monthly income of $1,000 (generally, this is the money left over after mandatory payroll deductions). They have two minor children. The husband is the higher earning spouse with a $600 monthly income. He has twenty percent physical custody time with both children.

We begin with the formula:

$$CS = K [HN - (H\%)(TN)]$$

Where:

CS is the child support amount.

HN is the net monthly disposable income of the higher earning parent (the husband in our example).

H% is the percentage of custody time the parent with the higher income has. If you have several children with different times, use the average. In our example, the husband has twenty percent custody time for both children.

TN stands for the total net monthly disposable income of both parents.

K is the amount of both parents' income set aside for child support, arrived at by the following computation:

K = One plus H% if the higher earning parent has fifty percent of less custody time, OR

K = Two minus H% if the higher earning parent has more than fifty percent custody time. Depending upon which case is applicable, and in our example the first case is, you then multiply the one plus H% times one of the following fractions, depending upon the net disposable income range:

If total net disposable income per month is:	Use the applicable fraction:
$0 to 800:	$0.20 + TN/16,000$
$801 to 6,666:	0.25
$6,667 to 10,000:	$0.10 + 1,000/TN$
Over $10,000:	$0.12 + 800/TN$

In our example, the .25 fraction applies because the total net is between $801 and $6,666.

We then arrive at a value for K:

K = (1 + 0.20) x 0.25.

K = 0.30.

Because our couple has two children, we must multiply the final result by one of the following values:

2 children	1.6
3 children	2
4 children	2.3

5 children	2.5
6 children	2.625
7 children	2.75
8 children	2.813

So let's work the formula: we have a couple with two children where husband is the higher-earning spouse with $600 and has twenty percent custody of their two children. The couple's total net disposable income is $1,000 per month:

$$CS = K [HN - (H\%)(TN)]$$

Where:

HN	=	$600
H%	=	20%
TN	=	$1,000
K	=	(1 + 0.20) x 0.25
K	=	.30

Then:

CS	=	.30 [$600 - (20%)($1,000)]
CS	=	.30 [$600 - $200]
CS	=	.30 ($400)
CS	=	$120

Because the parties have two children, we multiply CS ($120) times 1.6. CS then equals $192. Child support is thus $192 which husband must pay to wife.

If the resulting figure, in our example $192, were a negative number instead of a positive number, the low-earner spouse would pay that amount to the high-earner spouse.

When you have more than one child, child support must be allocated so that the support amount for the youngest child is the amount of support for one child, and the amount for the next youngest child is the difference between that amount and the amount for two children with similar allocations for additional children. This doesn't apply where there are different time-sharing arrangements for the children.

After reading through the above example, you may be convinced to let an attorney do the calculation for you on his or her computer. The attorney should be able to do the calculation quickly for a modest fee, provided you can explain the deductions on your paycheck and know the custody time for the children. Be sure to get a printout from the attorney so that you can take it with you to your hearing.

Don't forget that child care costs and medical insurance are added onto the child support after you have calculated it using the statutory formula. Uninsured medical expenses are usually divided between the parties half-and-half, unless their income gap is unusually wide.

Spousal Support (Alimony)

Spousal support can be given to either husband or wife, and, as stated before, if you and your spouse agree as to the amount, the judge will probably go along with it. Spousal support is unlike child support in that it is not mandatory and there is no specific amount the court must use if it does award it. In practice, however, the computer program also cranks out a suggested spousal support figure along with the child support figure. Because Family Code Section 4320 lists so many factors to be considered in determining spousal support, the judge has wide discretion. Refer to chapter 8 for a more complete discussion of the factors the judge considers.

Some counties have rules of thumb for spousal support, but these change with the whim of the legislature and the facts of each case. One rule of thumb is to take forty percent of the paying spouse's net income, then deduct any child support obligation and fifty percent of the net earning income of the receiving spouse. But a better rule of thumb is to go to court prepared to discuss the factors discussed in chapter 8.

Spousal support is based on actual earnings, but if a spouse has voluntarily reduced earnings to lessen support, the judge can use an *ability to earn* test. Also, *new mate income* (income earned by an ex-spouse's new wife or husband) is not considered in determining spousal support although it is does provide an argument that expenses are decreased because of the additional income. Sometimes, the parties will separate their divorce into two phases. The first phase declares them divorced (this is called *obtaining status*, meaning that you and your spouse will obtain the status of being divorced). The second phase, which will resolve the property and support issues, is reserved for a later hearing.

A word about insurance in connection with support: Life insurance is a way to make sure support payments continue, or to pay off the mortgage on the home where the kids are living if the paying spouse dies. The law gives the court discretion to order the paying spouse to purchase an annuity or life insurance, or even to set up a trust, to protect the supported spouse's needs. The court may also order the paying spouse to include the children as beneficiaries of his or her life insurance. Generally, the cost of insurance premiums will be part of the support award. In making such an order, the court must look at the entire circumstances. In many cases, the parties have barely enough to pay for shelter and food, and insurance or the setting up of a trust is a luxury. On the other hand, if the parties are young, term life insurance is relatively cheap.

WHICH PROCEDURE TO USE

Technically, there are two divorce procedures (*summary* and *regular*); however, we will refer to three procedures because of some differences in how you will handle certain situations. Therefore, we will discuss the following three procedures:

1. Summary divorce procedure.

2. Uncontested regular divorce procedure.

3. Contested divorce procedure.

> ***Residency requirement.*** Before you can use any procedure either you or your spouse must have lived in California for at least six months, and in the county where your divorce case is being filed for at least three months, immediately before filing your Petition with the court. (*Note:* If you don't meet these residency requirements and need to file immediately, an attorney may be able to guide you around this obstacle.)

SUMMARY DIVORCE PROCEDURE

The summary procedure uses a different set of forms from the regular uncontested and the contested. The uncontested and contested use the same basic forms, but the contested will require some additional steps and forms so it is treated as a separate procedure. Chapter 6 of this book describes the summary procedure, chapter 7 describes the uncontested regular procedure, and chapter 8 describes the contested divorce. You should read this entire book once before you begin filling out any court forms.

To be eligible for the summary procedure, you will have to be able to satisfy many requirements. Chapter 6 provides more details about the summary divorce procedure.

UNCONTESTED DIVORCE PROCEDURE

If you can't qualify for the summary procedure, you will have to use the uncontested procedure or contested procedure. The uncontested procedure is mainly designed for those who are in agreement, but can't use the summary procedure because there are children or substantial property involved. The uncontested procedure may also be used when your spouse does not respond to your Petition (form 3) or cannot be located. In other words, the uncontested procedure can be used whenever your spouse will not be fighting you. Chapter 7 will provide more details about the uncontested procedure.

CONTESTED DIVORCE PROCEDURE

The contested divorce procedure is necessary where you and your spouse can't agree. This may be the result of disagreement over custody of the children, the payment of child support or spousal support, the division of your property, or any combination of these items. The section of this book dealing with the contested procedure builds on the uncontested procedure section. So, you will first need to read chapter 7 to get a basic understanding of the forms and procedures, and then read chapter 8 for additional instructions on the contested situation. Be sure to read both chapters before you start filling out forms.

If your case becomes contested, it is also time to seriously consider getting a lawyer. If you don't think you can afford a lawyer, you may be able to require your spouse to pay for your lawyer. Find a lawyer who will give you a free or reduced-cost initial consultation. He or she will explain your options regarding lawyer's fees. See chapter 3 for more information about lawyers.

General Procedures 5

Family Law Facilitator Act

In 1996, the California Legislature created the Family Law Facilitator Act (which will be called "the Act" in the remainder of this section) to aid families that cannot afford a lawyer. The reason for the Act is that the "current system for obtaining child and spousal support orders is suffering because the family courts are unduly burdened with heavy case loads and do not have sufficient personnel to meet increased demands on the courts…"

The basis for the Act is the "compelling state interest in having a speedy, conflict-reducing system for resolving issues of child support, spousal support, and health insurance that is cost-effective and accessible to families that cannot afford legal representation."

Under the Act, each county must maintain an Office of the Family Law Facilitator which will help in various areas, including:

- ☛ child and spousal support
- ☛ health insurance
- ☛ nullity of marriage (annulment)
- ☛ custody
- ☛ domestic violence

- educational materials
- order enforcement
- completing forms
- preparing support schedules
- meetings with the spouses
- reviewing documents
- preparing formal orders consistent with the court's announced orders

This act is found in sections 10000 to 10012 of the Family Code, and all the courts in the state are required to implement the program. If you wish to find out more about the program, call the clerk of the superior court in your county to find out if the program has been implemented and whether you can take advantage of it.

In early 2000, the California Judicial Council released three videos and related brochures in the area of general divorce law (including legal separation and nullity), applications for restraining orders, and responses to applications for restraining orders. The videos and brochures are specifically designed to aid persons representing themselves in the divorce courts and will be sent to every Family Law Facilitator office in the county, as well as to related offices such as legal aid clinics, domestic violence clinics, victim witness assistance offices, and libraries. Although these materials were not available at the time this book went to press, they will no doubt be an excellent resource if you are representing yourself.

These videos are a direct response by the California Judicial Council to the fact that the great majority of child support cases in the courts are managed not by attorneys, but by persons representing themselves.

The California Judicial Council is the policy-making body of the California courts—the largest such system in the nation. The Council is led by the chief justice of the California Supreme Court, and is responsible for ensuring consistent, independent, impartial, and accessible administration of justice for all of the state's residents.

The California Judicial Council also recently created four new forms for simplifying the modification of support orders. Modifying judgments is beyond the scope of this book, but if you already have a divorce and think the support provisions should be changed, you may be interested in going to your local law library and looking at Family Code Section 3680 and Judicial Council forms 1285.30, 1285.31, 1285.32, and 1285.33.

AN INTRODUCTION TO LEGAL FORMS

Most of the forms in this book are adopted by the Judicial Council of California and their use is mandatory. Although most are self-explanatory, some can be confusing. If you cannot cope with these, you really need to consult a lawyer.

Do not tear the forms out of this book to file with the court. It is best to make photocopies of the forms and keep the originals blank to use in case you make mistakes or need additional copies.

You should type the information on the forms. If typing is not possible, *print* the information required in the forms but be sure your writing can be easily read or the clerk may not accept your papers for filing.

Caution: Some, if not all, of the counties require the use of black ink on the forms. Therefore, whenever you sign a form, or if you print the information instead of typing, be sure to use a pen with black ink. Local court rules up and down the state are in constant flux; it is therefore advisable to type the forms or call the clerk beforehand to find out if you can print on the forms.

Courts have various rules that have absolutely nothing to do with the law and which, if not observed, will land your documents back in your lap. The variety and novelty of these rules vary from court to court, requiring you to check with the clerk as to what is and is not required. Listed below are some of the more common practices:

1. Almost all courts require two-hole punching of documents at the top. You can buy a two-hole punch at any stationery store, along with two-prong fasteners and manila folders so you can build your own file.

2. Most courts require your original documents to be typed. If you don't have access to a computer or a typewriter, call the clerk to see if you may print the information.

3. The type size and style of the font you use to type your documents should be that on a standard typewriter. If you're using a computer for typing a document for which there is not a standardized form, such as a declaration or Marital Settlement Agreement, use a type size and font which is at least as large as "Courier standard pica" or "Courier 12-point" type. A font equivalent to Courier is permitted. Use double spacing on paper with numbers for each line as shown on form 28. Although one-and-a-half spacing is permitted, don't use it because it isn't normally done and it won't fit on the normal 28-line paper. You can, however, use single spacing for quoted material.

4. Use only one side of the paper.

5. Have an extra copy of the *face sheet* (the first page) of all documents presented for filing. This requirement isn't universal, but have an extra face sheet with you in addition to the other copies you want file stamped in order to avoid potential delay.

6. Although the state-wide Rules of Court do not always mandate use of the Judicial Council forms, like those supplied in the back of this book, use them in *all* cases anyway because the local courts will almost always require their use.

7. A very few courts (for example, San Diego County) require certain forms to be on a certain color paper. If you're in one of those jurisdictions, either pick up the forms from the clerk's office or use the form in the back of this book and copy it on the required color.

8. A few years ago, an environmentally conscious California Judicial Council adopted a rule requiring the use of recycled paper for legal

documents. The problem was that, at the time, most stationery stores didn't even stock recycled paper; and in those that did, there was no selection, it was very expensive, it wasn't the right color, and it contained only a percentage of recycled paper. Consequently, the rule wasn't, and still isn't, being enforced. Enforcement may also be difficult because some recycled paper is not so identified with a watermark. But the rule exists, and anyone filing a paper with the court, or serving a legal paper, certifies by the very act of filing or serving that recycled paper was used; however, there is no penalty for not using recycled paper.

9. Another practice you'll occasionally find is the use of *blue backers*, which is a blue, heavier, oversized paper that is attached after the last page of a document (such as you may have seen with a will), with its sides and bottom extending beyond the margins of the paper, and the top folding over the top of the document. The official name for these is *manuscript cover*. Few courts use blue backers, and when they are used, there is confusion as to which documents must have them. For example, Los Angeles once required them, but in early 1999 it made them optional. If you are dealing with one of the few courts that require them, you would not use blue backers for the official California Judicial Council forms unless your particular court requires. You'll know if the form is an official California Judicial Council approved form by looking at the bottom left of the form. The purpose of blue backers was to distinguish original documents from copies. Identify all originals by putting a self-sticking removable note stating "original" on the first page of all original documents. Another practice many courts now require is the typing of a brief identification of the document for all non-Judicial Council forms at the bottom of every page beneath the page number, such as, for example, "Ex-Parte Petition" or "Declaration."

Each form found in appendix B of this book is referred to by both the title of the form and a form number. Be sure to check the form number because some of the forms have similar titles. The form number is found in the top outside corner of the first page of each form. Also, a list of the forms, by both number and name, is found at the beginning of appendix B.

You will notice that the forms in appendix B have the same heading information in the top portion of the form. The first box contains your name, address, phone number, and fax number if you have one (unless you have an attorney, in which case your attorney's information will go here). After the words "Attorney for", type your name, then a comma followed by the phrase "In Propria Persona," which means that you are representing yourself. In the next box, type in the name of the county for the superior court where you reside, along with the court's address.

Next, you need to type your full name on the line marked "Petitioner," and your spouse's full name on the line marked "Respondent." Do not use nicknames or shortened versions of names. You should use the names as they appear on your marriage license, if possible. You won't be able to fill in the case number until after you file your Petition with the clerk. The clerk will assign a case number and will stamp it on your Petition and any other papers you file. You must fill in the case number on all papers you file later.

When completed, the top portion of your forms should look something like the example on the following page:

ATTORNEY OR PARTY WITHOUT ATTORNEY*(Name, state bar number, and address)*	FOR COURT USE ONLY
MARY D. NOUGH 3333 HALIFAX RD. GARDEN GROVE, CA 99999 TELEPHONE NO.: 714-000-0000 FAX NO.: 714-000-0000 ATTORNEY FOR *(Name)*: MARY D. NOUGH, In Propria Persona	

SUPERIOR COURT OF CALIFORNIA, COUNTY OF ORANGE
STREET ADDRESS: 341 The City Drive
MAILING ADDRESS: PO Box 14170
CITY AND ZIP CODE: Orange, CA 92868
BRANCH NAME: Lamoreaux Justice Center -- Family Law

MARRIAGE OF	
PETITIONER: MARY D. NOUGH	
RESPONDENT: BEAU E. NOUGH	CASE NUMBER:

PETITION FOR	CASE NUMBER:
[X] Dissolution of Marriage [ ] Legal Separation [ ] Nullity of Marriage [ ] AMENDED	0000000

At the end of most of the forms there will be places for you to fill in the date, sign your name, and type or print your name. This book contains forms for your convenience. Bear in mind, however, that official changes to these forms can occur twice a year. The clerk's office can tell you if a form has changed. Be aware also that a few courts require certain forms to be a particular color, and courts require they be printed so that the bottom of side one is the top of side two (court files are fastened at the top rather than at the side like this book). You can copy the forms in the book onto colored paper and in the manner required.

Be advised that the clerk's office follows the rules to the letter and will reject your papers even if a seemingly insignificant box that should be checked is not. This can be irritating but it does eliminate problems that could occur later because a box is not completed.

At some time during the divorce proceeding, you may need to make a *declaration* (a statement under penalty of perjury) to the court, either to further explain something or in connection with a court form that doesn't have sufficient space for the information required. This book provides for that eventuality with a general Declaration (form 27), and with an Additional Page (form 28). Both of these forms have the required data and perjury statement to pass court muster.

FILING WITH THE COURT CLERK

Once you have decided which forms you need and have them prepared, it is time to file your case with the court clerk. First, make at least three copies of each form (the original for the clerk, one copy for yourself, one for your spouse, and one extra just in case the clerk asks for two copies or you decide to hire an attorney later).

Filing is actually about as simple as making a bank deposit, although the following information will help things go smoothly. Call the court clerk's office. You can find the phone number under the county government section of your phone directory. Ask the clerk the following questions (along with any other questions that come to mind, such as where the clerk's office is located and what its hours are):

☞ How much is the filing fee for a dissolution of marriage?

☞ Does the court have any special forms (other than the official forms) that need to be filed with the Petition? (If there are special forms which are not in this book, obtain them from to the clerk's office. There may be a fee, so ask.)

☞ How many copies of the Petition and other forms do you need to file with the clerk?

Next, take your Petition, and any other forms you determine you need, to the clerk's office. The clerk handles many different types of cases, so be sure to look for signs telling you to which office or window to go. You should be looking for signs that say such things as "Family Court," "Family Division," "Filing," etc. If it's too confusing, ask someone where you file a petition for dissolution of marriage.

The clerk will examine the papers and then do one of two things: either accept them for filing (and either collect the filing fee or direct you to where to pay it), or tell you that something is not correct. If you're told something is wrong, ask the clerk to explain to you what is wrong and how to correct the problem. Although clerks are not permitted to give legal advice, the types of problems they spot often are minor and they can tell you how to make the necessary corrections. Often, it is possible to figure out how to correct it from the way they explain what is wrong.

When speaking to the personnel at the clerk's office, ask specific questions; do not make open-ended pleas for help or ask "Tell me how to do this" questions. The clerk will probably tell you that he or she cannot practice law and that you should get an attorney.

NOTIFYING YOUR SPOUSE

A basic sense of fairness requires that a person be notified of a legal proceeding that involves him or her, and you use the Summons—Family Law (form 1) to do this. If you are using the summary dissolution procedure you do not need to worry about the information in this section (your spouse will have to sign the petition, so it will be obvious that he or she knows about the divorce). However, in all other cases, you are required to notify your spouse that you have filed for divorce. This gives your spouse a chance to respond to your Petition. If you are unable to find your spouse (and therefore can't have him or her personally served), you will need to read chapter 10. The notice requirements as they relate to particular situations will be discussed in later chapters.

NOTICE OF
FILING THE
PETITION

> *Note:* This subsection does not apply to the summary dissolution. If you use the summary dissolution procedure, you do not need to use the Summons—Family Law (form 1).

The usual way to notify your spouse that you filed for a divorce is called *personal service*, which is where the sheriff, marshal, or someone else personally delivers the papers to your spouse. You, being a party to the case, are not permitted to serve your spouse. A friend or relative over eighteen years may serve your spouse.

Call the sheriff's or marshal's office in the county where your spouse lives, and ask how much it will cost to have him or her served with divorce papers and what forms of payment they accept (they may not accept personal checks). Note that form 1 is a summons for family law cases. If you obtain the form from the clerk, make sure you get the form designated Summons—Family Law, and not a summons pertaining to other types of legal matters. To complete the Summons—Family Law (form 1):

1. Complete the "Notice to Respondent" by typing in your spouse's name.

2. Type your name after "Petitioner's Name Is."

3. In item 1, type the name and address of the court as shown on page 69.

4. In item 2, type your name, address, and phone number.

5. In the bottom box under item 2, check "a." Your spouse is being served as an individual.

6. Take form 1 to the clerk's office, along with your other documents, (see chapter 7) and the clerk will issue the Summons (form 1) by affixing the clerk's signature to it. Remember that you must put in the case number on all other forms once the clerk assigns the number.

7. After your spouse is served with this Summons—Family Law (and the other documents discussed in Chapter 7), check "c" under item 2 if he or she was personally served, i.e., someone handing the papers to the spouse.

Warning: On the back of the Summons—Family Law (form 1) you'll see a notice in English and Spanish. It states that you have read the notice and that you must abide by the automatic restraining orders printed there. This applies to you and your spouse. If you violate them by taking the children out of the state without consent, by transferring any funds without consent, or in any other way, you are in contempt of court and exposed to both civil and criminal court sanction.

Once the Summons—Family Law is served, you should file the Proof of Service of Summons (form 2) with the clerk.

Look at form 2 now. Notice that item 1 states that several documents were served. We haven't discussed those documents yet, so be patient. We'll get to them in chapter 7.

Serve only copies of forms. Never serve the originals of the documents; keep those for filing with the court. If a friend or relative will serve your spouse, provide one copy of the documents to be served. If the sheriff's or marshal's office will serve the papers, it is best to go to that office with at least two sets of all papers. You can call ahead to find out the service fee and how it must be paid, *e.g.*, by check or cash. You'll have to write instructions as to the location of your spouse, and times that you expect your spouse to be present at the location. It is a good idea to give a picture of your spouse to the person doing the serving. After your spouse is served, you'll receive back the Proof of Service of Summons (form 2) from the marshal or sheriff for filing with the court. If a friend or relative serves the papers, he or she will need to complete the Proof of Service of Summons.

Note that this form shows four ways to serve your spouse. Method "a," personal service, is far and away the best method.

Method "b," refers to *substituted service*. You use this when several attempts have been made to personally serve your spouse, but he or she is obviously trying to duck service. If that's the situation, hire a registered process server (check the phone book or an attorney's office) who will do the service legally and complete the Proof of Service of Summons correctly.

Method "c," "mail and acknowledge service," is used when you know your spouse's address and believe he or she will sign a form acknowledging service and send it back. This form is called a Notice and Acknowledgment of Receipt (form 6). Although this is an easy way to serve the initial papers, provided your spouse cooperates and sends the signed form back, personal service is still the better way to go. The court's power over your spouse is limited if all you have is mail service, and your spouse doesn't file any response to the Petition or otherwise formally appear. Further discussion in this area requires explanation of the types of court jurisdiction and related concepts, which are beyond the scope of this book.

Complete the top portion of form 6 the same as all the others. Insert your spouse's name after "To:" (under the caption), then sign and date it in the middle of the page where indicated. Place an "x" in each applicable box at item 2, as applicable. You'd normally only place an "x" in the boxes for "A copy of the summons and of the Petition (Marriage) and;" and "Blank Confidential Counseling Statement (Marriage)." Send your spouse two copies of the form by first class mail (not certified or registered mail), one for your spouse's file and one to return to you with his or her original signature, together with a self-addressed stamped envelope. And don't forget to include copies of the documents you checked in item 2.

Your spouse enters two dates: when the form was received and when it was signed. Your spouse then signs and prints his or her name.

Service by this method is complete on the date it is signed at the bottom by your spouse, and the thirty-day response period begins to run from that date. Remember that you must also complete and file a Proof of Service of Summons (form 2), attach it to the Notice and Acknowledgment of Receipt (form 6) bearing your spouse's original signature, and then file both forms with the clerk. Don't forget to check box "2c" on the Proof of Service of Summons (form 2). It is recommended, for reasons beyond the scope of this book, that you use personal service whenever you can.

Method "d" can be used if your spouse is out of state. For this method to work, your spouse will obviously have to be cooperative. If your spouse is out of state and not cooperative, you'll probably need an attorney's assistance.

OTHER NOTICES

Once your spouse has been served with the initiating documents, namely the Summons—Family law (form 1), Petition (form 3), a blank Response (form 22), and a blank Confidential Counseling Statement (form 5), you may serve copies of other documents on your spouse by mail. Of course, you could still use the personal service method (having the documents handed to your spouse), but that is not required. You cannot mail the copies yourself nor can you hand the copies to your spouse because you are a party in the action, so have a friend, relative, or process serving company mail or personally serve them. You'll need to file a Proof of Service By Mail (form 29) or a Proof of Personal Service (form 33) which are different from the Proof of Service of Summons (form 2). The person who signs either Proof of Service must be the person who placed the documents in the mail or who personally handed the documents to your spouse. Fill out either proof of service completely but do not have the person who will serve it (either by mail or personally) sign or date it; then staple a filled out but unsigned and undated copy of the proof of service to the back of the copy of the document being served and have that copy served. The person who served the copy signs and dates the original proof of service after he or she has served the document(s). Then staple this original proof of service to the original document and file it, keeping a copy of the document to which is attached the signed and dated proof of service for your records. (This may sound unduly complicated but one cannot sign that he or she did something until after doing it.)

COURT
HEARING DATE

This discussion is a little premature, but since we're dealing with notices, it's probably appropriate here. You can get a date for the final hearing to get the divorce when you've completed all of the required documents (and there are many more than we've already discussed) by asking the clerk's office the procedure. Clerks are not allowed to give legal advice, but they will tell you what form or procedure their court uses to set a hearing date. Once you get a hearing date, make sure you notify your spouse of such date, time, place, and courtroom number in writing, and complete a Proof of Service By Mail (form 29) [*not* the

Proof of Service of Summons (form 2)] for filing with the court, along with the form you served by mail. If you want a hearing date for some immediate or temporary relief, you'll have to prepare an *order-to-show cause* or *motion* papers. That task is beyond the realm of this book, so an attorney will probably be necessary. The subject is briefly discussed in chapter 11 under the section Temporary Support and Custody.

Be aware that the clerk will not accept any papers for filing unless they are accompanied by a Proof of Service (form 29 or 33), which shows you have served your spouse with copies of the papers you want to file. The legal system requires all parties to notify the other parties of documents being filed.

Courtroom Manners

There are certain rules of procedure that are used in a court. These are really rules of good conduct, or good manners, and are designed to keep things orderly. Many of the rules are written down, although some are unwritten customs that have just developed over many years. They aren't difficult, and most of them do make sense. Following these suggestions will make the judge respect you for your maturity and professional manner, and possibly even make the judge forget for a moment that you are not a lawyer. It will also increase the likelihood that you will get the things you request.

RESPECT   Show respect for the judge. This basically means, don't make the judge angry at you. Be polite, and call the judge "Your Honor" when you speak to him or her, such as "Yes, Your Honor," or "Your Honor, I brought proof of my income." Although many lawyers address judges as "Judge," this is not proper. Many of the following rules also relate to showing respect for the court. This also means wearing appropriate clothing, such as a coat and tie for men and a dress for women. This especially means no T-shirts, blue jeans, shorts, or "revealing" clothing.

COURTESY	Whenever the judge talks, you listen. Even if the judge interrupts you, stop talking immediately and listen. Judges can become rather upset if you don't allow them to interrupt.
ONE AT A TIME	Only one person can talk at a time. Each person is allotted his or her own time to talk in court. The judge can only listen to one person at a time, so don't interrupt your spouse when it's his or her turn. And as difficult as it may be, stop talking if your spouse interrupts you. (Let the judge tell your spouse to keep quiet and let you have your say.)
TALK TO THE JUDGE, NOT YOUR SPOUSE	Many people get in front of a judge and begin arguing with the other party. They turn away from the judge, face their spouse, and argue as if they were in the room alone. This has several negative results: With both talking at once, the judge can't understand what either one is saying; they both look like fools for losing control; and the judge gets angry with both. So whenever you speak in a courtroom, look only at the judge. Try to pretend that your spouse isn't there. Remember, you are there to convince the judge that you should have certain things. You don't need to convince your spouse.
WAIT YOUR TURN	Talk only when it's your turn. The usual procedure is for you, as the Petitioner, to present your case first. When you are done saying all you came to say, your spouse will have a chance to say whatever he or she came to say. Let your spouse have his or her say. When your spouse is finished, you will get another chance to respond to what has been said.
STICK TO THE SUBJECT	Many people can't resist the temptation to get off the track and start telling the judge all the problems with their marriage over the past twenty years. This wastes time and aggravates the judge, so stick to the subject and answer the judge's questions simply and to the point.
KEEP CALM	Judges like things to go smoothly in their courtrooms. They don't like shouting, name calling, crying, or other displays of emotion. Generally, judges don't like family law cases because the parties get too emotionally charged. So give your judge a pleasant surprise by keeping calm and focusing on the issues.

SHOW RESPECT
FOR YOUR SPOUSE

Even if you don't respect your spouse, act like you do. All you have to do is refer to your spouse as "Mr. Smith" or "Ms. Smith" (using your spouse's correct name, of course.)

NEGOTIATING

It is beyond the scope of this book to fully present a course in negotiation techniques. However, a few basic rules may be of some help.

ASK FOR MORE
THAN YOU
WANT

Asking for more than you want always gives you some room to compromise by giving up a few things and ending up with close to what you really want. With property division, this means you will review your Schedule of Assets and Debts (form 8) and decide which items you really want, would like to have, and those about which you don't care much. Also try to figure out which items your spouse really wants, would like to have, and doesn't care much about either way. At the beginning, you will say that you want certain things. Your list will include: (a) everything you really wan;, (b) almost everything you'd like to have; (c) some of the things about which you don't care; and (d) some of the things you think your spouse really wants or would like to have. Once you find out what is on your spouse's list, you begin trading items. Try to give your spouse things that he really wants and that you don't care about in return for your spouse giving you the items you really care about and would like to have.

Child custody is sometimes used as a weapon by one of the parties in order to get something else, such as more of the property, or lower child support. If the real issue is one of these other matters, don't be concerned by a threat of a custody fight. In these cases, the other party probably doesn't really want custody and won't fight for it. If the real issue is custody, you won't be able to negotiate for it and will end up letting the judge decide anyway.

If child support is involved in your case, you should first work out what you think the judge will order based upon the child support guidelines discussed in chapter 4. Do this before discussing the matter with your spouse. If you will be paying child support, you may want to try for slightly less than the guideline calls for, but keep in mind that the judge will probably look at the schedule and ask questions if you and your spouse are agreeing to less. This doesn't mean the judge will reject your agreement, but you may need to offer an explanation as to why you are not following the guidelines. You can tell your spouse that there is little room for negotiation on child support, as the court will require it be set according to the guideline if you can't agree. If your spouse won't agree on something very close to the guidelines, give up trying to work it out and let the judge decide.

LET YOUR
SPOUSE START
THE BIDDING

There is an old saying about negotiations that the first person to mention a dollar figure loses. Whether it's a child support figure or the value of a piece of property, try to get your spouse to name the amount he or she thinks it should be first. If your spouse starts with a figure almost what you had in mind, it will be much easier to get to your figure. If your spouse begins with a figure far from yours, you know how far in the other direction to begin your bid in order to arrive at a compromise closer to what you really want.

GIVE YOUR
SPOUSE TIME TO
THINK AND
WORRY

Your spouse is probably just as afraid as you about the possibility of losing to the judge's decision and would like to settle. Don't be afraid to state your "final offer," then walk away. Give your spouse a day or two to think it over. Maybe he or she will call back and make a better offer. If not, you can always "reconsider" and make a different offer in a few days, but don't be too willing to do this or your spouse may think you will give in even more.

KNOW YOUR
BOTTOM LINE

Before you begin negotiating, you should try to set a point which you will not go beyond. For example, if you have decided that there are four items of property that you absolutely must have, and your spouse is only willing to agree to let you have three, it's time to end the bargaining session and go home.

REMEMBER
WHAT YOU'VE
LEARNED

By the time you've read this far you should be aware of two things:

1. The judge must divide your property equally.

2. The judge must use the child support guideline.

This awareness should give you an approximate idea of how things will turn out if the judge is asked to decide these issues, which should help you to set your bottom line on them.

SUMMARY DISSOLUTION PROCEDURE 6

CAN YOU USE THE SUMMARY DISSOLUTION PROCEDURE?

In certain circumstances, you may take advantage of California's *summary dissolution procedure*. In order to use this procedure, you must meet certain requirements which are listed below. If you qualify, this is a cheap and easy way to get your divorce, with one caution: make sure that both you and your spouse are ninety-nine percent sure you agree on this procedure. If either of you change your mind within the six-month waiting period, you've just wasted a lot of time.

REQUIREMENTS
The procedure requires only a few forms, and although there are many requirements as you can see from the following, they are clear and easy to understand. To qualify for the summary dissolution procedure, you and your spouse must meet the following requirements:

1. You and your spouse must have read the *Summary Dissolution Booklet* you will obtain from the court clerk.

2. You were married for no longer than five years.

3. No children were born to you and your spouse before or during the marriage.

4. You and your spouse have no adopted children under age eighteen.

5. The wife is not pregnant.

6. Neither of you own any part of any land or buildings.

7. Your community property is not worth more than $25,000, not including cars or car loans.

8. Neither of you has separate property worth more than $25,000, not including cars or car loans.

9. Your community obligations are less than $5,000, not including cars or car loans.

10. At least one of you has lived in California for the past six months or longer, and in the county where you are filing for dissolution for the past three months or longer.

11. You and your spouse have prepared and signed an agreement which states how you want your possessions and debts to be divided between the two of you (or which states that you have no community property or community obligations).

12. You have both signed the Joint Petition for Summary Dissolution of Marriage (form 23) and the other papers needed to carry out the agreement.

13. You both want to end the marriage because of serious and permanent differences.

14. You both have agreed to use the summary dissolution procedure rather than the regular dissolution procedure.

15. You are both aware of the following facts:

    a) There is a six-month waiting period, and that either of you can stop the divorce at any time during this period.

    b) The marriage will be ended only if, after the waiting period, one of you files with the county clerk a Request for Final Judgment on the designated court form.

    c) After the dissolution becomes final, neither of you has any right to expect money or support from the other, except for what is included in the Property Settlement Agreement (which is part of the *Summary Dissolution Booklet* you must obtain from the clerk and read); and,

d) By choosing the summary dissolution procedure, you both give up certain legal rights that you could have had if you had used the regular dissolution procedure, such as support, the right to have the court decide any disagreements, the right to an appeal, and the right to a new trial.

If you qualify under all of the above, you should go to the courthouse and pick up the necessary forms. Call first because sometimes the forms are located at another branch of the court. Ask for the *Summary Dissolution Booklet* and for the forms that you will need.

If you don't meet all of the above conditions, you may *not* use the summary dissolution procedure. However, you may still want to read this section, as it may help you understand the standard procedure better. If the only requirement you don't meet is that you can't agree on the division of your property, you may want to reconsider your position on the property. Read this chapter, and have your spouse read it. Then compare the summary dissolution procedure to the standard procedures in chapter 7 and chapter 8 of this book. Once you see how much easier the summary procedure is, you may want to try harder to resolve your differences over the property.

THE PROCEDURE Basically, the procedure is as follows:

☛ You and your spouse complete the Joint Petition for Summary Dissolution of Marriage (form 23), and attach the worksheets from the *Summary Dissolution Booklet*.

☛ You file form 23 with the court clerk.

☛ You and your spouse wait six months.

☛ You or your spouse file the Request for Judgment, Judgment of Dissolution of Marriage, and Notice of Entry of Judgment (form 24).

☛ The court grants your divorce without the need of a court hearing.

The following is a discussion of the forms used in the summary procedure and of the procedure itself. ***Caution:*** You should also be aware that, with the summary dissolution procedure, neither of you may receive spousal support and there is no appeal.

JOINT PETITION FOR SUMMARY DISSOLUTION OF MARRIAGE

The Joint Petition for Summary Dissolution of Marriage (form 23) is the form used to open your case and ask for a divorce. Complete form 23 as follows:

1. Complete the top portion of the form according to the instructions in chapter 5.

2. Fill in the marriage date for item 2.

3. Items 3 to 8 are reminders to you of the qualifications required to use this procedure.

4. Item 9 directs you to complete and attach copies of the worksheets on pages 9, 11, and 13 of the *Summary Dissolution Booklet* that you've picked up from the clerk's office. (Note: In various places in the *Summary Dissolution Booklet*, the qualifying dollar amounts for community property, separate property, and debts may be incorrect. In order to save printing and distribution costs, the state has not reprinted this booklet to show the increased correct numbers of $25,000 for community property, $25,000 for separate property, and $5,000 for community debts. You'll know the definitions of community and separate property after reading the *Summary Dissolution Booklet.* The fair market value is what you, as a willing seller, could get for the item from a willing buyer if you sold it. It's not what you think the item should be worth.)

5. In Item 10, check box "a" if you have no community assets or liabilities. If you have community assets or liabilities, check box "b," and type up a Property Settlement Agreement according to the

sample in the *Summary Dissolution Booklet* on pages 15 through 18. Then attach that agreement to the Joint Petition for Summary Dissolution of Marriage (form 23).

6. Check the box for item 12 if the wife wishes to have her former name restored and type in her complete former name.

7. In the box at the top of the second page, fill in your name and your spouse's name where indicated. The case number will be filled in when you file your papers and the clerk assigns a case number.

8. Item 16 asks for your mailing addresses.

9. Sign and date the form where indicated, signing exactly as your names appear on the front of the form.

That's all there is to it. There is a filing fee you'll have to pay, so if you didn't ask when you picked up the forms, call ahead to find out the amount and the acceptable forms of payment (cash, money order, or check). If the clerk will take a check, find out how the clerk wants it to read. After the clerk files and stamps your copies, give one copy to your spouse. You should sign the form in California, but if for some reason you need to sign it while out of the state, have your signature notarized.

REQUEST FOR JUDGMENT, JUDGMENT OF DISSOLUTION OF MARRIAGE, AND NOTICE OF ENTRY OF JUDGMENT

After six months and one day from the date of filing the Joint Petition for Summary Dissolution of Marriage (form 23), you can file the Request for Judgment, Judgment of Dissolution of Marriage, and Notice of Entry of Judgment (form 24). This is really three forms combined into one. To complete form 24:

1. Complete the top portion of the form according to the instructions in chapter 5.

2. In item 1, type in the date you filed the Joint Petition for Summary Dissolution of Marriage (form 23).

3. In item 3, check box "a" if you want your dissolution to be effective immediately. If you want your dissolution to be effective at a date later than the time you file it, you must check box "b," and type in the date you want it to become effective and the reason for wanting this date.

4. Sign your name, fill in the date, and type or print your name where indicated. Notice that this form need only be signed and dated by one spouse.

5. If the wife wants her former name restored and she didn't request it on the Joint Petition for Summary Dissolution of Marriage, she can do so now by checking the box for item 4, typing in her full former name, and signing where indicated.

6. Item 5 at the bottom of the form is for the judge to complete.

7. On the back of form, type in your names and case number in the boxes at the top, and both your and your spouse's address in the boxes shown.

Remember to make several copies of the original after you complete it. The clerk will want at least three copies and maybe more depending on the county. And don't forget to always have an extra copy for your files and for your spouse.

NOTICE OF REVOCATION OF PETITION FOR SUMMARY DISSOLUTION

The Notice of Revocation of Petition for Summary Dissolution (form 25) is self-explanatory. If, during the six-month waiting period, you and your spouse decide to get back together, or if either of you decide to use the standard divorce procedure, this is the form to use. This is the easiest of all of the forms. Simply type it as you did the other forms, and sign it, date it, and fill in your and your spouse's addresses at the bottom. Then take it to the clerk's office and file it. Take at least four copies with you. You don't need your spouse's signature to do this. Either spouse can revoke the summary dissolution procedure during the six months.

If you don't revoke the divorce during the six months, one of you must file the Request for Judgment, Judgment of Dissolution of Marriage, and Notice of Entry of Judgment (form 24). If you don't, the court may dismiss your case for lack of action on your part.

UNCONTESTED DIVORCE PROCEDURE 7

You no doubt have already begun to experience the emotional pangs of divorce. What you are now about to discover is that the legal process is not calming. Courts do not have uniform procedures, and what procedures they do have change frequently. New forms are added, others are modified. Each court layers its own rules over statewide rules. Judges establish personalized procedures for their particular courtroom. When you understand this, you'll understand why this book is only a guide, and why, in the following discussion, you are so often told to call the clerk's office for information about procedures.

There are two ways that a case can be considered *uncontested*. One is where you and your spouse reach an agreement on every issue in the divorce, but don't qualify for the summary procedure. To be in this situation you must be in agreement on the following points:

1. How your property is to be divided.

2. How your debts are to be divided.

3. Which of you will have custody of the children, and in what percentage of time.

4. How much child support is to be paid.

5. Whether any alimony is to be paid, and if so, how much and for how long a period of time.

The other type of uncontested case is where your spouse doesn't respond to your Petition (form 3). If your spouse is served (see chapter 5 for more information about service) and does not respond, you will need to file certain forms. If you cannot find your spouse, you will need to file several other forms (see chapter 10).

Most lawyers have had the following experience: A new client comes in saying she wants to file for divorce. She has discussed it with her husband, and it will be a "simple, uncontested" divorce. Once the papers are filed, the husband and wife begin arguing over a few items of property. The lawyer then spends a lot of time negotiating with the husband. After much arguing, an agreement is finally reached. The case will proceed in the court as uncontested, but only after a lot of contesting out of court. For purposes of this book, a *contested* case is one where you and your spouse will be doing your arguing in court and leaving the decision up to the judge. An *uncontested* case is one where you will do your arguing and deciding before court, and the judge will only be approving your decision.

You may not know if you are going to have a contested case until you try the uncontested route and fail. This section assists you in the uncontested case. Chapter 8 specifically discusses the contested case.

To begin your divorce, the following forms should be taken to the court clerk in all cases (see chapter 5 for filing instructions):

☐ Any required local forms (for example, see the sample Certificate of Assignment form at end of this chapter on pages 131-3).

☐ Summons—Family Law (form 1). The clerk issues this form so that you can serve a copy of it on your spouse.

☐ Petition (form 3).

☐ Confidential Counseling Statement (form 5). In those counties requiring it, file this form.

Local forms are those required by individual counties. For example, Los Angeles County requires a cover sheet and calls it a Certificate of

Assignment. Orange County and some others require a *Child Information Handbook* (obtain a copy from the clerk) to be served on your spouse. Some courts have an individual information sheet they want served. San Diego County requires certain forms to be on different color paper. In larger counties, such as Los Angeles County, each of the different branch superior courts within the same county may have different local forms, and even different procedures. Ask the clerk if there are any special local forms needed.

Other official forms, some mandatory and some depending upon your situation, will also need to be filed. These include:

- ☐ Request to Enter Default (form 13).
- ☐ Declaration for Default or Uncontested Dissolution or Legal Separation (form 14).
- ☐ Declaration Regarding Service of Declaration of Disclosure and Income and Expense Declaration (form 10).
- ☐ Appearance, Stipulation and Waivers (form 12).
- ☐ Schedule of Assets and Debts (form 8).
- ☐ Income and Expense Declaration (form 9).
- ☐ Proof of Service of Summons (form 2).
- ☐ Wage and Earnings Assignment Order (form 21).
- ☐ Judgment (form 18).
- ☐ Notice of Entry of Judgment (form 20).
- ☐ Stipulation to Establish or Modify Child Support and Order (form 16).
- ☐ Marital Settlement Agreement (MSA) (form 17).

These and other additional forms are found in appendix B and are discussed as appropriate in this book.

These forms can be tricky. Fill them out *completely* and *carefully*. Have someone else check them over before you take them to the court clerk for filing, just in case you forgot to check a box or fill in a blank. That omission could be enough for the clerk to reject the document. These forms will be discussed in detail later.

Once you complete and file the necessary forms, you have the choice of either:

1. delivering or mailing your papers to the court and getting your Judgment back in the mail, or

2. appearing before the judge to get your Judgment.

If you choose to go to court, you'll first have to apply for a court date. Local practice may vary, so be sure to ask the clerk's office for the procedure to obtain your Judgment.

To get your Judgment by either method, your forms will have to be in order. It might actually be faster to get a court date than to submit papers by mail because if the clerk rejects them for some reason, you'll have to correct and resubmit them. That could take longer than if you just waited for your court date. Of course, if you appear on your court date and the judge finds your papers are incomplete or incorrect, you'll have the same problem. However, you probably have a better chance of getting the problem fixed right then and there because the judge has more power and discretion than the clerk and would like to clear your case from the calendar.

As mentioned above, some courts require a *cover sheet* to be filed with your Petition. You'll have to call the clerk in your particular county to find out if a cover sheet is required. If it is, you can obtain the form from the clerk. The sample beginning on page 131 is a cover sheet used in Los Angeles County, called a Certificate of Assignment.

SUMMONS—FAMILY LAW

The Summons—Family Law (form 1) will need to be completed with the original issued by the court clerk and a copy served on your spouse along with the Petition. See chapter 5 for information on completing form 1 and serving your spouse.

PETITION

The Petition (form 3) must be completed in all cases. This is the paper you file to begin your case. The Petition should be accompanied by a Confidential Counseling Statement (form 5) if required by your court. The Petition may also be accompanied by other forms depending upon your situation. The following instructions for form 3 are based on the assumption that you and your spouse are in agreement on everything.

To complete the Petition (form 3):

1. Complete the top portion of the form according to the instructions in chapter 5.

2. In the "Petition For" box, check the box for "Dissolution of Marriage." Do not check the box for "Amended" unless you've made a substantial error and are refiling the Petition.

3. In item 1, check the box that applies. Check both boxes if both of you satisfy the residency requirements.

4. In item 2, provide the requested information. The date of separation is when you definitely decided to divorce, even though you may still be living in the same place as your spouse. It would be wise for the two of you to agree in writing as to the date of separation. That's the date you decided to divorce; it is not the date you and your spouse temporarily separated to test the marriage. The separation date affects the community property value of a pension or other fund where the community property interest is from date of marriage to date of separation. The separation date is the date after which you and your spouse's earnings and debt are no longer community earnings or debt. An attorney's advice is recommended if there are separation-date issues.

5. In item 3, check either "a" or "b," and provide the requested statistical information if you check "b."

6. If there are minor children of the marriage, note that item "3c" requires you to complete the Declaration Under Uniform Child Custody (form 4) You will note that item "3d" refers to a "voluntary declaration of paternity" form. Such a form is not applicable to married parents; it is used primarily by social workers at the hospitals to establish paternity for children born out of wedlock. If you have such a form, it would have been completed before you were married, usually at the hospital at the time your child was born. If the father signed the form at the hospital and did not rescind it within a short time thereafter, and he is now the spouse in the divorce case, he cannot deny being the father.

7. Check the box next to item 4, and type under "Item" those pieces of property that you claim are your separate, not community, property. If there is not enough space, check the box marked "in Attachment 4," and attach a page containing this information, labeling it "Attachment 4 to Petition." If your spouse claims certain property as separate, list that property and type either "Petitioner" or "Respondent" under the "Confirm to" section. (Remember, the Petitioner is the spouse who files the Petition.) "Confirm to" means that you agree that the property listed belongs to you or your spouse as his or her separate property.

8. Fill out the top portion on the back of the form just like you did the other forms.

9. In item 5, check box "a" if there are no assets or obligations for the court to divide. In other words, you have no community property. If you do have community property, you should check box "b" or "c." Check box "b" if you and your spouse have written, or will write, a Marital Settlement Agreement (MSA) (form 17) in which you divide the community property. Check box "c" if you do not have, and do not intend to have, a written MSA. If there is enough room below item 5 for you to list the assets and obligations that

need dividing, list them in that space. If you need more space check the box marked "in Attachment 5." Then list the assets and obligations on an Additional Page (form 28), label it "Attachment 5 to Petition," and staple it to the Petition. Be sure to fill in the case title and number at the top of the Additional Page.

10. In item 6, check boxes "a" and "(1)," indicating you are requesting dissolution of your marriage based on the ground of irreconcilable differences. Checking those two boxes permits the court to grant you a divorce.

11. Item 7, boxes "a" through "i:" References to "children" are to the minor children of your marriage and to those still unborn if the wife is pregnant. It does not include stepchildren or children eighteen years of age and older. However, the duty of support continues for an unmarried child who (1) has reached eighteen; *and* (2) is a full-time high school student; *and* (3) is not self-supporting; in which case support will continue until the time the child completes the twelfth grade or attains the age of nineteen years, whichever occurs first. Check these boxes as follows:

Item "a:" Check the box under "Joint." Legal custody refers to the decision-making aspects of child rearing, such as religious training, medical decisions, special needs, and the like. Routinely, both spouses jointly participate in these decisions unless there are extraordinary problems, such as physical or substance abuse, or total disinterest by one parent. If a special problem exists, check the box for the spouse that will retain sole legal custody. Remember that the legislature's dictate to the courts in this area of law is the health, safety, and welfare of the children.

Item "b:" This box has major psychological implications. If you check physical custody for one spouse, then the other spouse is necessarily reduced to having only visitation rights with the children. Do you as a parent want a court order stating that you as father or you as mother shall only be permitted to "visit" your own children? It may be best to check joint physical custody even though the actual custody time is not equal. Child support can still be based on the actual percentage of time with the children and the spouses' respective incomes, so there's no harm in doing this. On the other hand, if you or your spouse do not have a problem with making one spouse the primary custodial parent, indicate that.

Item "c:" This box relates to the above discussion. If you decide that one spouse will have physical custody, then the other necessarily has visitation rights. Check the box so indicating that. The "Supervised for" language refers to situations where a parent has a drinking or drug problem, or a history of abusing the children, or some other negative that would put the children in danger were they to see such parent alone. If this is applicable, the court is going to want to know the facts because it is the best interests of the children the court is obligated to protect. The proceeding can still proceed as uncontested, but you may well have to appear in court if the "Supervised for" or "No Visitation for" is checked to explain things to the judge.

Item "d:" Check this box if the two of you had children together before your marriage and parentage was established by a voluntary declaration of paternity as discussed in number 6 above and pertaining to item "3d" on the front of this form.

Item "e:" If you have decided that one spouse will pay spousal support, check the box showing which spouse will pay. Note that the form states payment will be by wage assignment. This is mandatory unless you and your spouse agree otherwise. Wage assignment means nothing other than having the spousal support payment coming directly from the paying spouse's employer. This can benefit both spouses because it eliminates arguments over if and when payments were made. Child support will also be paid by wage assignment. A wage assignment is not a garnishment or an indication of bad credit. It is a method of making support payments that at the same time eliminates any question as to amount or date paid.

Item "f:" Ignore this item. You don't have an attorney so there are no attorney's fees.

Item "g:" Check this box if you and your spouse agree that you will *not* pay spousal support to your spouse.

Item "h:" Check this box if you checked item 4 or item "5c" above.

Item "i:" If the petitioner wants her or his former name restored, check this box and type in the full former name.

12. Item 8 is a notice about child support and item 9 is a verification that you have read the restraining orders on the Summons-Family Law (form 1). Be sure that you read and understand the restraining orders. At the bottom of the form, you'll see a notice about reviewing your will, insurance, etc. It's good advice, take it, unless you want your ex and his or her new spouse to collect your insurance proceeds.

13. Date and sign the form where indicated at the bottom. Above the dotted line marked "(Type or Print Name of Attorney)," type or print your name with the phrase "In Pro Per" (short for "In Propria Persona") after it. That phrase simply means you are acting as your own attorney. Your Petition is now ready for filing.

DECLARATION UNDER UNIFORM CHILD CUSTODY JURISDICTION ACT (UCCJA)

The Declaration Under Uniform Child Custody Jurisdiction Act (UCCJA) (form 4) must be completed and attached to the Petition (form 3) if there are minor children of the marriage.

Form 4 is straightforward and needs no explanation. If you must use form 4, file it along with the Petition. (Note also that this is the form referred to in the Petition in item 3c.) You would ordinarily not keep the address of the children confidential unless you had a good reason. The word *declarant* means you.

CONFIDENTIAL COUNSELING STATEMENT

Most courts use the Confidential Counseling Statement (form 5). Fill in the top portion of the form according to the instructions in chapter 5, then simply check the appropriate box to indicate whether or not you want counseling. You usually have the opportunity for one free consultation, even before filing any papers. If you wish, get the number from the clerk's office and schedule an appointment, with or without your spouse, but try to bring your spouse with you.

STARTING YOUR DIVORCE PROCEEDING

The documents mentioned above are all that are required to get the divorce going. Before you have your spouse served, be sure you have:

☐ Completed the Summons—Family Law (form 1).

☐ Completed and filed the Petition (form 3).

☐ Completed and filed the Confidential Counseling Statement (form 5).

☐ Completed and filed the Declaration Under Uniform Child Custody Jurisdiction Act (UCCJA) (form 4).

☐ Completed and filed any other documents required by the court.

☐ Had the clerk issue the Summons—Family Law (form 1).

You now need to serve these documents on your spouse. See the section in chapter 5 on "Notifying Your Spouse" for details on how to go about having your spouse served.

PRELIMINARY DECLARATION OF DISCLOSURE

Sometimes one spouse may feel inclined to hide certain property, despite the restraining orders referred to on the back of the Summons—Family Law (form 1). To avoid this, the law requires both spouses to voluntarily reveal to the other all property he or she has, both separate and community, on the Declaration of Disclosure (form 7). There are both a *preliminary* and a *final* Declaration of Disclosure. They are the same form, but are served at different times, the final version being used for updating purposes.

Although you and your spouse may waive the final Declaration of Disclosure, you may not waive the preliminary Declaration of Disclosure. Each spouse must serve the other with the preliminary Declaration of Disclosure within sixty days from the date you serve your spouse with the initial documents [the Summons—Family Law (form 1), Petition (form 3), Confidential Counseling Statement (form 5), and any local forms]. You can also serve form 7 with the initial papers. Both spouses owe a duty of fair dealing and full disclosure to the other. If a spouse is found to have deliberately hidden property or to have disclosed it without sufficient particularity, the court can prevent the noncomplying spouse from presenting evidence on issues that should have been covered in the Declaration of Disclosure and sanction such noncomplying spouse with a money penalty. Because the Code requires this be done by a legal motion, you may want to contact an attorney if you find yourself in this situation.

Neither the preliminary nor final Declaration of Disclosure is filed with the court, but the Declaration Regarding Service of Declaration of Disclosure and Income and Expense Declaration (form 10) is filed. Form 10 is brief and contains only two items: Whether you are the respondent or petitioner, and when and how you served the final Declaration of Disclosure on your spouse. Note that only form 10 is filed; you do *not* file with it any other documents or information. The preliminary Declaration of Disclosure forms must be exchanged between you and your spouse.

To complete the Declaration of Disclosure (form 7):

1. Complete the top portion of the form according to the instructions in chapter 5.

2. Check box 1 and complete and attach the Schedule of Assets and Debts (form 8).

3. Check box 2 and complete and attach the Income and Expense Declaration (form 9).

4. Check box 3 and write and attach a statement as the form requires. As an example, if a home is involved and you know of information that would affect its valuation, you must disclose it.

5. Check box 4 and write and attach a statement as to any information you have that would affect a community obligation. For example, if a community debt is really more (or less) than what appears, you must disclose this.

6. Check box 5 and write and attach a statement if you know of any investment opportunity that arose since your separation.

If you have no information that applies under boxes 3, 4, and 5, indicate that fact on the form itself beneath the item. For example, if you have no information of any investment opportunity in Item 5, write "I have no knowledge of any investment opportunity since separation." Then sign, print your name, and serve it on your spouse.

The Declaration of Disclosure (form 7) is really only a cover sheet for two other documents and three statements, all made under penalty of perjury. These will be discussed below.

SCHEDULE OF ASSETS AND DEBTS

The Schedule of Assets and Debts (form 8) is a four-page form, the first three pages relating to assets and the last page for debts. You must (1) list all your property, separate and community; (2) indicate under the column "Sep. Prop." whether any separate property is husband's "H" or wife's "W" (leave this column blank if the item is community property); (3) show the approximate date you obtained the property; (4) show the gross fair market value (*gross* means without deducting for any debt against it); and (5) show the amount of the debt against it.

Complete the Schedule of Assets and Debts (form 8) as follows:

1. Complete the top portion of the form according to the instructions in chapter 5.

2. Under item 1, list all real property, and attach a copy of the deed, with its legal description and latest lender's statement.

3. Under item 2, list all *special* furniture separately. If your furniture, appliances, and furnishings are pretty ordinary, don't list every bed and table and use a garage-sale value for all of it. (If you or your spouse want to list everything to avoid an argument later, that's fine.)

4. Under item 3, identify valuable items and use the fair market value, not what you paid for it and not what you could possibly get for it; its value is what a willing seller could get from a willing buyer today. Do not list inexpensive costume jewelry or drug store watches.

5. Under item 4, describe your cars and boats and attach a copy of the pink slip, if you have it, or the registration, and show the value and loans.

6. Under items 5, 6, and 7, identify the financial institution and the account number and attach the latest statement.

7. Items 8 and 9 are self-explanatory.

8. For item 10, call your insurance agent to find out the cash surrender value of any life insurance you have. If the policy has a value, attach a copy of the declaration page of the policy and the information you obtained from the agent.

9. Item 11 is self-explanatory, but be complete.

10. Under items 12 and 13, you may need to contact your company's pension department or the administrator of the plan you have at work. Retirement accounts are community property for that portion of the time worked from marriage to time of separation. You may be surprised at the large value. These include profit

sharing plans, 401(k) plans, defined benefit plans, etc. If either of you have a substantial retirement account, you should seek professional advice as to these items.

11. Item 14 is asking for the value of any money owed you from someone else.

12. For item 15, you must attach the IRS K-1 partnership form and/or the IRS Schedule C form included in your income tax return. All business interests should be described here including corporations, limited liability companies, or any other interest.

13. Under item 16, list any other assets not mentioned.

14. If you need more space to list everything, use attachment pages and label each attachment page with the name and number of your case. For any such pages, total the two right-hand columns and write the totals in item 17.

15. In item 18, write in the totals for the two right-hand columns.

16. On page 4 of the form, list your debts under the appropriate headings in items 19 through 24. The only item requiring explanation is item 21, "Support Arrearage." If you are behind in spousal or child support payments from a previous marriage, list the amounts here. You need to attach a copy of the court order showing the support to be paid and a statement showing the arrearage dates and amounts. If you need more space to list everything, use attachment pages and label each attachment page with the name and number of your case. For any such pages, total the "Total Owing" column and write the total in item 25. In item 26, write in the total for this column.

17. Check the box for item 27 if you have attached any additional pages, and write in the number of additional pages.

18. Fill in the date, print your name, and sign you name where indicated at the bottom of page four.

If you don't have all of the information for this preliminary Declaration of Disclosure, put "unknown." If your spouse has all the paperwork and it's not accessible to you, try to get it. The law requires diligence to complete this form, and the fact that the information is not handy in your top dresser drawer doesn't excuse you.

INCOME AND EXPENSE DECLARATION

The Income and Expense Declaration (form 9) is the second form that must be attached to the preliminary Declaration of Disclosure.

> *Note:* There is a Financial Statement (Simplified) (form 11) that can be used instead of form 9 if you qualify. This simplified form is self-explanatory and the instructions for using it are printed on the reverse side of the form. Your income must be from certain sources and you need to attach proof. Read the instructions on form 11 in appendix B to see if you qualify to use it instead of form 9. Even if you qualify, you may want to use the Income and Expense Declaration (form 9) anyway, as form 9 does not require proof of income and your case may be delayed if you use form 11 and the court later decides you need to use form 9.

The Income and Expense Declaration is long, but not difficult. It does not require the proof documents that the simplified form does and does not have the risk of delay if you used the simplified form when you shouldn't have. To complete the Income and Expense Declaration (form 9):

1. Complete the top portion of the first page according to the instructions in chapter 5.

2. Note that the forms have labels at the bottom, such as "Income Information," "Expense Information," etc. Complete Steps 1 and 2 on the first page, then go to the "Income Information" page. Note that the amounts on this page for items 1, 2, and 3 are annual amounts, not monthly; but the amounts for items 4 through 16 are monthly amounts, not annual.

3. Item 1 refers to your gross income, which is your wage before any deductions, and includes bonuses, commissions, and overtime. If you are self-employed, attach a schedule showing gross receipts less expenses such as inventory and salaries. Item 2 is self-explanatory. Include everything other than the exclusions listed. Item 3 asks you to add all your income and then divide it by 12 to get a monthly gross amount, which you put on line "4a."

4. For items 5, 6, and 7, enter the actual tax you pay according to actual exemptions, not necessarily what you have told your employer to deduct each pay period.

5. Items 8, 9, and 10 are the actual deductions for those items.

6. In item 11, enter the mandatory, not voluntary, contributions deducted from your pay.

7. Item 12 refers to support payments you are paying for a previous marriage or relationship.

8. For items 13 through 16, do what the form says to do.

9. The information required for items 17 through 21 has probably been gathered for the Schedule of Assets and Debts form, so enter the totals. You can also state "see Schedule of Assets of Debts" in item 21 and enter the total. The form requires you to attach a copy of your three most recent pay stubs.

The following items (10 through 14) refer to the "Expense Information" page of form 9. Remember that all amounts are monthly.

10. Don't forget to complete the box at the very top.

11. In item "1a," list yourself and anyone else living in your home who has expenses you are paying for; for example, a child or parent. If such person earns income, list the gross income.

12. In Item "1b," list all persons living in your home for whose expenses you do not pay. If such person has income, provide that and the other information asked.

13. Item 2 is a listing of your monthly expenses. List them as required. Note that item "2o" calls for the total of the installment payments listed in Item 3.

14. In item 4, list the costs you have paid. The rest of item 4 is not applicable because you are representing yourself, so put "N/A" on the signature line for the attorney.

The following items (15 through 18) refer to the "Child Support Information" page of form 9 and must be completed if child support is an issue.

15. Item 1 as to health insurance is self-explanatory.

16. Item 2 is important because the percentage entered here is a major factor in the amount of child support the court will order unless you and your spouse have agreed to an amount.

17. In item 3, note that child care costs are in addition to child support. If you show uninsured health care costs, educational or other special needs, or child visitation expenses, you need to show details.

18. Item 4 addresses extraordinary and catastrophic situations. You need to show the details and attach any documents supporting your claims.

When you have completed pages 2, 3, and 4, go back to page 1 and complete the balance of that form by inserting the totals asked. Then, as before, date it, and print and sign your name where indicated.

SERVING YOUR SPOUSE

You must serve your spouse with a copy of your preliminary Declaration of Disclosure (form 7), the attached Schedule of Assets and Debts (form 8), and Income and Expense Declaration (form 9). Service can be by mail. Complete and file the Declaration Regarding Service of Declaration of Disclosure and Income and Expense Declaration (form 10) to show that you complied with the law by serving your spouse with the preliminary Declaration of Disclosure (form 7). For your own records in case you are challenged, complete and keep in your file the original Proof of Service By Mail (form 29) that you used in mailing the Declaration of Disclosure to your spouse. (Refer to the section Other Notices in chapter 5.)

WHEN YOUR SPOUSE WON'T COOPERATE

So what happens if your spouse won't exchange the Declaration of Disclosure (form 7) with you? You then need to make a record of your attempt to get him or her to exchange the form. You do that by mailing a copy of your Declaration of Disclosure to your spouse's last known address, and at least one certified *and* one regular letter informing your spouse of his or her legal duty to serve you with his or her preliminary Declaration of Disclosure. Then, using the Declaration (form 27), write a statement as to what you've done to try to get your spouse to comply and file it with the court. The purpose for doing this is to anticipate a judge's question as to why both Declaration of Disclosure forms weren't exchanged. The last paragraph of the statement must state: "I declare under penalty of perjury under the laws of the state of California that the above is true and correct. Executed at _____ (*city*), California on _____, _____ (*date*)." Then sign it. Form 27 already has this required information. If you need more space, use an Additional Page (form 28) and label it "Attachment to Declaration," typing the case name and number at the top of the Additional Page.

FINAL DECLARATION OF DISCLOSURE

The final Declaration of Disclosure (form 7) may be waived by you and your spouse if you have a Marital Settlement Agreement (MSA) (form 17), or if the divorce is a default divorce (i.e., where your spouse either doesn't respond to the Petition, or responds but doesn't show up at court on the trial date). Remember, however, that you must have served the *preliminary* Declaration of Disclosure on your spouse because that requirement is not waived.

The final Declaration of Disclosure is the same as the preliminary Declaration of Disclosure, except that the "final" updates the "preliminary." If your case becomes contested, both you and your spouse need to serve the final Declaration of Disclosure on each other not later than forty-five days before the first assigned trial date. If your case is uncontested, but you and your spouse do not waive the final Declaration of Disclosure in the Marital Settlement Agreement (MSA) (form 17) or in the Declaration for Default or Uncontested Dissolution (form 14), you both need to exchange your final Declaration of Disclosure forms at the time you prepare your MSA. Neither the preliminary nor the final Declaration of Disclosure is filed with the court, but each of you must file a Declaration Regarding Service of Declaration (form 10) for the *preliminary* Declaration of Disclosure in any event.

Stipulation for Child Support

Some courts require a Stipulation to Establish or Modify Child Support and Order (form 16) and some do not. A helpful clerk may answer your questions about the forms required.

Generally, the Marital Settlement Agreement (MSA) (form 17) replaces form 16. The word *stipulation* means *agreement*, and there is no need for two agreements where one will suffice. Nevertheless, some courts require both of these forms. Complete the Stipulation To Establish or Modify Child Support and Order (form 16) as follows:

1. Complete the top portion of the forms according to the instructions in chapter 5.

2. In item 1, check box "a," and enter the net incomes of both spouses (you already determined this on the Income and Expense

Declaration (form 9). If you have an attorney friend who has one of the computer programs certified by the courts, you may check box "b" instead, and attach the printout.

3. Check the appropriate boxes, and enter the information for items 2 and 3 in detail, making sure it corresponds to the information you entered for hardship on the Income and Expense Declaration (form 9).

4. If you know the amount from the support guidelines, which you can obtain from an attorney who has one of the computer programs, fill in this amount in item 4, along with the name of the person who will be paying support (you or your spouse).

5. Check item 5 if you and your spouse agree to the amount determined by the guideline.

6. Check item 6, and not item 5, if you and your spouse do not agree to the guideline amount and wish a different amount. Enter the amount you do agree to.

7. Complete the item 7 boxes as applicable, remembering to total all amounts contributing to the child support in the box "(7c)."

8. Fill in the names and case number called for in the box at the top of the second page of the form.

9. Item 8 is self-explanatory as to health insurance.

10. For item 9, it is recommended that the Wage and Earnings Assignment Order (form 21) not be stayed. A wage assignment eliminates potential disagreement and potential attorney's fees later by having the support paid directly by the payor's employer to the payee spouse. Arguments over missed or late support payments are eliminated with a wage assignment. Make it easy and let the employer make the payments. A wage assignment won't work, of course, if the payor spouse is self-employed.

11. The balance of the form is self-explanatory, but don't forget to date the form, print your name and sign it, and type "In Pro Per" after your name so the court knows you're representing yourself.

Marital Settlement Agreement (MSA)

The Marital Settlement Agreement (MSA) (form 17) is the document in which you and your spouse state your agreement regarding matters such as property division, spousal support, child support, custody, and visitation. (For simplification, this form will be referred to as an MSA in this section.) You will note that form 17 contains optional provisions for you to choose from by checking a box. It is more common for the MSA to be prepared individually, rather than using a form. This check-the-box format may, or may not, be acceptable to the court in your county. It would be advisable for you to re-type form 17, using only those provisions that apply to your agreement.

The following information will help you to either fill-out form 17 or type an original MSA using form 17 as a guideline:

1. In the first, unnumbered paragraph, type in the date, the wife's name, and the husband's name on the three blank lines.

2. In paragraph 1, type in the date of your marriage.

3. In paragraph 2, type in the date you and your spouse agree is the separation date.

4. In paragraph 3, fill in the county and case number.

5. In paragraph 4, check the first box if no children were born or adopted during your marriage. If you have children, check the second box and type in their names and birthdates.

6. In paragraph 5, type in your and your spouse's social security numbers on the appropriate lines.

7. In paragraph 6, check the box beside the statement that reflects your situation. If you check the second box, type in a brief description of the health problem or problems.

8. In paragraph 7, type in the names of employers and monthly income for you and your spouse on the appropriate lines.

9. In paragraphs 13 through 16, list your and your spouse's community and separate property in the appropriate paragraphs. If real property is included, type the complete address and full legal description. If the legal description is lengthy, make a clear copy of it and attach it to the MSA, stating in the appropriate paragraph of the MSA that "the legal description to this property is attached as Exhibit A and incorporated herein by this reference." The legal description may be found on the deed.

The real property is often the only substantial asset and if there are children, you may want to arrange that one spouse remain in the home with the children until a later time, if it makes economic sense. If you do so agree, include a clause in the MSA that the house will be sold at some date in the future and the proceeds divided evenly. During the time one spouse remains in the home with the children, that spouse would normally pay the upkeep of the home, including mortgage, taxes, and insurance. However, the cost of a capital improvement, such as a new roof or other major repair would normally be divided equally between the parties. If there is substantial equity in the home, you may want to seek the help of an attorney for the drafting of this particular issue.

10. List the wife's debts in paragraph 18, dividing them into the three categories listed, and list the husband's debts similarly in paragraph 19.

11. Regarding paragraph 22, if either you or your spouse has substantial retirement or other employee benefits, remember that such benefits are community property to the extent they were earned during the marriage to the time of separation. These include IRAs, 401(k)s, 403(b)s, pension plans, and Keoghs, SEPs, and others. If the value is substantial, talk to an attorney and see an actuary so you know the community property value. Half of the community value is yours. Any such item must be included in the MSA and must be the subject of an additional court order, called a *QDRO* (which stands for *Qualified Domestic Relations Order*). This QDRO is then sent to the administrator of the plan or account, who in turn takes

the appropriate community property interest out of the employee spouse's account and creates an account for the other spouse. As you have probably guessed, this is an area for which you'll need an attorney. These retirement plans are often worth much more than you'd think, and you won't really know what its value is unless you get professional help. It is often the largest asset of the marriage.

12. In paragraph 23, check the box for the sub-paragraph that reflects your agreement regarding spousal support, and fill in any other items that need completing in the sub-paragraph you select. As of January 1994, the legislature defined a reasonable period of time for spousal support as "one-half the length of the marriage," but did not deprive the judge of discretion to order a greater or lesser period of time. But when the parties intelligently agree between themselves as to spousal support, such agreement will normally stand. Note also that life insurance may be used as a support tool. However, as you get into more exotic conditions, you will want to have the agreement reviewed by an attorney.

13. In paragraph 24, check the box for the sub-paragraph that reflects your agreement regarding child custody and fill in any other items that need completing in the sub-paragraph you select. Note that form 17 has a standard visitation schedule in the event you and your spouse don't agree as to what is reasonable. If you wish to have a different schedule, you will need to re-type the form and insert the schedule you desire.

14. In paragraph 25, check the appropriate boxes and fill in the information required to reflect your agreement on child support.

15. You and your spouse will need to date and sign the MSA before a notary public. *Be sure to have your signatures notarized.* You will note that there are two notary spaces in the event that you and your spouse do not sign at the same time and place.

A word of caution: if you and your spouse are going to get "fancy" with how support is to be paid, or with how certain property is to be divided, have a lawyer look over your agreement. The last thing you want is to have to return to court because no one knows what a certain provision means, or worse, you want to change it because you didn't foresee the legal consequences of the fancy provision.

Remember that in an MSA, you and your spouse can divide your property any way you want. If you don't agree, and leave it to the court to divide, the court must divide the property equally and will perhaps divide it in a way you don't want. The judge would much prefer to have you settle everything yourself and just present the completed Judgment for his or her signature.

As of July 1, 1999, a new rule made it mandatory that the MSA be attached to and filed with the new Judgment form (form 18) which now has a box to check for attaching the MSA. All you need to do is check box 4i of the Judgment and attach the MSA to it. [Although that was the procedure used by most courts previously, a few courts, notably Los Angeles, required the provisions of the MSA to be retyped in the mandatory language a judge would use in an order (for example, "Respondent shall pay to Petitioner the sum of…") and attached to the Judgment as additional pages of the Judgment itself. The MSA was then attached as an exhibit to the Judgment.]

To resolve your issues, unless you have no community property, no children, no community debts, and no support issues, you'll need an MSA. That's the only way your case can be settled, unless, of course, you go to trial and get a Judgment or stipulate to a Judgment at the hearing.

REQUEST TO ENTER DEFAULT

Your spouse is required to file a Response within thirty days after being served with a copy of the Summons—Family Law (form 1) and Petition (form 3). If your spouse does not file a Response within this time period, you may seek a *default* by filing a Request to Enter Default (form 13). This form is used in either of the following situations:

1. Your spouse is personally served and fails to file a Response within thirty days (and you do not give an extension of time).

2. You can't locate your spouse.

Once a default is entered, it prevents your spouse from participating further in your divorce case.

In many cases, provided the two of you have agreed on everything, the default of your spouse will be by agreement to save the Response filing fee. If you and your spouse are not in agreement, but for whatever reason he or she doesn't bother to respond to the Summons—Family Law (form 1) and Petition (form 3) within the thirty days, you can file the Request to Enter Default (form 13).

Once the clerk enters your spouse's default, your spouse cannot contest the proceeding and you can go ahead with the forms you need to complete your case and get your divorce. (Note that because your defaulted spouse could obtain an attorney to try to set aside the default, it makes more sense to let your spouse file a response even if it is late.)

Bear in mind once again that different counties have different policies. There are some subtle traps that could throw you off track if you proceed by default. For example, if you are the husband/petitioner and your wife wants her maiden name back, you would check the box on the Judgment form that accomplishes this. But if you and your wife agree to proceed by way of default to save the response filing fee, your papers might be bounced by the clerk because your wife would be asking the court to change her name when she has not appeared in the case, and if she appears in the case, a response filing fee is due. Some courts will accept your wife's signature on the judgment without requiring a response fee. You and your spouse may also wish to *stipulate* (agree) to something after the default has been entered. In that case the court may not accept the agreement unless the response filing fee is paid.

Exactly what triggers the clerk to ask for a response filing fee varies from county to county. Certainly, the response filing fee is due if your spouse files a Response (form 22). But sometimes your spouse agrees that the divorce can proceed by default because you've agreed on everything and he or she wants to save the response filing fee, which is approximately $190.

Even if your spouse doesn't file a Response, he or she may still have to pay the response fee. As an example, if your spouse signs a Marital Settlement Agreement (MSA) in San Diego and San Francisco county, your spouse would not have to pay the fee, but in Orange County your spouse would have to pay the fee. Bottom line: You need to call the clerk to find out the policy.

Often it is more efficient, even when you and your spouse have no disagreement, to have the other spouse file a Response and pay the response filing fee. This eliminates traps and encourages exchange of required documents such as the preliminary Declaration of Disclosure forms. But, because the Response makes the matter contested, you would both have to sign and file the Appearance, Stipulation, and Waiver (form 12) when you request your Judgment to tell the court that your matter is really uncontested. Form 12 is explained later in this chapter.

When the Judgment, with the MSA, is ready to be submitted to the court for signature granting the divorce, you would file an Appearance, Stipulation, and Waiver (form 12) with the Judgment, which tells the court that both of you agree the action may now proceed as an uncontested, as opposed to a default, divorce. This eliminates a trial and also permits you to obtain your divorce without a court appearance, if you so choose, by filing all the papers with the court clerk.

Opinions differ on this, and how best to proceed may depend on local practice. If there is little property and no substantial issues, you may want to proceed by default just to avoid having one spouse pay the Response fee. But if you decide to proceed by default, or must proceed by default because your spouse has not filed a Response, complete the Request to Enter Default (form 13) as follows:

1. Complete the top portion of the form according to the instructions in chapter 5.

2. For items 2 and 3, check the applicable boxes. If you do not attach the Income and Expense Declaration (form 9) and the Property Declaration (form 15), you must explain why in items (1) through (5). If there are no issues of support, property, custody, or attorney's fees, you don't need to attach these forms. If there are such issues, but all issues are addressed in a Marital Settlement Agreement (MSA), you would only need to attach the Income and Expense Declaration forms. (However, you may want to check with the clerk to confirm local policy.) Item (6) refers to a paternity proceeding so leave it blank.

    If the form requires you to attach the documents, remember that the preliminary Declaration of Disclosure already includes this information, so all you need to do is attach an updated Income and Expense Declaration. The Property Declaration is very similar to the Schedule of Assets and Debts. Simply transfer the information from one form to the other and state in the last two columns of the Property Declaration your proposal as to who gets what. Then sign and print your name and date it.

3. Item 3, "Declaration," requires you to give the clerk a copy of the form (with any attachments) and an envelope with sufficient postage on it addressed to respondent's last known address, or to respondent's attorney if he or she has one, unless you served your spouse by publication. (Refer to chapter 10 for more information on publication.) Use the court clerk's address for the return address or the envelope because the clerk will do the mailing.

> ### *Caution*
>
> To avoid rejections by the clerk's office, note that there are four places where you date it, print your name, and sign.
>
> Your spouse has thirty days to file a Response, so you cannot file a Request to Enter Default until the next day—the thirty-first day. And if the thirtieth day falls on a weekend or court holiday, the time is extended to the next court day. Be aware also that your spouse may have filed the Response but neglected to serve you with a copy. Check the court file before you file the Request to Enter Default to make sure.

4. On the back of the form in item 4, check the box at the top waiving costs and disbursements, and enter the date, your printed name, your signature, and the place you signed.

5. In item 5, sign, print, date, and fill in the place you sign just as above, provided your spouse in not in the military. If you don't know if your spouse is in the military, refer to the section below on "Military Service Considerations."

File the form and any attachments with the clerk and provide the clerk with two copies for mailing back to respondent and to you. Don't forget the stamped envelopes, one addressed as item three states and the other addressed to you. Type the clerk's return address on the envelopes, as stated under no. 3 above.

DECLARATION FOR DEFAULT OR UNCONTESTED DISSOLUTION

The Declaration for Default or Uncontested Dissolution (form 14) is used when your spouse either defaults (doesn't file a Response to the Summons—Family Law and Petition), or you and your spouse agree on all issues. In either of these two cases, you can seek a Judgment without having to go to court. If your spouse has defaulted, you can file this form with the Request to Enter Default (form 13) above, the proposed Judgment (form 18), and the Notice of Entry of Judgment (form 20). In the second case where your spouse has not defaulted (has filed a Response) but the two of you agree on all issues, you file the Declaration for Default or Uncontested Dissolution (form 14) with the Appearance, Stipulation, and Waivers (form 12), which states that your spouse agrees to no longer contest any issues.

If you already filed the Request to Enter Default (form 13) and received a copy back showing the default was entered, attach a copy to the Declaration for Default or Uncontested Dissolution or Legal Separation (form 14) so the clerk makes no mistake that the default was in fact entered. When you and your spouse are not seeking support, the procedure should work well. However, if support is an issue, you might want to get a court date. The reason is that if the judge reviewing your papers has a question about the matter, especially child support, and you've chosen this *declaration* route rather than a hearing, the judge can't get an answer. Also, the clerk may return your entire package because you've forgotten to check a box on one of the forms.

In either case, your papers will be sent back to you for correction and resubmission or with a note to set the matter for a court hearing. Either way, you'll have to resubmit your papers and go back to the end of the line (normally). Result: More delay. Conclusion: If you feel confident your documents are in order and the support agreed to is at or near guideline, try using the Declaration for Default or Uncontested Dissolution or Legal Separation. Otherwise, get a court date and appear. Even though you appear, you may still get sent home with directions to resubmit. But you've got a chance the judge will permit you to make changes on the spot or give oral evidence to overcome some deficiency.

Complete the Declaration for Default or Uncontested Dissolution or Legal Separation (form 14) as follows:

1. Complete the top portion of the form according to the instructions in chapter 5.

2. Check the box in the caption area for "Dissolution."

3. In Item 3, check the box for "Petition."

4. In Item 4, check "a" if your spouse has not filed a Response and you have already filed the Request to Enter Default (form 13). Check "b" if your spouse has filed a Response to the Petition and you filed the Appearance, Stipulation, and Waivers (form 12), which tells the court that your spouse has agreed not to contest any issues.

5. In item 5, you must check either "a" or "b." If you do not have a Marital Settlement Agreement (see MSA form 17), you must check either box "b(1)" or "b(2)." The "Stipulated Judgment" box at "5a" is checked when you or your spouse show up in court on the day of the trial but settle the case before the trial begins. You'd then write up your settlement on a stipulated judgment form available in the courtroom and take it to the judge to sign.

6. In item 6, complete the boxes as applicable. If you become confused, refer to chapter 7 and review the sections on Preliminary Declaration of Disclosure and Final Declaration of Disclosure. You would normally leave box "a" blank and check box "c" if you have an MSA, and box "b" if you don't.

7. If you have custody and visitation issues, make sure your proposed Judgment addresses them and check the boxes for items 7 and 8.

8. In item 9, ignore the "Family Support" box unless you've talked with an attorney and know what you're doing. If spousal support is an issue, attach a current Income and Expense Declaration (form 9), unless you've already filed it, and check at least one of the boxes. You'd check box "a" if you don't want spousal support now or in the future; box "b" if you don't want spousal support now but may want it later; and "c" if you've covered the subject in the MSA (which is part of the Judgment). If the concepts confuse you, review the spousal support sections in chapter 4.

9. Items 10 through 13 are self-explanatory. The only box needing some clarification is box "d" in item 13. If your spouse intentionally

reduces his gross income to pay less child or spousal support, and you can prove it, the court may order support based not your spouse's actual earnings but rather on the amount he or she has the ability to earn. Remember that *gross* income is income before any deductions and *net* income is the income after taxes and all other mandatory deductions.

10. Item 14 would only be checked if you checked box "3d" on the Petition (see above discussion in paragraph 6 under Petition in this chapter).

11. Leave the item 15 box blank because you do not have an attorney.

12. Items 16, 17, 18, and 19 are self-explanatory.

13. Do not check box 20. This box would only be checked if you need an immediate judgment (after the six-month mandatory wait) stating that you are no longer married and are keeping all other issues (such as property, custody, and support) open to be decided later. This separating of issues, called *bifurcation*, is beyond the scope of this book because bifurcation requires a motion to the court and raises many legal issues with respect to preserving property rights. If you need bifurcation, talk to an attorney.

14. Ignore box 22, which is for legal separations.

15. Date, sign, and print your name where indicated.

Note: If you are asking for a custody order in a default where your spouse has not been served by personal service and has not appeared in the case, you should file a certified copy of the birth certificates of all children with the clerk.

APPEARANCE, STIPULATION, AND WAIVERS

The Appearance, Stipulation, and Waivers (form 12) requires a response fee to be paid with it if your spouse hasn't filed a Response (form 22). Form 12 is used when local court policy requires a response fee if a

Marital Settlement Agreement (MSA) is to filed with, or as part of, the Judgment. As mentioned in the discussion on the MSA, some courts require a response fee and some don't when an MSA is filed with the Judgment. If your county requires the fee, your spouse files the Appearance, Stipulation, and Waivers (form 12) instead of the Response, and pays the fee. The concept is that you must pay for the right to have a court consider your requests. Because your spouse is asking the court to consider requests made in the MSA, he or she must pay (in counties requiring it). Form 12 is also used when the case changes from contested to uncontested. For example, you and your spouse disagreed on several issues so your spouse filed a Response. But now you both agree on all issues. The two of you would then sign and file form 12, telling the court the case can proceed as uncontested and that you're waiving your right to a trial. Form 12 has other waivers also, which you and your spouse should be sure to read and understand before signing.

To complete the Appearance, Stipulation and Waivers (form 12):

1. Complete the top portion of the form according to the instructions in chapter 5, and check box 1 if your spouse has not filed a Response.

2. Check box 2 only if your spouse has already filed a Response. (If he or she has, no additional filing fee is paid.)

3. Check box 3 only if your spouse is in the military and is waiving his rights as a member of the military.

4. Check box 4. Presumably the reason you're both filing this form is that you've resolved all differences.

5. Check box 5 because you've got no *triable* issues.

6. Check box 6. A commissioner, although not a judge, is appointed on the basis of ability and experience, and will be able to handle uncontested matters. It will also speed things along because a judge may not be available.

7. Check box 7 if you and your spouse have signed a Marital Settlement Agreement (MSA).

8. Check box 8 if you're submitting the Judgment at a later time with or without the Marital Settlement Agreement (MSA).

9. Check box 9 if you and your spouse have signed a Marital Settlement Agreement (MSA).

10. Leave box 10 blank. This refers to a separate action and procedure called Petition to Establish Parental Relationship, which is outside the scope of this book.

11. If you and your spouse are agreeing to something not covered in items 1 through 9, check box 10 and specify your agreement.

12. Sign and date the form.

MILITARY SERVICE CONSIDERATIONS

If you know for sure your spouse is *not* in the military, you date, sign, and enter the place where you signed, in item 5 of the Request to Enter Default (form 13) as stated above. But what if you don't know for sure and can't really sign item 5 of the Request to Enter Default? Then don't sign item 5. The clerk should still enter the default under the law. The only problem is that if your spouse is active in the military, he or she may be able to set aside (void) the default judgment pursuant to the 1940 Soldiers' and Sailors' Civil Relief Act, and you'd have to start over.

Don't get confused: the default you obtain from the clerk after filing the Request to Enter Default is different from the default judgment. The default here pertains to your spouse not responding to the Petition within the time allowed. Even though you have the default, you must still obtain the Judgment, referred to in such case as a *default* Judgment.

If you cannot state unequivocally that your spouse is not in the military, you could file a statement showing facts that would support a reasonable presumption that your spouse is not in the military.

Maybe you don't have a clue whether your spouse is in the service, but you want to protect against a possible setting aside of the Judgment if it turns out he or she is in the military. In that case, use the Memorandum of Request for Military Service Status (form 26) to find out if your spouse is active in the military and where. If your spouse isn't active in the military, you can sign Item 5 on the Request to Enter Default or file the negative responses from the military service branches. You might want to call the military branches beforehand to determine if there is any fee for them sending the information.

You will need to make seven copies of the Memorandum of Request for Military Service Status (form 26) and mail one to each of the seven addresses listed on the form. Be sure to enclose a stamped envelope addressed to yourself with each one. Each branch will then check its records, and send you a written statement as to whether or not your spouse is in that branch. If a response shows your spouse to be in the military, you can send him or her notice of the divorce and try to reach an agreement so you can use the uncontested procedure. If such attempts fail, you should contact an attorney.

JUDGMENT

Caution: Court clerks' offices throughout California are being unnecessarily burdened by both attorneys and persons doing their own divorces who neglect to attach to the Judgment the two forms which the Judgment (form 18) at item 4h clearly states must be attached; these are the Notice of Rights and Responsibilities (form 19) and Information Sheet on Changing a Child Support Order (form 38). Without these attachments, your Judgment will be returned to you without the judge's signature. Additionally, the Judgment requires you to submit a third form, called the Child Support Case Registry Form (form 37). This form does not have to be submitted at the time you submit the Judgment, but you must do so within ten days of the Judgment date. This form is not "filed" (simply hand it to the clerk) so DO NOT attach it to the Judgment. None of these forms are required, naturally, if you have no child support issues. (See discussion below.)

The Judgment (form 18) officially tells the world you are divorced. It contains all of the terms you and your spouse agreed to, or what the judge orders. If a provision isn't in the Judgment, you can't enforce it in court. An oral agreement you have with your spouse carries no weight.

The Judgment shows the effective date of your divorce, which cannot be earlier than six months and a day from the date you served your spouse with the Summons—Family Law. (For example, if you served your spouse on October 22, 1999, your divorce would not be effective until April 23, 2000.) You can request a later effective date if the date is crucial for some reason, such as qualifying for your spouse's social security or for tax reasons.

Your judgment will consist of the Judgment (form 18) with various attachments and the Marital Settlement Agreement (MSA) (form 17) if you have one. As of July 1, 1999, the Judgment form was revised to include a box to check if you are attaching a Marital Settlement Agreement (MSA). This new mandatory form will eliminate the practice of some courts requiring the MSA to be retyped into mandatory "judge" language and included within the Judgment itself, and also requiring the MSA to be attached to the Judgment as an exhibit. (The MSA is discussed in chapter 7.)

The July 1st revision to the Judgment form has numerous attachments, and attachments to attachments. Some of the attachments are merely information sheets and most won't be applicable if you and your spouse have an MSA. An important change, item 1 on the first page relating to "personal conduct restraining orders," requires a short digression here.

There are two types of restraining orders: personal conduct orders and property orders. The July 1st revisions removed personal conduct restraining orders from the divorce procedure and made them an exclusive and separate action under the Domestic Violence Protection Act (sections 6200 to 6390 of the Family Code) because of heightened concern over domestic violence. This book does not explain personal conduct restraining orders because they are no longer part of the procedure to obtain a divorce. They are now a separate procedure to protect a spouse from physical violence while obtaining a divorce. There is no need to cover the area in this book because an excellent informational booklet entitled *Domestic Violence Restraining Orders Instruction Booklet* with forms is available free from the court clerk. Refer to chapter 11 under the heading "Protecting Yourself, Your Children, and Your Property" for more information regarding this subject. Any personal conduct restraining orders obtained, however, are attached to the Judgment form.

Property restraining orders, on the other hand, are still part of the divorce procedure and will usually be effective only while the divorce is pending. Such orders relate to restraining the spouses from dealing with any of their property and whether one spouse must leave the family residence.

Complete the Judgment (form 18) as follows:

1. Complete the top portion of the form according to the instructions in chapter 5.

2. In the "Judgment" box, check the box for "Dissolution." If you and your spouse have agreed on a particular date for the divorce, which is after six months and a day from time of service, enter it after the words "Date marital status ends:." You may want a specific date for social security eligibility or tax reasons. If you don't, leave it blank.

   If you want a particular date, include it (for example, "We hereby agree on the date of November 1, 2000, for marital status to end") in the Appearance, Stipulation, and Waivers (form 12), and the Marital Settlement Agreement (MSA) (form 17), if you have one. Unfortunately, your spouse will have to pay the response filing fee in order for you to file the Appearance, Stipulation, and Waivers form. It is strongly suggested that if you opt to get your divorce by filing the documents with the clerk, instead of appearing in court, that you attach a large note to your papers that you want the particular divorce date indicated and give the reason.

3. In item 1, leave the boxes blank unless you have previously obtained personal conduct restraining orders under the Domestic Violence Prevention Act, as discussed immediately above and in chapter 11.

4. In Item 2, check the box for "default or uncontested" if you opted for the court hearing method, and the other box if you are going to file everything with the clerk's office and avoid a court appearance. Leave all the other boxes blank, except check box "2c" if you want a court hearing.

5. In Item 3, after the colon, enter the date your spouse was served with the Summons—Family Law (form 1) or the date he or she filed a response to the Summons—Family Law. Check the box marked "Respondent was served with process" if you filled in the date your spouse was served with the Summons—Family Law. Check the box marked "Respondent appeared," if you filled in the date your spouse filed a Response.

6. Check item "4a" and box "(1)." If you don't need a particular date, leave the space after the colon blank. If you want a particular date, type the date after the colon. (Skip items "4b," "4c," "4d," and "4e.")

7. In Item "4f," check the box for a former name being restored and type it in full.

8. In Item "4g," check the box.

9. Check item "4h" if the Judgment provides for child support, and attach (staple) the Notice of Rights and Responsibilities (form 19) and the Information Sheet on Changing a Child Support Order (form 38) to the Judgment. If you don't attach these forms, the clerk will probably reject the Judgment. The third form, Child Support Case Registry Form (form 37) is NOT attached to the Judgment, but rather submitted to the clerk separately. Note that it does not have to be submitted at the time of filing the Judgment, but can be submitted within 10 days from the date of the Judgment.

If there is a change of information on the registry form (form 37), you must update a new form and provide it to the clerk within ten days of the change. This is confidential information and the form is not "filed," meaning it is not included in your public courthouse file but sent to a state agency for informational purposes. Use the instruction sheet (pages 3 and 4) of the form to complete it. Both you and your spouse must each file a separate form.

10. Items "4i" through "4m" refer to several forms as follows:

☞ Marital Settlement Agreement (form 17)

☞ Child Custody and Visitation Order Attachment (form 39)

☞ Supervised Visitation Order (from 40)

☞ Child Support Information and Order Attachment (form 41)

☞ Non-Guideline Child Support Findings Attachment (form 42)

☞ Stipulation to Establish or Modify Child Support and Order (form 16)

☞ Spousal or Family Support Order Attachment (form 43)

Wouldn't it be nice if you could ignore all these attachments? Well, you can—provided you and your spouse complete a Marital Settlement Agreement (MSA) (form 17). These attachment forms need only be completed if you don't have an MSA or a stipulated judgment. (If you've forgotten what a stipulated judgment is, refer to the chapter 7 section entitled "Declaration for Default of Uncontested Dissolution.") With an MSA, you're not asking the judge to step in the ring with you and your spouse and referee against low blows, biting and gouges and then decide the match. Instead, you and your spouse agree to both win without even stepping inside the stadium, so you never give the judge the chance to decide your match. Having a stranger sort out the delights and detritus from your years of wedded bliss may not be the best way to go anyway, although sometimes it can't be avoided. And when it can't, the judge will decide your match with the help of the above attachment forms.

Notice boxes "4k," "4l," and "4m" on the left side of the Judgment form, each of which states that "...is ordered as set forth in the attached...." On the right side of the form, there are several choices for each item and the first choice for each is a box for Marital settlement agreement. If you have an MSA, you would check any of the items "k," "l," or "m" that apply and the corresponding box on the right for the MSA, and then you'd be done after checking the "Notice" box in the middle and counting the number of attached pages for item 5.

On the other hand, if you don't have an MSA, and you have issues of custody, visitation, and support, you must check the box on the right for the attachments that apply and complete them according to the instructions below. You should know that there is a free booklet available from the clerk's office entitled *Domestic Violence Restraining Orders Instruction Booklet*, which, although applying only to personal conduct restraining orders, contains forms identical to forms 39 to 43 in this book with specific instructions for completing them. It would be an additional aid but should not be necessary with the description provided below.

11. Check item 4i at the top of page two if you and your spouse signed a Marital Settlement Agreement (form 17).

12. It is unlikely you would check item "4j." A stipulation (agreement) for judgment is used when you and your spouse do not have a Marital Settlement Agreement and are contesting issues; then when the two of you show up at the courthouse on the trial date, you agree to everything without trial. You would then complete the stipulation for judgment form available inside the courtroom. However, you would still have to prepare the formal Judgment (form 18) and file it at the court later, along with the above attachment forms.

13. If item "4k" applies, check the box and also the box on the right side of the form for "Marital settlement agreement" and attach the MSA. If you don't have an MSA, you'd check the box for the Child

Custody and Visitation Order Attachment and complete that form (form 39). Remember that what you're doing here is completing formal proposed orders for the judge to sign after you've appeared in front of the judge and presented your case. You would take form 39 to court with you, completed to your liking; the judge could then change it to his liking based on your testimony. Or if your spouse is present, you both could agree to a visitation schedule and check box "2e(iv)," attaching the schedule as "Attachment 2e(iv)."

14. If item "4l" applies, check the box and also the box on the right side of the form for "Marital settlement agreement," leaving the other boxes blank. The Non-Guideline Child Support Findings Attachment (form 42) box would be checked and the form attached only if you don't have an MSA and the child support ordered by the judge is different from the computer-generated guideline amount. If you do have an MSA, you must include in it the required language justifying the non-guideline support. The MSA (form 17) in this book contains the required language. You would take the form to court with you, completed to your liking; the judge could then change it to his liking based on your testimony.

15. If item "4m" applies, check the box and also the box on the right side of the form for "Marital settlement agreement." Also check the box for the Notice. Leave the other boxes blank. As in item "4k" above, if you don't have an MSA, check the box for Spousal or Family Support Order Attachment (form 43) and complete it. You would take the form to court with you, and the judge could change it based on your testimony. Supply your and your spouse's gross and net incomes and check the appropriate box if either of you receive public assistance. Also check the proper boxes in item 4, leave the box for item "4c" blank, and check boxes for items 5 and 6.

16. Leave item "n" box blank, unless you and your spouse bore a child together before marriage and parentage has been established either by a voluntary declaration of paternity or thorough a previous legal

action you brought. (Refer to paragraph 6 of the section entitled Petition in chapter 7.)

WAGE AND EARNINGS ASSIGNMENT ORDER

The Wage and Earnings Assignment Order (form 21) is mandatory for all child and spousal support orders. This form is served on the paying spouse's (obligor) employer who must by law withhold the support amount up to fifty percent of the obligor's wages and send it to you (the receiving spouse or obligee). It is up to you as the obligee spouse to have the order served on the employer, which you can do by mail. Once it is served, the employer has ten days in which to process the order. Even if you can't locate the employer, you still must submit this form with the Judgment so that you'll have it when you do locate the present or future employer. Although you can agree with your spouse to ask the court to *stay* (hold) the order on certain grounds, the court will remove such stay upon your declaration that the payments have been late.

It is probably better for both of you not to ask for a *stay*. By law, the employer may not in any way impair the employee spouse's status with the company. The regular payment by the employer of the support establishes a record for the support payments for both spouses, and eliminates argument as to whether a payment was missed or late.

Complete the Wage and Earnings Assignment Order (form 21) as follows:

1. Complete the top portion of the form according to the instructions in chapter 5.

2. Check the box under the title of the form only if you are modifying a previous order.

3. Complete "To the Payor" by typing in the paying spouse's full name and birthdate.

4. In item 1, check the appropriate box and enter the amount of support ordered by the court; then total the amounts at "1c."

5. In item 2, type in your name and address.

6. Skip item 3, unless back support is included.

7. Skip item 5, unless you are modifying a previous order.

8. Item 8 will normally be blank.

9. Skip item 9, unless back support is included.

NOTICE OF ENTRY OF JUDGMENT

The purpose of the Notice of Entry of Judgment (form 20) is to establish when the Judgment was entered in the records of the court. Complete the Notice of Entry of Judgment (form 20) as follows:

1. Complete the top portion of the form according to the instructions in chapter 5.

2. Check the box in item 1.

3. In the box showing the "Effective date of termination of marital status," leave it blank and let the clerk fill in the date.

4. Type in your name and address and that of your spouse in the two boxes at the bottom of the form.

Also supply the clerk with two stamped envelopes with the clerk's address as the return address, one should be addressed to you and the other addressed to your spouse. If you don't know your spouse's address, type in the last known address.

SUPERIOR COURT OF CALIFORNIA, COUNTY OF LOS ANGELES

SHORT CASE TITLE	CASE NUMBER
	FAMILY AND PROBATE CASE COVER SHEET- CERTIFICATE OF GROUNDS FOR ASSIGNMENT TO DISTRICT

This form is required in all new Family and Probate cases in the Los Angeles Superior Court.

This form is not required in Abandonment, Sole Custody & Emancipation cases.
Please file those cases at Children's Court.

I. Fill in the requested information and estimated length of hearing expected for this case:

MINOR CHILDREN INVOLVED? ☐YES ☐NO   HOW MANY? _____   TIME ESTIMATE: _____ ☐HOURS/☐DAYS.

II. Select the correct district (3 steps):

① Under Column ① below, check the one type of action which best describes the nature of this case.

② In Column ② below, circle the reason for your choice of district that applies to the type of action you have checked.

Applicable Reasons for Choosing District (See Column② below)

1. May be filed in Central District.
2. District where one or more of the parties reside.
3. District where proposed ward/conservatee resides.
4. Child is held within the district.
5. District where petitioner resides.
6. District where decedent resided.
7. Decedent resided out of state - held property in District.
8. Child resides or decedent parent's probate would be filed in district.

③ Fill in the information requested on page 3 in item III; complete item IV. Sign the certificate.

---

① Type of Action (Check only one)	② Applicable Reasons - See Above
Marriage/Custody/Support Matters	
☐ A5520 Regular Dissolution of Marriage	1., 2.
☐ A5525 Summary Dissolution of Marriage	1., 2.
☐ A5530 Nullity of Void or Voidable Marriage	1., 2.
☐ A5510 Legal Separation	1., 2.
☐ A6135 Foreign Support Order	1., 2.
☐ A6136 Foreign Custody Order	1., 2., 4.
☐ A6137 Reciprocal Enforcement of Support - Initiating Petition	1.
☐ A6139 Reciprocal Enforcement of Support - Registration of Foreign Support	1.
☐ A6122 Domestic Violence Restraining Order (Civil Harassment - use Civil Cover Sheet)	1., 2.
☐ A6600 Habeas Corpus Petition - Child Custody	1., 4.
Other Family Case	
☐ A6080 Determination of Parentage/Paternity (Non-governmental)	1., 4., 8.
☐ A6111 Approval of Minor's Contract (6751 Family Code)	1.
☐ A6130 Other Family Complaint or Petition (Specify):_____	1., 2., 4., 8.
Adoption Matters (Submit Central District Filings at Children's Court)	
☐ A6101 Agency Adoption	1., 5.
☐ A6102 Independent Adoption	1., 5.
☐ A6103 Adult Adoption	1., 5.
☐ A6104 Stepparent Adoption	1., 5.

FAMILY AND PROBATE CASE COVER SHEET -
CERTIFICATE OF GROUNDS FOR ASSIGNMENT TO DISTRICT

* LASC Rule 2.0(d)

Page 1 of 3 pages

B537

SHORT TITLE.		CASE NUMBER

① Type of Action (Check only one)		
Decedent Estates		
☐ A6210	Petition for Probate of Will - Letters Testamentary	1., 6., 7
☐ A6211	Petition for Probate of Will - Letters of Administration	1., 6., 7.
☐ A6212	Petition for Letters of Administration	1., 6., 7.
☐ A6213	Petition for Letters of Special Administration	1., 6., 7.
☐ A6214	Petition to Set Aside Small Estate (6602 Prob. Code)	1., 6., 7.
☐ A6215	Spousal Property Petition	1., 6., 7.
☐ A6216	Petition for Succession to Real Property	1., 6., 7.
☐ A6217	Summary Probate (7660 Prob. Code)	1., 6., 7.
☐ A6218	Petition re Real Property of Small Value (13200 Prob. Code)	1., 6., 7.
Conservatorship/Guardianship/Trust Matters		
☐ A6230	Petition for Conservatorship of Person and Estate	1., 3., 5.
☐ A6231	Petition for Conservatorship of Person only	1., 3., 5.
☐ A6232	Petition for Conservatorship of Estate only	1., 3., 5.
☐ A6243	Petition for Conservatorship of Spouse who Lacks Capacity	1., 3., 5.
☐ A6233	Petition for Approval of Medical Treatment without Consent	1., 3., 5.
☐ A6240	Petition for Guardianship of Person and Estate	1., 3., 5.
☐ A6241	Petition for Guardianship of Person only	1., 3., 5.
☐ A6242	Petition for Guardianship of Estate only	1., 3., 5.
☐ A6254	Trust Proceedings Petition	1., 5.
Other Probate Court Matters		
☐ A6260	Petition for Compromise of Minor's Claim - no civil case filed (3500 Prob. Code)	1., 5.
☐ A6180	Petition to Establish Fact of Birth, Death or Marriage	1., 5.
☐ A6200	Other Probate Matter (Specify):_____	1., 2.

③ III. Choose the district: Enter the address of the party or decedent residence, property, or other circumstance you have circled in Column ② as the proper reason for filing in the district you selected.

REASON: CHECK THE NUMBER YOU CIRCLED IN ② WHICH APPLIES IN THIS CASE		ADDRESS:
☐1. ☐2. ☐3. ☐4. ☐5. ☐6. ☐7. ☐8.		
CITY:	STATE: ZIP CODE:	

IV. Certificate/Declaration of Assignment: The undersigned hereby certifies and declares that the above entitled matter is properly filed for assignment to the _____District of the Los Angeles Superior Court under § 392 et seq., Code of Civil Procedure, 2300 et seq. of the Family Code, 2200 and 7000 et seq. of the Probate Code, and Rule 2(b), (c) and (d) of this court for the reason checked above. I certify and declare under penalty of perjury under the laws of the State of California that the foregoing is true and correct and this declaration was executed on_____.
                                                                              (date)

_____
SIGNATURE OF ATTORNEY/FILING PARTY)

4	**FAMILY AND PROBATE CASE COVER SHEET -** **CERTIFICATE OF GROUNDS FOR ASSIGNMENT TO DISTRICT**	LASC Rule 2.0(d) Page 2 of 3 pages

New Family/Probate Case Filing Instructions

This cover sheet form is required so that the court can assign your case to the correct court district for filing and hearing. It satisfies the requirement for a certificate as to reasons for authorizing filing in the district, as set forth in Los Angeles Superior Court Local Rule 2 (d). It must be completed and submitted to the court along with the original Complaint or Petition in **ALL** Family or Probate cases filed in any district (including the Central District) of the Los Angeles County Superior Court.

> **PLEASE HAVE THE FOLLOWING DOCUMENTS COMPLETED AND READY TO BE FILED IN ORDER TO PROPERLY COMMENCE YOUR NEW COURT CASE:**

1. Original Complaint or Petition.

2. If filing a Paternity or other Family Complaint or Petition for Dissolution, Legal Separation or Nullity, a completed Summons form for issuance by the Clerk (Summons forms available at the Forms Counter).

3. This "Family and Probate Case Cover Sheet" form (Superior Court Form Number 4 , revised 7/99), completely filled out.

4. Payment in full of the filing fee or an Order of the Court waiving payment of filing fees in forma pauperis (fee waiver application forms available at the Filing Window)

5. Except when applying for orders restraining or enjoining violence or harassment, plaintiffs or petitioners who are minors under 18 years of age and otherwise not emancipated must have an Order of the Court appointing an adult as a guardian ad litem to act on their behalf (Guardian ad Litem Application and Order forms available at the Forms Counter).

6. Additional copies of documents presented for endorsement by the Clerk and return to you.

* With the exception of personal injury (including wrongful death) and property damage cases, Labor Commissioner Appeals, and those types of actions required to be filed in the Central District by Local Court Rule 2(b), all civil actions, including family and probate actions, may be optionally filed either in the Central District, or in whichever other district the rule would allow them to be filed. When a party elects to file an action in Central District which would also be eligible for filing in one or more of the other districts, this form must still be submitted with location and assignment information completed.

4 | **FAMILY AND PROBATE CASE COVER SHEET - CERTIFICATE OF GROUNDS FOR ASSIGNMENT TO DISTRICT** | LASC Rule 2.0(a)
Page 3 of 3 pages
B537

CONTESTED DIVORCE PROCEDURE 8

PROCEDURE DIFFERENCES FROM UNCONTESTED DIVORCE

This book cannot turn you into a trial lawyer. It is risky to try to handle a contested case yourself. There are many differences between a contested and an uncontested case. In an uncontested case the judge will usually go along with what you and your spouse have decided. In a contested case you need to prove that you are entitled to what you are asking. This means you need a longer time for the hearing, you need to present evidence, and you may need witnesses.

You may have to send out subpoenas (which are discussed in the next section of this chapter) or even hire a private investigator. You will need to assure that your spouse is properly notified of any court hearings, and that he or she is sent copies of any papers you file with the court.

When it becomes apparent that you have a contested divorce, it is probably time to consider hiring an attorney, especially if child custody is involved. If you are truly ready to go to war over custody, you will want to get professional assistance. You can predict a contested case when your spouse is fighting you every inch of the way, or when he or she hires an attorney.

On the other hand, you shouldn't assume that you need an attorney just because your spouse has hired one. Sometimes it is easier to deal with the attorney than with your spouse. The attorney is not as emotionally involved and may see your settlement proposal as reasonable. So discuss things with your spouse's attorney first and see if things can be settled. You can always hire your own lawyer if your spouse's isn't reasonable. Just be cautious about signing any papers until you are certain you understand what they mean. You should have an attorney review any papers prepared by your spouse's lawyer before you sign them.

You will not prepare the Judgment (form 18) until after the hearing with a contested case because you won't know what it should contain until the judge decides.

COLLECTING INFORMATION

The court rules require each party serve on the other the preliminary Declaration of Disclosure (form 7) (see chapter 7 for a detailed discussion of form 7). If your spouse is not cooperating and will not provide the forms, you may have to try to get the information yourself. You will need to have the information available at the hearing. This will require you to get subpoenas issued. You can make a motion to compel your spouse to give you the documents, but now you are getting into a more complicated matter, and will have to research the law and procedures at the local law library. It may be easier to check with an attorney.

The *preliminary* and *final* Declaration of Disclosure (form 7) are relatively new forms and are designed to eliminate or reduce the need for spouses to serve interrogatories, document production requests, subpoenas, and other forms of discovery. *Discovery* is a legal term meaning legal process to obtain information about the other party's personal and business affairs. Before California had the preliminary and final Declaration of Disclosure forms, discovery was the only way to obtain information from a reticent spouse.

Of course, you may still have to rely on formal discovery if your spouse refuses to cooperate. In cases with substantial assets where you don't trust your spouse, you will want to subpoena the information directly from the source, such as your spouse's bank or employer. You'll probably need a lawyer's help for this.

PROPERTY AND DEBTS

The judge looks at your property and debts and must divide the community property equally. At the same time, the judge will confirm any separate property to the spouse owning it. Just to review: *community property* is all property acquired by you and your spouse during marriage, other than gifts or inheritances. *Separate property* is all property you had before marriage or after separation (and gifts and inheritances received at any time). If the property is part separate and part community, as for example, retirement benefits from a job you had both before and during marriage, only that portion earned between the date of your marriage and the date of your separation is community property. In that case, depending upon the type of retirement plan, you may need an actuary to figure how much is community and how much is separate.

PROPERTY DECLARATION

You'll need to complete another form, called the Property Declaration (form 15). But this one you've already completed for the most part. Look at the Schedule of Assets and Debts (form 8) that you and your spouse had to serve on each other with a Declaration of Disclosure (see chapter 7). The Property Declaration (form 15) will be the same, updated to the time of the hearing, along with a proposed property division. The judge will use that form to divide the property. In most cases, the property can't be divided exactly even. For example, if your major asset is your home, the judge can't very well give half to you and half to your spouse. What happens is that the judge would order the house sold and the proceeds divided equally.

If you have very young children and the house payment is approximately equal to what the custody spouse would have to pay for rent anyway, you might want an order where the custody spouse and the children live in the house for a period of time, say until the children reach a certain age, and then the house would be sold and the proceeds divided. In the meantime, the spouse living in the home would pay normal maintenance expenses and the mortgage payment.

If you get to this level of complication, you might want an attorney's help unless you and your spouse can fashion a reasonable order. Remember that the judge cannot give you legal advice and, in addition, has a huge, daily calendar of cases.

Note: You won't need form 15 if you and your spouse have completed a Marital Settlement Agreement (MSA) (form 17). If you've done that, your case is no longer contested.

Notice that the Property Declaration (form 15) is much the same as the Schedule of Assets and Debts (form 8), except it includes the net value and your proposal for division. If you need continuation pages, use form 28. You must use separate forms for the community property and the separate property. Complete the forms just as you did the Schedule of Assets and Debts, but this time distribute the amount in the third column (the net fair market value), in either the petitioner's or the respondent's column.

In dividing the property, consider:

- ☛ What you really want
- ☛ What you'd like to have
- ☛ What you don't care about either way
- ☛ What your spouse really wants
- ☛ What your spouse would like to have
- ☛ What your spouse doesn't care about either way

Start a list of what each of you should end up with, using the categories listed above. You will eventually end up with a list of things you can probably get with little difficulty (you really want and your spouse doesn't care), those which you'll fight over (you both really want), and those which need to be divided but can probably be easily divided equally (you both don't really care).

At the hearing, the judge will probably try to get you to work out your disagreements, but he won't put up with arguing for very long. In the end, he will arbitrarily divide the items you can't agree upon, or he may order you to sell those items and equally divide the money you get.

For the few items that are really important to you, it may be necessary to prove why you should get them. It will help if you can convince the judge of one or more of the following:

1. You paid for the item out of your own earnings or funds.

2. You are the one who primarily uses that item.

3. You use the item in your employment, business, or hobby.

4. You are willing to give up something else you really want in exchange for that item (of course, you will try to give up something from your "don't care" or your "like to have" list).

5. The item is needed for your child (assuming you will have custody).

The best thing you can do is make the division reasonably fair and equal, regardless of how angry you are at your spouse. Even if the judge changes some of it to appear fair to your spouse, you will most likely get more of what you want if you do offer a few suggestions. (No, this is not an exception to the negotiating rule of letting your spouse make the first offer because at this point you are no longer just negotiating with your spouse. You are now negotiating with the judge. You are trying to impress the judge with your fairness—not trying to convince your spouse.)

Special problems arise if a claim of separate property becomes an issue. This may be in terms of your spouse trying to get your separate property, or in terms of you trying to get property you feel your spouse is wrongly claiming to be separate.

It is also a good idea to have documents that prove the property you claim to be separate property is actually separate property. These would be papers showing that:

☞ You bought the item before you were married (such as dated sales receipts).

☞ You inherited the item as your own property (such as certified copies of wills and probate court papers).

☞ You got the property by exchanging it for property you had before you got married, or for property you received as a gift or through an inheritance (such as a statement from the person you made the exchange with, or some kind of receipt showing what was exchanged).

If you want to get at assets your spouse is claiming are separate assets, you will need to collect the following types of evidence:

☞ Papers showing that the community helped pay for the asset (such as a check from a community property bank account, or from your separate account if you and your spouse had previously agreed in writing that you would maintain a separate property bank account). For example, suppose your spouse owned a house before marriage and during the marriage some of the mortgage payments or repairs were made with community property money (or with your separate account money if you had a separate account). The community is entitled to reimbursement of such contribution to your spouse's separate property. (In such case, you would be entitled to one-half of the reimbursement because community property is owned fifty-fifty by you and your spouse.) You are also entitled to reimbursement for funds from your separate account provided it wasn't a gift. You would need to bring to court copies of the cancelled checks showing such payments.

☞ Papers showing that the asset was improved, or increased in value, during your marriage. *Example 1:* Your spouse owned the house before you were married. During your marriage, you and your spouse added a family room to the house. This will enable you to make a claim for some of the value of the house.

Example 2: Your spouse owned the house before you were married. The day before you got married, the house was worth $85,000. Now the house is appraised at $115,000. You can claim part of the $30,000 of increased value if the community (you or your spouse using community property funds) made some of the mortgage payments.

Caution: This area becomes very complex and often requires the help of an accountant as well as that of an attorney.

In order to make a claim on what would otherwise appear to be your spouse's separate property, you need to ask for it in your Petition (form 3). The judge will probably announce who gets what at the end of the hearing. Take notes of the order if you can keep up. Also ask the court clerk for a copy of the *minute order*. The minute order will contain the judge's ruling unless it is complicated. In that case, ask the court clerk or the court reporter for a copy of the transcript of that part of the hearing where the judge issued the order. It'll take a few days and you'll have to pay for the transcript, but at least you'll have the exact order. When you're sure you have the order right, prepare the Judgment and have your spouse sign it. Then you'll have to take it to the judge's clerk for the judge's signature. Complete the Judgment as described in chapter 7.

CHILD CUSTODY AND VISITATION

Generally, if you are the wife, the odds are in favor of you getting custody. But don't depend on it. Start out by reviewing the guidelines the judge will use to decide the custody question. These can be found in chapter 4. For each item listed in that section, write down an explanation of how that item applies to you. This will be your argument when you have your hearing with the judge.

Many custody battles revolve around the moral fitness of one or both of the parents. If you become involved in this type of a custody fight, you should consult a lawyer. Charges of moral unfitness (such as illegal drug use, child abuse, and immoral sexual conduct) can require long court hearings involving the testimony of many witnesses, as well as the hiring of private investigators. For such a hearing, you will require the help of an attorney who knows the law, what questions to ask witnesses, and the rules of evidence.

However, if the only question is whether you or your spouse has been the main caretaker of the child, you can always have friends, neighbors, and relatives come into the hearing to testify on your behalf. It may not be necessary to have an attorney. But if you need to subpoena unwilling witnesses to testify, you will probably need one.

The judge's decision regarding custody will have to be placed into the Judgment.

CHILD SUPPORT

In California, as in most states, the question of child support is a matter of a mathematical calculation. Getting the guideline child support amount depends upon the accuracy of the income information presented to the judge. If you feel fairly sure that the information your spouse presents is accurate, or that you have accurate information about his or her income, there isn't much to argue. The judge will simply take the income information provided, determine the amount of custody time each spouse has, use a computer to calculate the amount to be paid, and order that amount to be paid.

In most cases, there isn't much room to argue about the amount of child support, so there usually isn't a need to get an attorney. If you claim your spouse has not provided accurate income information, it will be up to you to prove this to the judge by showing the income information you have obtained from your spouse's employer or other source of income.

The areas open for argument are whatever special needs are claimed by the party asking for child support and whether the party paying child support has other children he or she is obligated to support. Once again, it will be necessary for that party to provide proof of the cost of these special needs by producing billing statements, receipts, or other papers to show the amount of these needs.

Refer to chapter 4 for a more complete discussion on child support. The judge's decision regarding child support will have to be put into the Judgment. Read chapter 7 for instructions on preparing the Judgment.

SPOUSAL SUPPORT (ALIMONY)

A dispute over spousal support (alimony) may require a lawyer, especially if there is a request for permanent alimony because of a disability. Such a claim may require the testimony of expert witnesses (such as doctors, accountants, and actuaries).

In setting spousal support, the judge looks at criteria in Family Code section 4320. Generally, the categories are:

1. The standard of living during the marriage, taking into consideration the marketable skills of the supported party and the job market for such skills, expenses for training to further develop such skills, and the need for any retraining to acquire other more marketable skills

2. The supported party's impairment of his or her earning capacity by the period devoted to domestic duties

3. The extent to which the party seeking support contributed to the attainment of an education, training, a career, or a license of the supporting party

4. The supporting party's ability to pay

5. The needs of each party based on the standard of living during the marriage

6. The obligations, assets, and separate property of each party

7. The duration of the marriage and age and health of the parties

8. The ability of the supported party to work without unduly interfering with the needs of the dependent children in the custody of supported party

9. The immediate tax consequences, if any

10. The balance of the hardships of each party

11. The goal that the supported party shall be self-supporting within a reasonable period, with "reasonable period" defined as one-half the length of the marriage

12. Any other factors the judge considers fair

Note that number 11 implies that spousal support will generally be for a period determined by one-half the length of the marriage. For example, if you were married for ten years, the period for paying spousal support would be five years. This was a rule of thumb which the California legislature made law in 1996. Remember, however, that unless you and your spouse agree differently, the judge must retain the power to award spousal support indefinitely in marriages of long duration (ten years or more).

After considering the above criteria, and if your spouse makes lots of money, and if you sacrificed your career to help him or her, you might want to talk to an attorney because some substantial support might be at stake.

You should also bring to the hearing documentation and witnesses that can support your claim to spousal support.

THE COURT HEARING 9

PREPARATION

To set a court hearing date, you'll have to pick up a form from the clerk's office because these forms vary from court to court. For example, Los Angeles uses what it has designated "Form 41," also called a Request for Trial Setting. San Diego, San Francisco, and most other courts use an At-Issue Memorandum form. All the forms are similar in that they inform the court that the case is ready for trial and ask for a time estimate. When you file that form, the clerk will normally send out a notice of the trial date to you and your spouse. To be on the safe side, it is recommended that you also notify your spouse in writing of the trial date, time, and place. You can do that with a letter, but make sure you complete a Proof of Service by mail (form 29) after you mail it. Then take the letter and attached proof of service to the court hearing just in case your spouse doesn't show up. If the clerk's notice is missing from the court file, you'll have your notice ready and the matter won't have to be continued because there's no proof your spouse had notice of the hearing.

When you go to court, bring:

☐ Your entire file, organized so you can locate papers quickly if asked to do so

☐ Your three most recent pay stubs and copies of your recent income tax returns

☐ Others papers showing the financial condition of yourself and your spouse, including his or her pay stubs

☐ The Judgment (form 18) filled out to the extent the information is available and at least four copies

☐ The Notice of Entry of Judgment (form 20) filled out to the extent the information is available, along with four copies

☐ The Marital Settlement Agreement (MSA) (form 17) if you and your spouse have completed one

☐ Declaration Regarding Service of Declaration of Disclosure and Income and Expense Declaration (form 10) for both the preliminary and final Declaration of Disclosure (form 7), with a copy of each if you haven't already filed them with the clerk

All of these forms were previously discussed. Sometimes the clerk's office makes a mistake and the judge doesn't have all of the papers you filed in the court file. That's why you need to bring copies of all the papers you have filed to prove they've been filed.

THE HEARING

Your hearing will probably take place in one of the smaller courtrooms, not like those you see on television or in the movies. The judge calls your case by name (*e.g.*, "Smith versus Smith"). Normally, a listing of the cases scheduled will be posted outside the courtroom door. Whether it is or isn't, make sure you check in and tell the bailiff or clerk inside the courtroom that you're present and ask what number your case is on the docket. When the judge (or commissioner) calls your case, he or she will look over your papers and start asking you questions. Or he or she may ask you, as the petitioner, to present your case. Styles among judges vary.

Before the judge calls your case, the clerk will review your papers and tell you if there is something missing. Hopefully, you'll be able to fix any problem. The judge may review your papers before you get to say anything and point out various legal deficiencies, if any exist. Whatever style you confront, answer courteously. Don't be afraid to speak up and ask the judge if he could call your case at the end of his calendar (later that morning or afternoon) to give you time to obtain a missing document. If it would take longer than that, or if you left the papers at home, ask the judge if you could bring the papers to him the next day. Your goal is to get the case finished without the judge continuing it.

Assuming your papers are in order, the judge will eventually ask you four general questions:

1. Have you been a resident of the California for at least six months and of the county for at least three months?

2. Have irreconcilable differences arisen in your marriage?

3. Are those differences irremediable?

4. Would any kind of counseling save the marriage?

You must answer "yes" to the first three, and "no" to the last. Those are the four magic answers that get you a divorce in California. Gone are the days where you had to prove extreme cruelty, infidelity, or the like.

If you have updated the income and expense statement, be sure to file it with the courtroom clerk. All of your financial information should be current as of the time of the hearing.

If there are issues you and your spouse have not been able to agree upon, tell the judge about them and present your proposed solution. If you've prepared a proposed Judgment (form 18) because you don't have any complicated issues for the judge to rule on, and the judge rules the way you'd expect, you can give the judge the original and four copies at the end of the hearing. You'll also need the Notice of Entry of Judgment (form 20), along with two stamped envelopes (one addressed to you and the other to your spouse). Make sure the return address on the envelopes is the clerk's address, not yours. If the judge rules differently from how you've prepared the Judgment and the difference is slight, ask the judge if you can make the correction right on the form. If the difference is major, you'll have to go home and re-type it, and then submit it through the clerk's office. Make certain you have the judge's order correct. You'll also need the completed Wage and Earnings Assignment Order (form 21), with at least two copies to give to the judge's clerk along with the Judgment. Remember, you have to serve the file-stamped Wage and Earnings Assignment Order signed by the judge on your spouse's employer.

If the unexpected occurs, such as your spouse testifying to something you were not prepared for, ask the judge for a continuance so you can get an attorney. The judge may not go along with your request (believing it should have been made before the hearing got underway), but try it anyway. If you're granted a continuance, go get a lawyer.

This book is not designed to get you through a contested divorce with substantial issues. If your divorce involves significant property disputes or major opposing positions as to income and expenses in connection with spousal or child support, the money you'll pay to an attorney could be well spent. This book can give you a quick overview for simple divorces, but don't be fooled into thinking that reading this book or spending a few weekends in the law library will keep you from harm's way inside a courtroom.

Caution: Don't think that once you're in a courtroom, the court officers will watch out for your interests. That's not how it works. The judge is sworn to make decisions based on the law and the evidence you present. If you and your spouse can't agree between yourselves, and decide to let the judge figure it all out, understand that the judge doesn't know you're the most fair person alive and your spouse the most greedy. In fact, the judge may even get the two of you confused.

PUBLIC ASSISTANCE

If you expect child support and receive public assistance, you must contact the Family Support Division of the local district attorney's office in
your county. Child support payments will be made to the enforcement
office, which will in turn pay you. New forms to cover this area are
frequently generated, and the court will not hear your case unless the
district attorney's office, who will be a participant in the case, is
contacted. That office will help you with public assistance requirements
for the Wage and Earnings Assignment Order (form 21) and the other
court forms, including the Judgment.

When You
Can't Find
Your Spouse

10

Your spouse has run off and you have no idea of where he or she might be. So how do you have the sheriff or marshal deliver a copy of your summons and other papers to your spouse? The answer is, you can't. Instead of personal service you will use a method of giving notice called *service by publication*, which can be complicated.

The Diligent Search

The court will only permit service by publication when you can't locate your spouse. This includes the situation where the sheriff or marshal has tried several times to personally serve your spouse, but it appears that your spouse is hiding to avoid being served. First, you'll have to show that you can't locate your spouse by letting the court know what you've done to try to find him or her. In making this search, you should try the following:

☛ Check the phone book and directory assistance in the area where you live

☛ Check directory assistance in the area where you last knew your spouse to be living

☛ Ask friends and relatives who could know where your spouse might be

☛ Check with the post office where he or she last lived to see if there is a forwarding address (you can ask by mail if it is too far away)

☛ Check records of the tax collector and property assessor to see if your spouse owns property

☛ Write to the Department of Motor Vehicles to see if your spouse has any car registrations

☛ Check with any other sources you know that may lead you to a current address (such as landlords, prior employers, etc.)

☛ Check the registrar of voters.

☛ Investigators are also available but a fee is required

If you do come up with a current address, go back to personal service by the sheriff or marshal, but if not, continue with this procedure.

PREPARING AND FILING COURT PAPERS

Once you've made a diligent search, you need to tell the court what you have done to try to find your spouse, and request the court's permission to publish. This is done by filing an *ex parte* (meaning "without notice to the other party") application for a court order permitting you to publish the Summons—Family Law (form 1) in the newspaper instead of serving it on your spouse personally. Along with the *ex parte* application, you need to file a declaration stating your efforts to find your spouse.

Before you do any of the above, call the newspaper in the city of your spouse's last known address and ask if it is certified for legal advertising in that area and how much it costs. Shop around if there are other newspapers of general circulation in that particular area. Rates vary greatly. The newspaper may even have some forms you can use, and sometimes the person in charge of the legal advertising may help you with the procedure.

You first need to determine if your local court has forms. If so, use the court's forms. If not, use the Ex Parte Application for Publication of Summons Order; Declaration of Petitioner in Support Thereof; Memorandum of Points and Authorities (form 35) and Order for Publication of Summons (form 36) from appendix B. You will need to call the clerk and ask about the local ex-parte procedure for publication orders. Follow the clerk's instructions.

Form 35 is a combined application and declaration. Be careful with the declaration portion of form 35 (this is the third and fourth page). A declaration normally contains information from your own personal knowledge, not from what someone has told you. This is important because, although you must declare your efforts to locate your spouse, you may also need another declaration from the person you may have hired to try to find your spouse. Because declarations must be on personal knowledge, such a third person should also complete a declaration showing his or her attempts to serve your spouse. For such a third person, use the Declaration (form 27).

To complete the Ex Parte Application for Publication of Summons Order; Declaration of Petitioner in Support Thereof; Memorandum of Points and Authorities (form 35):

Page 1:

1. Type in your name, address, phone number, and fax number (if you have one) where indicated at the top of the form.

2. Type in your name after the words "Attorney for." The phrase "In Propria Persona" means that you are acting as your own attorney.

3. On the lines indicated, type in the county and division of the court, the case number, your name after the word "Petitioner," and your spouse's name after the word "Respondent." The clerk will fill in the lines marked "Date," "Time," and "Dept."

4. In the first paragraph, type in your name after the word "Petitioner," your spouse's name after the word "Respondent," and the name of the newspaper you intend to publish the Summons—Family Law in on the third line. This should be a newspaper of general circulation in the area of respondent's last known address.

Page 2:

5. In the third paragraph, type in the date your Petition was filed.

6. In the last paragraph, type in your name.

7. Type in the date and your name on the appropriate lines and sign your name on the line marked "(Petitioner's signature)."

Page 3:

8. Type in your name after the words "Declaration of" and in the blank in the first paragraph.

9. In the second paragraph, type in your spouse's name in the first blank, and the date you first tried to have your spouse served in the second blank.

10. In the blank at the beginning of the third paragraph, type in the name of the newspaper where you intend to publish. On the lines after that paragraph, type in a brief explanation of why that newspaper is most likely to give notice to your spouse. This might be something like: "Said newspaper circulates in the area where Respondent was last known to have resided."

11. On the lines after the last paragraph on this page, type in a list of all of your efforts to serve your spouse under all of the normal service procedures under the Code of Civil Procedure, sections 415.10 to 415.40.

Page 4:

12. On the lines after the first paragraph on this page, type in a list of the things you have done to try to locate your spouse. Specifically state how, when, and where you attempted to locate your spouse. Such efforts should include the items listed on pages 151 and 152

above. Include all the detail. Remember that service by publication is a last resort, and is usually unlikely to actually give notice to the respondent. For that reason, the judge will want to know that you've exercised reasonable diligence in your search. Courts expect to see very diligent efforts to locate your spouse because if the Summons—Family Law is served by publication it is unlikely that your spouse will ever know about the dissolution. You don't need to notarize these papers, as long as your declaration includes the last paragraph: "I declare under penalty of perjury under the laws of the state of California that the above is true and correct. Executed at _____, California, on _____, _____."

13. On the lines in the last paragraph on this page, type in the city where you signed this form and the date you signed it. Then sign your name on the line marked "Petitioner."

You will also need to be prepared with an order for the judge to sign, permitting you to publish the Summons—Family Law. Form 36 is provided for this purpose in the event your court does not have its own form. To complete the Order for Publication of Summons (form 36):

1. Complete the top portion of the form with the same information you filled in on form 35.

2. In the first paragraph, type in your name after the word "Petitioner," and your spouse's name on the two lines after the word "Respondent."

3. In the second paragraph, type in your spouse's name in the blank after the word "Respondent," the name of the newspaper in the second blank, and the name of the county or city in which the newspaper is published in the third blank.

4. In the last paragraph, type your spouse's name in the blank after the word "Respondent." The judge will fill in the date and sign the form.

PUBLISHING

After you obtain a copy of the Order for Publication of Summons (form 36) signed by the judge, you will need to send or deliver it and a copy of the Summons—Family Law (form 1) to the newspaper for publishing. There are certain publication requirements. For example, the Summons—Family Law must be published at least once a week for four successive weeks, and there should be five days between the successive publications. The thirty days that your spouse has to file a Response to your Summons—Family Law begins to run on the twenty-eighth day after the first day of publication.

If you don't have the money to pay for the publication, there are alternatives the court can authorize to avoid the publication expense, but you must demonstrate your indigence to the court. For more information on this, refer to the section in chapter 11 titled "When You Can't Afford Court Costs."

SPECIAL CIRCUMSTANCES 11

WHEN YOU CAN'T AFFORD COURT COSTS

If you can't afford to pay the filing fee and other costs associated with the divorce, you will need to file an Application for Waiver of Court Fees and Costs (form 30). In order to qualify for a waiver, or partial waiver, of the filing fee and costs, you must be *indigent*. If you are indigent, your income is probably low enough for you to qualify for public assistance (welfare).

> *Caution:* Before you file form 30, ask the court clerk for information on what is required to be declared indigent. You can be held in contempt of court for giving false information on this form. The clerk's office will have an *Information Sheet* on waiver of court fees and costs.

The Application for Waiver of Court Fees and Costs is self-explanatory and requires detailed financial information.

If the judge approves your application, he or she will issue an order declaring you indigent and waiving filing fees and other court costs. You will need to show a copy of this order to the court clerk so that you will be allowed for file your Petition (form 3) without paying the filing fee. You will also need to provide a copy of this order to the sheriff's or marshal's office so that you can have your spouse served without paying the service fee. However, if you need to publish a service of summons in a newspaper, you will still need to pay the newspaper's fee. The waiver of fees applies only to fees charged by government agencies such as the court and sheriff's office. It does not require any private person or company to provide you with free services.

Protecting Yourself, Your Children, and Your Property

Some people have three special concerns when getting prepared to file for a divorce: Fear of physical attack by their spouse, fear that their spouse will take the children and go into hiding, and fear that their spouse will try to take community property and hide it. There are additional legal papers you can file if you feel you are in any of these situations.

Protecting Yourself

The California legislature, being especially sensitive to domestic violence, has tried to streamline procedures to protect the abused spouse. The legislature removed personal conduct restraining orders from the divorce context and put them into a separate legal procedure. This book does not cover that area of law because it is not directly related to obtaining a divorce and there is an excellent informational booklet on the subject with forms available free from clerks' offices. It is called the "Domestic Violence Restraining Orders Instruction Booklet" and was written by the Judicial Council for the general public. Some courts have domestic violence clinics, and the clerks will always steer you to help if you have a domestic violence problem. The law is found in the "Domestic Violence Prevention Act," sections 6200 to 6390 of the Family code. Lawyers are helpful in this area, but may not be needed because of the many free resources available. Because the booklet may be a little overwhelming (ninety-eight pages), some courts have designated clerks to help persons complete the forms.

PROTECTING
YOUR
CHILDREN

If you fear physical violence directed at your children, you can use the same procedures you would use for protecting yourself from violence. If you are worried that your spouse may try to kidnap your children, you should make sure that the day care center, baby-sitter, relative, or whomever you leave the children with at any time, is aware that you are in the process of a divorce and that the children are only to be released to you personally (not to your spouse or to any other relative, friend, etc.). A public school may not be willing to prevent your spouse or someone else from picking up your child unless you obtain a temporary custody order stating your child is only to be released to you or someone you designate (see the following section of this chapter on "Temporary Support and Custody").

To prevent your spouse from taking the children out of the United States, you can apply for a passport for each child. Once a passport is issued, the government will not issue another. So get their passport and lock it up in a safe deposit box. (This won't prevent them from being taken to Canada or Mexico, where passports are not required, but will prevent them from being taken overseas.) You can also file a motion to prevent the removal of the children from the state and to deny passport services, but this may involve a level of complexity that an attorney is better equipped to handle.

PROTECTING
YOUR PROPERTY

If you genuinely fear that your spouse will try to remove money from bank accounts, try to hide important papers showing what property you own, or try to hide items of property, you may want to take this same action before your spouse can. However, you can make a great deal of trouble for yourself with the judge if you do this to try to get these assets for yourself. So, make a complete list of any property you do take and be sure to include these items in your Schedule of Assets and Debts (form 8). You may need to convince the judge that you only took these items temporarily, in order to preserve them. Do not spend any cash you take from a bank account or sell or give away any items of property you take. Any cash should be placed in a separate bank account, without your spouse's name on it, and kept separate from any other cash you have. Any papers, such as deeds, car titles, stock or bond certificates, etc., should be placed in a safe deposit box without your spouse's name on it. The idea is not to take these things for yourself, but to get them in a safe place so that your spouse can't hide them and deny they ever existed.

If your spouse is determined and resourceful, there is no guaranteed way to prevent the things discussed in this section from happening. All you can do is put as many obstacles in his or her way as possible and rely on legal remedies for the improper actions.

TEMPORARY SUPPORT AND CUSTODY

If your spouse has left you with the children, the mortgage, and monthly bills and is not helping you financially, then you may want to consider asking the court to order the payment of support for you and the children immediately while the divorce is pending. Of course, if you were the only person bringing in income and have been paying all the bills, don't expect to get any temporary support.

You will need to prepare an order to show cause for temporary support and custody, and other papers, including your declaration which sets forth all your reasons for the request.

ORDER TO
SHOW CAUSE

It is possible for you, if you have the time and industry, to go to the law library and research how to do an OSC (meaning "order to show cause"). However, although the forms required are generally uniform, some courts may still have local forms and varying procedures.

It is urged that you get an attorney if you need an *order to show cause* (OSC). OSC litigation requires a working knowledge of both law and procedure, and someone unfamiliar and unschooled in this area should prepare for frustration and for the prospect of hiring an attorney. Following is a brief overview of this area.

The purpose of an OSC is to obtain quick legal relief when you and your spouse cannot come to an interim agreement on an immediate need such as support, custody, or living arrangements. The OSC is an order issued by the court to your spouse to show cause why your requested order should not be granted.

An even faster procedure is available, called *ex parte orders*, when you need to get relief now and you cannot even wait for the formal notice time required for an OSC hearing to elapse. Ex parte procedure differs from court to court and you'll have to call the court clerk. *Ex parte* refers to having a court hearing without notice to your spouse. In practice, courts require some kind of notice, usually by telephone a certain number of hours before the hearing, unless notice would pose a danger.

The fact that this book discusses ex parte and OSC matters is not meant to imply that you'll be able to do an ex parte or OSC without an attorney. This discussion is only to make you aware they're available and point you in the right direction.

Although another procedure called *notice of motion* can sometimes be used in lieu of an OSC, the OSC procedure is most often used and is therefore recommended. Firstly, you need to serve the appropriate papers on your spouse. You can serve them initially by personal service, along with the Summons—Family Law (form 1), Petition (form 3), and Confidential Counseling Statement (form 5), or, if you have already served your spouse with the initial papers, you can serve the OSC papers by mail with proof of service.

To complete the Order to Show Cause (form 31):

1. Complete the top portion of the form according to the instruction in chapter 5.

2. Check the box relating to the type of relief you are requesting. If none of the boxes apply, check the "Other" box and type in the subject matter.

3. In item 1, provide the name of your spouse.

4. Complete item "2a" after you obtain the date, time, and department or room number from the clerk. The hearing date must be at least

fifteen calendar days from the time you serve your spouse. If service is by mail, notice time is increased to twenty days. Complete "2b" as applicable. Check box "2c" if applicable; you and your spouse will be required to attend mediation if you have issues of custody or visitation.

5. In item 3, "(1)" to "(5)," check the boxes showing the documents you are serving on your spouse with the OSC. You'll recognize "(1)" and "(3)" from previous sections in this book. Item "(4)" refers to written legal arguments citing particular law where the relief requested is not standard and requires legal support. You'd check item "3b" if the judge reduces the time required for notice of the hearing, and you'd check items "3c" and "3d" if you are serving any ex parte or temporary restraining orders with the OSC.

The portion of form 31 titled "Application for Order and Supporting Declaration" must be attached to the first page. Complete it as follows:

1. Items 1 through 4 refer to custody and support. Complete them as applicable. The "To be ordered pending the hearing" line in bold refers to ex parte requests (above).

2. Complete items 5 through 7 as applicable. Bear in mind that accompanying this form must be your declaration (see item 10 on back of form) setting forth in clear, vivid, language facts and circumstances supporting why you need such relief. The facts and circumstances must be based on your personal knowledge, not on what someone has told you or what you think.

3. Item 8 refers requesting a shortened period of time for notice of the OSC.

4. Item 9 refers any other relief you need right away and not indicated on the form.

5. Check both boxes at item 10 and type the reasons why you need the requested relief (see no. 2 directly above) on an attached declaration unless you type what you want to say in the space provided.

Some courts don't permit you to testify at the hearing and consider your OSC request solely on the written documents. For that reason, your declaration must be graphic, persuasive, and convincing.

If you are trying to get an order before the hearing on the OSC, you also need to attach the Temporary Orders (form 32) to the OSC form. You complete this form as applicable, bearing in mind that whatever relief you ask for must be supported with specific details based on first-hand knowledge. The same declaration you typed for the Application for Order and Supporting Declaration portion of form 31 is used for this form because all these forms are filed together.

The purpose of your declaration is to provide the court with hard-hitting facts as to why the orders are urgent and necessary. Don't hold back, but be truthful.

If you are seeking any financial relief, you need to complete and file with these papers the Income and Expense Declaration (form 9) and if appropriate, the Property Declaration (form 15). Bring to the hearing other financial information you may have, such as W-2 forms, the last three wage statements for you and your spouse if you have them, and the most recent federal and state income tax returns, loan applications during the past two years, and if a sole proprietor, copies of 1099 forms, profit and loss statements, and balance sheets.

After you file the forms with the clerk and obtain the hearing date, you must serve the papers on your spouse so that he or she has fifteen days notice if personally served, or twenty days notice if served by mail. Note that item 3 on the Order to Show Cause (form 31) requires you to serve blank forms also, for the convenience of the person you are serving. If you are seeking ex parte relief, and have given the telephonic notice required, the clerk will direct you to a particular courtroom. Remember that if you do seek ex parte relief, you must bring to the courtroom your written declaration stating that you attempted to contact, or did contact, your spouse, providing the details such as the telephone numbers you called, who you spoke with, when you called, that you fully informed such person of the nature of the hearing and of the time and place of the hearing. Also, don't forget to file the proof of service of all of the documents after you've served your spouse.

After the hearing, you'll need to prepare the court's order. But since your need is immediate, you must ask the judge, if he or she grants your request, to make the order effective now and not wait until you can prepare a written order and return it to the judge.

The form used for the order is the Findings and Order after Hearing (form 34) with the same attachment forms (forms 39 through 43) used for the Judgment (form 18). These attachment forms are described in the discussion on Judgment in chapter 7, so refer to those pages for instructions on completing them. There is one additional attachment used exclusively for the Order to Show Cause hearing, namely the Property Order Attachment (form 44). This form is an order for property restraining orders and mirrors the requests you made in items 6 and 7 of the Application for Order and Supporting Declaration which is part of the Order to Show Cause form (form 31).

Once the orders are approved by the judge, you need to have them served on your spouse and then complete and file a Proof of Personal Service (form 33). Review the section Other Notices in chapter 5.

Further detail in this area is beyond any useful purpose this book could serve. The above discussion will, at most, only introduce you to this area and give you some idea of what's involved when you speak with an attorney about it.

TAXES

As you are no doubt aware, the United States income tax code is complicated and ever-changing. Therefore, it is impossible to give detailed legal advice with respect to taxes in a book such as this. Any such information could easily be out of date by the time of publication.

Therefore, it is strongly recommended that you consult a tax expert about the tax consequences of a divorce. A few general concerns are discussed in this chapter to give you an idea of some of the tax questions that can arise.

FILING TAX RETURNS

Generally, married persons will pay less income tax by filing a joint return than by filing separate returns. Your filing status as being married or single is determined as of the end of the year. Thus, if your divorce is pending and you are separated from your spouse as of the end of the year, you can both agree to file a joint return.

TAXES AND FAMILY SUPPORT

We've discussed spousal support and child support previously. Sometimes, however, because of tax laws, these two kinds of support are combined into one payment called *family support*. To understand the significance of the term *family support*, you must understand that spousal support is deductible by the payor and taxable to the payee. That is, if you receive spousal support, you have to declare it as income on your tax return, but your spouse can deduct it from income on his or her return. Child support, on the other hand, is not deductible or taxable.

Some time ago, the tax law was that if you did not call a support payment "child support," even though it decreased when a child reached age eighteen, it was considered spousal support. So if the combined spousal and child support amounts were labeled "family support," without allocation between the two, the payor spouse would deduct the entire amount of the family support on his or her taxes as if it were all spousal support. This often benefited both parties, because if the payor spouse was in a high income-tax bracket and the payee spouse in a low bracket, a deduction for substantial spousal support reduced the payor's tax considerably, while barely nudging the payee spouse's tax. The ex-spouses could then agree to split the savings with the result that the payor spouse could pay more spousal support and still have a larger net income.

The agreement would provide that as the children reached eighteen, the family support amount would decrease by the amount of the child support the payor spouse would otherwise be paying.

The Internal Revenue Service (IRS) soon labeled family support as disguised child support, and said that if a reduction in family support is associated with a contingency relating to a child, it's presumed to all be child support. The IRS applies two tests:

1. If the support is reduced within six months before or after the child's eighteenth birthday, it will be considered child support.

2. Where there is more than one child and more than one reduction in child support, and the two reductions are within one year before or after the two children reach an age which is the same between eighteen and twenty-four.

There are arguments that may get around these tests, but we then enter territory way beyond the scope of this book. This issue is mentioned only to help you identify an issue which you may want to bring to an attorney.

TAXES AND PROPERTY DIVISION

You and your spouse may be exchanging title to property as a result of your divorce. Generally, there will not be any tax to pay as the result of such a transfer. However, whoever gets the property will be responsible for any capital gain tax when the property is sold.

The IRS has issued numerous rulings about how property is to be treated in divorce situations. You need to be especially careful if you are transferring tax shelters or other complicated financial arrangements.

TAXES AND DEPENDENTS

There are simple tax rules regarding child dependents. Whoever has custody gets to claim the children on his or her tax return (unless both parents file a special IRS form agreeing to a different arrangement each year). If you are sharing physical custody, the parent with whom the child lives for the most time during the year is entitled to claim the child as a dependent.

The IRS form to reverse this must be filed each year. Therefore, if you and your spouse have agreed that you will get to claim the children (even though you don't have custody), you should get your spouse to sign an open-ended form which you can file each year, so that you don't have to worry about it each year. A phone call to the IRS can help you get answers to questions on this point.

If Your Spouse Also Files for Divorce

It really makes no difference which spouse files first, unless your spouse has residence in a different county. In that case, it would be more convenient for you if you had filed first in your own county. But other than that, the only effect is psychological. You must answer the Summons—Family Law and Petition within thirty days, just as your spouse would. The other forms discussed in the book apply to both parties.

You answer the Summons—Family Law with the Response (form 22). Look at the Petition (form 3). You'll see it is the same form as the Response other than for the caption, which is "Response" rather than "Petition." Complete the Response according to the same instructions in this book for the Petition. The fee for filing the Response varies from county to county. For example, in Los Angeles it is $192, in Orange County $188. Fees change often, even during the year, so you must call the clerk to find out what the fee is at the time you're ready to file your documents. Please refer to the discussion on the Petition in chapter 7; the same instructions are applicable to the Response.

In situations where your spouse has the children and you find yourself served with divorce papers from another state, get an attorney—fast.

APPENDIX A
CALIFORNIA STATUTES

The following are excerpts from the *California Family Code* and the *California Code of Civil Procedure* relating to property distribution, spousal support (alimony), and child support. These are not the only provisions relating to these subjects, and it is strongly recommended that you review all sections of these codes.

CALIFORNIA STATUTES

FAMILY CODE

3020. (a) The Legislature finds and declares that it is the public policy of this state to assure that the health, safety, and welfare of children shall be the court's primary concern in determining the best interest of children when making any orders regarding the custody or visitation of children. The Legislature further finds and declares that the perpetration of child abuse or domestic violence in a household where a child resides is detrimental to the child.

(b) The Legislature finds and declares that it is the public policy of this state to assure that children have frequent and continuing contact with both parents after the parents have separated or dissolved their marriage, or ended their relationship, and to encourage parents to share the rights and responsibilities of child rearing in order to effect this policy, except where the contact would not be in the best interest of the child, as provided in Section 3011.

(c) Where the policies set forth in subdivisions (a) and (b) of this section are in conflict, any court's order regarding custody or visitation shall be made in a manner that ensures the health, safety, and welfare of the child and the safety of all family members.

4050. In adopting the statewide uniform guideline provided in this article, it is the intention of the Legislature to ensure that this state remains in compliance with federal regulations for child support guidelines.

4052. The court shall adhere to the statewide uniform guideline and may depart from the guideline only in the special circumstances set forth in this article.

4055. (a) The statewide uniform guideline for determining child support orders is as follows: CS = K (HN - (H%) (TN)).

(b) (1) The components of the formula are as follows:

(A) CS = child support amount.

(B) K = amount of both parents' income to be allocated for child support as set forth in paragraph (3).

(C) HN = high earner's net monthly disposable income.

(D) H% = approximate percentage of time that the high earner has or will have primary physical responsibility for the children compared to the other parent. In cases in which parents have different time-sharing arrangements for different children, H% equals the average of the approximate percentages of time the high earner parent spends with each child.

(E) TN = total net monthly disposable income of both parties.

(2) To compute net disposable income, see Section 4059.

(3) K (amount of both parents' income allocated for child support) equals one plus H% (if H% is less than or equal to 50 percent) or two minus H% (if H% is greater than 50 percent) times the following fraction:

Total Net Disposable

Income Per Month	K
$0-800	0.20 + TN/16,000
$801-6,666	0.25
$6,667-10,000	0.10 + 1,000/TN
Over $10,000	0.12 + 800/TN

For example, if H% equals 20 percent and the total monthly net disposable income of the parents is $1,000, K = (1 + 0.20) X 0.25, or 0.30. If H% equals 80 percent and the total monthly net disposable income of the parents is $1,000, K = (2 - 0.80) X 0.25, or 0.30.

(4) For more than one child, multiply CS by:

2 children	1.6
3 children	2
4 children	2.3
5 children	2.5
6 children	2.625
7 children	2.75
8 children	2.813
9 children	2.844
10 children	2.86

(5) If the amount calculated under the formula results in a positive number, the higher earner shall pay that amount to the lower earner. If the amount calculated under the formula results in a negative number, the lower earner shall pay the absolute value of that amount to the higher earner.

(6) In any default proceeding where proof is by affidavit pursuant to Section 2336, or in any proceeding for child support in which a party fails to appear after being duly noticed, H% shall be set at zero in the formula if the noncustodial parent is the higher earner or at 100 if the custodial parent is the higher earner, where there is no evidence presented demonstrating the percentage of time that the non-custodial parent has primary physical responsibility for the children.

(7) In all cases in which the net disposable income per month of the obligor is less than one thousand dollars ($1,000), the court shall rule on whether a low-income adjustment shall be made. The ruling shall be based on the facts presented to the court, the principles provided in Section 4053, and the impact of the contemplated adjustment on the respective net incomes of the obligor and the obligee. Where the court has ruled that a low-income adjustment shall be made, the child support amount otherwise determined under this section shall be reduced by an amount that is no greater than the amount calculated by multiplying the child support amount otherwise determined under this section by a fraction, the numerator of which is 1,000 minus the obligor's net disposable income per month, and the denominator of which is 1,000. If a low-income adjustment is allowed, the court shall state the reasons supporting the adjustment in writing or on the record and shall document the amount of the adjustment and the underlying facts and circumstances.

(8) Unless the court orders otherwise, the order for child support shall allocate the support amount so that the amount of support for the youngest child is the amount of support for one child, and the amount for the next youngest child is the difference between that amount and the amount for two children, with similar allocations for additional children. However, this paragraph does not apply to cases where there are different time-sharing arrangements for different children or where the court determines that the allocation would be inappropriate in the particular case.

(c) In the event a court uses a computer to calculate the child support order, the computer program shall not automatically default affirmatively or negatively on whether a low-income adjustment is to be applied. If the low-income adjustment is applied, the computer program shall not provide the amount of the low-income adjustment. Instead, the computer program shall ask the user whether or not to apply the low-income adjustment, and if answered affirmatively, the computer program shall provide the range of the adjustment permitted by paragraph (7) of subdivision (b).

4056. (a) To comply with federal law, the court shall state, in writing or on the record, the following information whenever the court is ordering an amount for support that differs from the statewide uniform guideline formula amount under this article:

(1) The amount of support that would have been ordered under the guideline formula.

(2) The reasons the amount of support ordered differs from the guideline formula amount.

(3) The reasons the amount of support ordered is consistent with the best interests of the children.

(b) At the request of any party, the court shall state in writing or on the record the following information used in determining the guideline amount under this article:

(1) The net monthly disposable income of each parent.

(2) The actual federal income tax filing status of each parent (for example, single, married, married filing separately, or head of household and number of exemptions).

(3) Deductions from gross income for each parent.

(4) The approximate percentage of time pursuant to paragraph (1) of subdivision (b) of Section 4055 that each parent has primary physical responsibility for the children compared to the other parent.

4057. (a) The amount of child support established by the formula provided in subdivision (a) of Section 4055 is presumed to be the correct amount of child support to be ordered.

(b) The presumption of subdivision (a) is a rebuttable presumption affecting the burden of proof and may be rebutted by admissible evidence showing that application of the formula would be unjust or inappropriate in the particular case, consistent with the principles set forth in Section 4053, because one or more of the following factors is found to be applicable by a preponderance of the evidence, and the court states in writing or on the record the information required in subdivision (a) of Section 4056:

(1) The parties have stipulated to a different amount of child support under subdivision (a) of Section 4065.

(2) The sale of the family residence is deferred pursuant to Chapter 8 (commencing with Section 3800) of Part 1 and the rental value of the family residence in which the children reside exceeds the mortgage payments, homeowner's insurance, and property taxes. The amount of any adjustment

pursuant to this paragraph shall not be greater than the excess amount.

(3) The parent being ordered to pay child support has an extraordinarily high income and the amount determined under the formula would exceed the needs of the children.

(4) A party is not contributing to the needs of the children at a level commensurate with that party's custodial time.

(5) Application of the formula would be unjust or inappropriate due to special circumstances in the particular case. These special circumstances include, but are not limited to, the following:

(A) Cases in which the parents have different time-sharing arrangements for different children.

(B) Cases in which both parents have substantially equal time-sharing of the children and one parent has a much lower or higher percentage of income used for housing than the other parent.

(C) Cases in which the children have special medical or other needs that could require child support that would be greater than the formula amount.

4057.5. (a) (1) The income of the obligor parent's subsequent spouse or nonmarital partner shall not be considered when determining or modifying child support, except in an extraordinary case where excluding that income would lead to extreme and severe hardship to any child subject to the child support award, in which case the court shall also consider whether including that income would lead to extreme and severe hardship to any child supported by the obligor or by the obligor's subsequent spouse or nonmarital partner.

(2) The income of the obligee parent's subsequent spouse or nonmarital partner shall not be considered when determining or modifying child support, except in an extraordinary case where excluding that income would lead to extreme and severe hardship to any child subject to the child support award, in which case the court shall also consider whether including that income would lead to extreme and severe hardship to any child supported by the obligee or by the obligee's subsequent spouse or nonmarital partner.

(b) For purposes of this section, an extraordinary case may include a parent who voluntarily or intentionally quits work or reduces income, or who intentionally remains unemployed or underemployed and relies on a subsequent spouse's income.

(c) If any portion of the income of either parent's subsequent spouse or nonmarital partner is allowed to be considered pursuant to this section, discovery for the purposes of determining income shall be based on W2 and 1099 income tax forms, except where the court determines that application would be unjust or inappropriate.

(d) If any portion of the income of either parent's subsequent spouse or nonmarital partner is allowed to be considered pursuant to this section, the court shall allow a hardship deduction based on the minimum living expenses for one or more stepchildren of the party subject to the order.

(e) The enactment of this section constitutes cause to bring an action for modification of a child support order entered prior to the operative date of this section.

4058. (a) The annual gross income of each parent means income from whatever source derived, except as specified in subdivision (c) and includes, but is not limited to, the following:

(1) Income such as commissions, salaries, royalties, wages, bonuses, rents, dividends, pensions, interest, trust income, annuities, workers' compensation benefits, unemployment insurance benefits, disability insurance benefits, social security benefits, and spousal support actually received from a person not a party to the proceeding to establish a child support order under this article.

(2) Income from the proprietorship of a business, such as gross receipts from the business reduced by expenditures required for the operation of the business.

(3) In the discretion of the court, employee benefits or self-employment benefits, taking into consideration the benefit to the employee, any corresponding reduction in living expenses, and other relevant facts.

(b) The court may, in its discretion, consider the earning capacity of a parent in lieu of the parent's income, consistent with the best interests of the children.

(c) Annual gross income does not include any income derived from child support payments actually received, and income derived from any public assistance program, eligibility for which is based on a determination of need. Child support received by a party for children from another relationship shall not be included as part of that party's gross or net income.

4059. The annual net disposable income of each parent shall be computed by deducting from his or her annual gross income the actual amounts attributable to the following items or other items permitted under this article:

(a) The state and federal income tax liability resulting from the parties' taxable income. Federal and state income tax deductions shall bear an accurate relationship to the tax status of the parties (that is, single, married, married filing separately, or head of household) and number of dependents. State and federal income taxes shall be those actually payable (not necessarily current withholding) after considering appropriate filing status, all available exclusions, deductions, and credits. Unless the parties stipulate otherwise, the tax effects of spousal support shall not be considered in determining the net disposable income of the parties for determining child support, but shall be considered in determining spousal support consistent with Chapter 3 (commencing with Section 4330) of Part 3.

(b) Deductions attributed to the employee's contribution or the self-employed worker's contribution pursuant to the Federal Insurance Contributions Act (FICA), or an amount not to exceed that allowed under FICA for persons not subject to FICA, provided that the deducted amount is used to secure retirement or disability benefits for the parent.

(c) Deductions for mandatory union dues and retirement benefits, provided that they are required as a condition of employment.

(d) Deductions for health insurance or health plan premiums for the parent and for any children the parent has an obligation to support and deductions for state disability insurance premiums.

(e) Any child or spousal support actually being paid by the parent pursuant to a court order, to or for the benefit of any person who is not a subject of the order to be established by the court. In the absence of a court order, any child support actually being paid, not to exceed the amount established by the guideline, for natural or adopted children of the parent not residing in that parent's home, who are not the subject of the order to be established by the court, and of whom the parent has a duty of support. Unless the parent proves payment of the support, no deduction shall be allowed under this subdivision.

(f) Job-related expenses, if allowed by the court after consideration of whether the expenses are necessary, the benefit to the employee, and any other relevant facts.

(g) A deduction for hardship, as defined by Sections 4070 to 4073, inclusive, and applicable published appellate court decisions. The amount of the hardship shall not be deducted from the amount of child support, but shall be deducted from the income of the party to whom it applies. In applying any hardship under paragraph (2) of subdivision (a) of Section 4071, the court shall seek to provide equity between competing child support orders. The Judicial Council shall develop a formula for calculating the maximum hardship deduction and shall submit it to the Legislature for its consideration on or before July 1, 1995.

4060. The monthly net disposable income shall be computed by dividing the annual net disposable income by 12. If the monthly net disposable income figure does not accurately reflect the actual or prospective earnings of the parties at the time the determination of support is made, the court may adjust the amount appropriately.

4061. The amounts in Section 4062, if ordered to be paid, shall be considered additional support for the children and shall be computed in accordance with the following:

(a) If there needs to be an apportionment of expenses pursuant to Section 4062, the expenses shall be divided one-half to each parent, unless either parent requests a different apportionment pursuant to subdivision (b) and presents documentation which demonstrates that a different apportionment would be more appropriate.

(b) If requested by either parent, and the court determines it is appropriate to apportion expenses under Section 4062 other than one-half to each parent, the apportionment shall be as follows:

(1) The basic child support obligation shall first be computed using the formula set forth in subdivision (a) of Section 4055, as adjusted for any appropriate rebuttal factors in subdivision (b) of Section 4057.

(2) Any additional child support required for expenses pursuant to Section 4062 shall thereafter be ordered to be paid by the parents in proportion to their net disposable incomes as adjusted pursuant to subdivisions (c) and (d).

(c) In cases where spousal support is or has been ordered to be paid by one parent to the other, for purposes of allocating additional expenses pursuant to Section 4062, the gross income of the parent paying spousal support shall be decreased by the amount of the spousal support paid and the gross income of the parent receiving the spousal support shall be increased by the amount of the spousal support received for as long as the spousal support order is in effect and is paid.

(d) For purposes of computing the adjusted net disposable income of the parent paying child support for allocating any additional expenses pursuant to Section 4062, the net disposable income of the parent paying child support shall be reduced by the amount of any basic child support ordered to be paid under subdivision (a) of Section 4055. However, the net disposable income of the parent receiving child support shall not be increased by any amount of child support received.

4062. (a) The court shall order the following as additional child support:

(1) Child care costs related to employment or to reasonably necessary education or training for employment skills.

(2) The reasonable uninsured health care costs for the children as provided in Section 4063.

(b) The court may order the following as additional child support:

(1) Costs related to the educational or other special needs of the children.

(2) Travel expenses for visitation.

4065. (a) Unless prohibited by applicable federal law, the parties may stipulate to a child support amount subject to approval of the court. However, the court shall not approve a stipulated agreement for child support below the guideline formula amount unless the parties declare all of the following:

(1) They are fully informed of their rights concerning child support.

(2) The order is being agreed to without coercion or duress.

(3) The agreement is in the best interests of the children involved.

(4) The needs of the children will be adequately met by the stipulated amount.

(5) The right to support has not been assigned to the county pursuant to Section 11477 of the Welfare and Institutions Code and no public assistance application is pending.

(b) A stipulated agreement of child support is not valid unless the district attorney has joined in the stipulation by signing it in any case in which the district attorney is providing services pursuant to Section 11475.1 of the Welfare and Institutions Code. The district attorney shall not stipulate to a child support order below the guideline amount if the children are receiving assistance under the Aid to Families with Dependent Children (AFDC) program, if an application for public assistance is pending, or if the parent receiving support has not consented to the order.

(c) If the parties to a stipulated agreement stipulate to a child support order below the amount established by the statewide uniform guideline, no change of circumstances need be demonstrated to obtain a modification of the child support order to the applicable guideline level or above.

4071. (a) Circumstances evidencing hardship include the following:

(1) Extraordinary health expenses for which the parent is financially responsible, and uninsured catastrophic losses.

(2) The minimum basic living expenses of either parent's natural or adopted children for whom the parent has the obligation to support from other marriages or relationships who reside with the parent. The court, on its own motion or on the request of a party, may allow these income deductions as necessary to accommodate these expenses after making the deductions allowable under paragraph (1).

(b) The maximum hardship deduction under paragraph (2) of subdivision (a) for each child who resides with the parent may be equal to, but shall not exceed, the support allocated each child subject to the order. For purposes of calculating this deduction, the amount of support per child established by the statewide uniform guideline shall be the total amount ordered divided by the number of children and not the amount established under paragraph (8) of subdivision (b) of Section 4055.

(c) The Judicial Council may develop tables in accordance with this section to reflect the maximum hardship deduction, taking into consideration the parent's net disposable income before the hardship deduction, the number of children for whom the deduction is being given, and the number of children for whom the support award is being made.

4320. In ordering spousal support under this part, the court shall consider all of the following circumstances:

(a) The extent to which the earning capacity of each party is sufficient to maintain the standard of living established during the marriage, taking into account all of the following:

(1) The marketable skills of the supported party; the job market for those skills; the time and expenses required for the supported party to acquire the appropriate education or training to develop those skills; and the possible need for retraining or education to acquire other, more marketable skills or employment.

(2) The extent to which the supported party's present or future earning capacity is impaired by periods of unemployment that were incurred during the marriage to permit the supported party to devote time to domestic duties.

(b) The extent to which the supported party contributed to the attainment of an education, training, a career position, or a license by the supporting party.

(c) The ability to pay of the supporting party, taking into account the supporting party's earning capacity, earned and unearned income, assets, and standard of living.

(d) The needs of each party based on the standard of living established during the marriage.

(e) The obligations and assets, including the separate property, of each party.

(f) The duration of the marriage.

(g) The ability of the supported party to engage in gainful employment without unduly interfering with the interests of dependent children in the custody of the party.

(h) The age and health of the parties.

(i) The immediate and specific tax consequences to each party.

(j) The balance of the hardships to each party.

(k) The goal that the supported party shall be self-supporting within a reasonable period of time. A "reasonable period of time" for purposes of this section generally shall be one-half the length of the marriage. However, nothing in this section is intended to limit the court's discretion to order support for a greater or lesser length of time, based on any of the other factors listed in this section and the circumstances of the parties.

(l) Any other factors the court determines are just and equitable.

4323. (a) (1) Except as otherwise agreed to by the parties in writing, there is a rebuttable presumption, affecting the burden of proof, of decreased need for spousal support if the supported party is cohabiting with a person of the opposite sex. Upon a determination that circumstances have changed, the court may modify or terminate the spousal support as provided for in Chapter 6 (commencing with Section 3650) of Part 1.

(2) Holding oneself out to be the husband or wife of the person with whom one is cohabiting is not necessary to constitute cohabitation as the term is used in this subdivision.

(b) The income of a supporting spouse's subsequent spouse or nonmarital partner shall not be considered when determining or modifying spousal support.

(c) Nothing in this section precludes later modification or termination of spousal support on proof of change of circumstances.

10000. This division shall be known and may be cited as the Family Law Facilitator Act.

10001. (a) The Legislature finds and declares the following:

(1) Child and spousal support are serious legal obligations. The entry of a child support order is frequently delayed while parents engage in protracted litigation concerning custody and visitation. The current system for obtaining child and spousal support orders is suffering because the family courts are unduly burdened with heavy case loads and do not have sufficient personnel to meet increased demands on the courts.

[subsections (a)(2)-(4) and (b) omitted]

10002. Each superior court shall maintain an office of the family law facilitator. The office of the family law facilitator shall be staffed by an attorney licensed to practice law in this state who has mediation or litigation experience, or both, in the field of family law. The family law facilitator shall be appointed by the superior court.

10005. (a) By local rule, the superior court may designate additional duties of the family law facilitator, which may include, but are not limited to, the following:

(1) Meeting with litigants to mediate issues of child support, spousal support, and maintenance of health insurance, subject to Section 10012. Actions in which one or both of the parties are unrepresented by counsel shall have priority.

(2) Drafting stipulations to include all issues agreed to by the parties, which may include issues other than those specified in Section 10003.

(3) If the parties are unable to resolve issues with the assistance of the family law facilitator, prior to or at the hearing, and at the request of the court, the family law facilitator shall review the paperwork, examine documents, prepare support schedules, and advise the judge whether or not the matter is ready to proceed.

(4) Assisting the clerk in maintaining records.

(5) Preparing formal orders consistent with the court's announced order in cases where both parties are unrepresented.

(6) Serving as a special master in proceedings and making findings to the court unless he or she has served as a mediator in that case.

(7) Providing the services specified in Division 15 (commencing with Section 10100). Except for the funding specifically designated for visitation programs pursuant to Section 669B of Title 42 of the United States Code, Title IV-D child support funds shall not be used to fund the services specified in Division 15 (commencing with Section 10100).

(b) If staff and other resources are available and the duties listed in subdivision (a) have been accomplished, the duties of the family law facilitator may also include the following:

(1) Assisting the court with research and any other responsibilities which will enable the court to be responsive to the litigants' needs.

(2) Developing programs for bar and community outreach through day and evening programs, videotapes, and other innovative means that will assist unrepresented and financially disadvantaged litigants in gaining meaningful access to family court. These programs shall specifically include information concerning underutilized legislation, such as expedited child support orders (Chapter 5 (commencing with Section 3620) of Part 1 of Division 9), and preexisting, court-sponsored programs, such as supervised visitation and appointment of attorneys for children.

10007. The court shall provide the family law facilitator at no cost to the parties.

10008. (a) Except as provided in subdivision (b), nothing in this chapter shall be construed to apply to a child for whom services are provided or required to be provided by a district attorney pursuant to Section 11475.1 of the Welfare and Institutions Code.

(b) In cases in which the services of the district attorney are provided pursuant to Section 11475.1 of the Welfare and Institutions Code, either parent may utilize the services of the family law facilitator that are specified in Section 10004. In order for a custodial parent who is receiving the services of the district attorney pursuant to Section 11475.1 of the Welfare and Institutions Code to utilize the services specified in Section 10005 relating to support, the custodial parent must obtain written authorization from the district attorney. It is not the intent of the Legislature in enacting this section to limit the duties of district attorneys with respect to seeking child support payments or to in any way limit or supersede other provisions of this code respecting temporary child support.

CODE OF CIVIL PROCEDURE

415.40. A summons may be served on a person outside this state in any manner provided by this article or by sending a copy of the summons and of the complaint to the person to be served by first-class mail, postage prepaid, requiring a return receipt. Service of a summons by this form of mail is deemed complete on the 10th day after such mailing.

415.50. (a) A summons may be served by publication if upon affidavit it appears to the satisfaction of the court in which the action is pending that the party to be served cannot with reasonable diligence be served in another manner specified in this article and that:

(1) A cause of action exists against the party upon whom service is to be made or he or she is a necessary or proper party to the action; or

(2) The party to be served has or claims an interest in real or personal property in this state that is subject to the jurisdiction of the court or the relief demanded in the action consists wholly or in part in excluding the party from any interest in the property.

(b) The court shall order the summons to be published in a named newspaper, published in this state, that is most likely to give actual notice to the party to be served and direct that a copy of the summons, the complaint, and the order for publication be forthwith mailed to the party if his or her address is ascertained before expiration of the time prescribed for publication of the summons. Except as otherwise provided by statute, the publication shall be made as provided by Section 6064 of the Government Code unless the court, in its discretion, orders publication for a longer period.

(c) Service of a summons in this manner is deemed complete as provided in Section 6064 of the Government Code.

(d) Notwithstanding an order for publication of the summons, a summons may be served in another manner authorized by this chapter, in which event the service shall supersede any published summons.

APPENDIX B

FORMS

Be sure to read the section "An Introduction to Legal Forms" in chapter 5 before you begin using the forms in this appendix. The instructions for a particular form may be found by looking in the index. Instead of removing forms, make photocopies to use for both practice worksheets and the forms you will file with the court. The blank forms can then be used to make more copies in the event you make mistakes or need additional copies.

TABLE OF FORMS

The following forms are included in this appendix:

FORM 1: SUMMONS—FAMILY LAW 179

FORM 2: PROOF OF SERVICE OF SUMMONS. 181

FORM 3: PETITION. 183

FORM 4: DECLARATION UNDER UNIFORM CHILD CUSTODY JURISDICTION ACT (UCCJA) . . 185

FORM 5: CONFIDENTIAL COUNSELING STATEMENT (MARRIAGE). 187

FORM 6: NOTICE AND ACKNOWLEDGMENT OF RECEIPT. 189

FORM 7: DECLARATION OF DISCLOSURE 191

FORM 8: SCHEDULE OF ASSETS AND DEBTS 193

FORM 9: INCOME AND EXPENSE DECLARATION 197

FORM 10: DECLARATION REGARDING SERVICE OF DECLARATION OF DISCLOSURE
          AND INCOME AND EXPENSE DECLARATION. 201

FORM 11: FINANCIAL STATEMENT (SIMPLIFIED) 203

FORM 12: APPEARANCE, STIPULATION AND WAIVERS 205

FORM 13: REQUEST TO ENTER DEFAULT 207

FORM 14: DECLARATION FOR DEFAULT OR UNCONTESTED DISSOLUTION OR
LEGAL SEPARATION 209

FORM 15: PROPERTY DECLARATION 211

FORM 16: STIPULATION TO ESTABLISH OR MODIFY CHILD SUPPORT AND ORDER 215

FORM 17: MARITAL SETTLEMENT AGREEMENT (MSA) 217

FORM 18: JUDGMENT 229

FORM 19: NOTICE OF RIGHTS AND RESPONSIBILITIES 231

FORM 20: NOTICE OF ENTRY OF JUDGMENT 233

FORM 21: WAGE AND EARNINGS ASSIGNMENT ORDER 235

FORM 22: RESPONSE 237

FORM 23: JOINT PETITION FOR SUMMARY DISSOLUTION OF MARRIAGE 239

FORM 24: REQUEST FOR JUDGMENT, JUDGMENT OF DISSOLUTION OF MARRIAGE, AND
NOTICE OF ENTRY OF JUDGMENT 241

FORM 25: NOTICE OF REVOCATION OF PETITION FOR SUMMARY DISSOLUTION 243

FORM 26: MEMORANDUM OF REQUEST FOR MILITARY SERVICE STATUS 245

FORM 27: DECLARATION 247

FORM 28: ADDITIONAL PAGE 249

FORM 29: PROOF OF SERVICE BY MAIL 251

FORM 30: APPLICATION FOR WAIVER OF COURT FEES AND COSTS 253

FORM 31: ORDER TO SHOW CAUSE 255

FORM 32: TEMPORARY ORDERS 259

FORM 33: PROOF OF PERSONAL SERVICE 261

FORM 34: FINDINGS AND ORDER AFTER HEARING 263

FORM 35: EX PARTE APPLICATION FOR PUBLICATION OF SUMMONS ORDER; DECLARATION OF
PETITIONER IN SUPPORT THEREOF; MEMORANDUM OF POINTS AND AUTHORITIES . . 265

FORM 36: ORDER FOR PUBLICATION OF SUMMONS—FAMILY LAW 269

FORM 37: CHILD SUPPORT CASE REGISTRY FORM 271

FORM 38: INFORMATION SHEET ON CHANGING A CHILD SUPPORT ORDER 275

FORM 39: CHILD CUSTODY AND VISITATION ORDER ATTACHMENT 277

FORM 40: SUPERVISED VISITATION ORDER 279

FORM 41: CHILD SUPPORT INFORMATION AND ORDER ATTACHMENT 281

FORM 42: NON-GUIDELINE CHILD SUPPORT FINDINGS ATTACHMENT 283

FORM 43: SPOUSAL OR FAMILY SUPPORT ORDER ATTACHMENT 285

FORM 44: PROPERTY ORDER ATTACHMENT 287

SUMMONS—FAMILY LAW   *CITACION JUDICIAL—DERECHO DE FAMILIA*

NOTICE TO RESPONDENT *(Name)*:
AVISO AL DEMANDADO (Nombre):

FOR COURT USE ONLY *(SOLO PARA USO DE LA CORTE)*

> **You are being sued.** *A usted le estan demandando.*

PETITIONER'S NAME IS:
EL NOMBRE DEL DEMANDANTE ES:

CASE NUMBER: *(Número del Caso)*

You have **30 CALENDAR DAYS** after this Summons and Petition are served on you to file a Response (form 1282) at the court and serve a copy on the petitioner. A letter or phone call will not protect you. If you do not file your Response on time, the court may make orders affecting your marriage, your property, and custody of your children. You may be ordered to pay support and attorney fees and costs. If you cannot pay the filing fee, ask the clerk for a fee waiver form. If you want legal advice, contact a lawyer immediately.	*Usted tiene **30 DIAS CALENDARIOS** después de recibir oficialmente esta citación judicial y petición, para completar y presentar su formulario de Respuesta (Response form 1282) ante la corte. Una carta o una llamada telefónica no le ofrecerá protección. Si usted no presenta su Respuesta a tiempo, la corte puede expedir órdenes que afecten su matrimonio, su propiedad y que ordenen que usted pague mantención, honorarios de abogado y las costas. Si no puede pagar las costas por la presentación de la demanda, pida al actuario de la corte que le dé un formulario de exoneración de las mismas (Waiver of Court Fees and Costs). Si desea obtener consejo legal, comuníquese de inmediato con un abogado.*

NOTICE *The restraining orders on the back are effective against both husband and wife until the petition is dismissed, a judgment is entered, or the court makes further orders. These orders are enforceable anywhere in California by any law enforcement officer who has received or seen a copy of them.*

AVISO *Las prohibiciones judiciales que aparecen al reverso de esta citación son efectivas para ambos cónyuges, tanto el esposo como la esposa, hasta que la petición sea rechazada, se dicte una decisión final o la corte expida instrucciones adicionales. Dichas prohibiciones pueden hacerse cumplir en cualquier parte de California por cualquier agente del orden público que las haya recibido o que haya visto una copia de ellas.*

1. The name and address of the court is: *(El nombre y dirección de la corte es)*

2. The name, address, and telephone number of petitioner's attorney, or petitioner without an attorney, is:
   (El nombre, la dirección y el número de teléfono del abogado del demandante, o del demandante que no tiene abogado, es)

[SEAL]

Date *(Fecha)*: _____   Clerk *(Actuario)*, by _____ , Deputy

NOTICE TO THE PERSON SERVED: You are served
a. ☐ as an individual.
b. ☐ on behalf of respondent
   under: ☐ CCP 416.60 (minor)   ☐ CCP 416.90 (individual)
          ☐ CCP 416.70 (ward or conservatee)   ☐ other:
c. ☐ by personal delivery on *(date)*:

(Read the reverse for important information)
(Lea el reverso para obtener información de importancia)

Form Adopted by Rule 1283
Judicial Council of California
1283 [Rev. January 1, 1995]

SUMMONS
(Family Law)

Family Code, §§ 232, 233, 2040, 7700
Calif. Rules of Court, rule 1216

WARNING: California law provides that, for purposes of division of property upon dissolution of marriage or legal separation, property acquired by the parties during marriage in joint form is presumed to be community property. If either party to this action should die before the jointly held community property is divided, the language of how title is held in the deed (i.e., joint tenancy, tenants in common, or community property) will be controlling and not the community property presumption. You should consult your attorney if you want the community property presumption to be written into the recorded title to the property.

ADVERTENCIA: Para los efectos de la división de bienes al momento de una separación legal o de la disolución de un matrimonio, las leyes de California disponen que se presuman como bienes de la sociedad conyugal aquélles adquiridos en forma conjunta por las partes durante el matrimonio. Si cualquiera de las partes de esta acción muriese antes de que se dividan los bienes en tenencia conjunta de la sociedad conyugal, prevalecerá el lenguaje relativo a la tenencia de los derechos de propriedad contenido en la escritura—como, por ejemplo, copropiedad con derechos de sucesión (joint tenancy), tenencia en comun (tenants in common) o bienes de la sociedad conyugal (community property)—y no la presunción de que los bienes son de la sociedad conyugal. Usted debe consultar a su abogado o abogada si desea que la presunción de que los bienes son de la sociedad conyugal se especifique en el título de propiedad inscrito.

STANDARD RESTRAINING ORDERS—FAMILY LAW
PROHIBICIONES JUDICIALES ESTANDARES—DERECHO DE FAMILIA

STANDARD FAMILY LAW RESTRAINING ORDERS

Starting immediately, you and your spouse are restrained from

1. removing the minor child or children of the parties, if any, from the state without the prior written consent of the other party or an order of the court;
2. cashing, borrowing against, canceling, transferring, disposing of, or changing the beneficiaries of any insurance or other coverage including life, health, automobile, and disability held for the benefit of the parties and their minor child or children; and
3. transferring, encumbering, hypothecating, concealing, or in any way disposing of any property, real or personal, whether community, quasi-community, or separate, without the written consent of the other party or an order of the court, except in the usual course of business or for the necessities of life.

You must notify each other of any proposed extraordinary expenditures at least five business days prior to incurring these extraordinary expenditures and account to the court for all extraordinary expenditures made after these restraining orders are effective. However, nothing in the restraining orders shall preclude you from using community property to pay reasonable attorney fees in order to retain legal counsel in the action.

PROHIBICIONES JUDICIALES ESTANDARES—DERECHO DE FAMILIA

A usted y a su cónyuge se les prohibe

1. *que saquen del estado al hijo o hijos menores de las partes, si los hay, sin el consentimiento previo por escrito de la otra parte o sin una orden de la corte; y*
2. *que cobren en efectivo, usen como colateral para préstamos, cancelen, transfieran, descontinúen o cambien los beneficiarios de, cualquier póliza de seguro u otras coberturas de seguro, inclusive los de vida, salud, automóvil e incapacidad mantenido para el beneficio de las partes y su hijo o hijos menores; y*
3. *que transfieran, graven, hipotequen, escondan o de cualquier otra manera enajenen cualquier propiedad mueble o inmueble, ya sean bienes de la sociedad conyugal, quasi conyugales o bienes propios de los cónyuges, sin el consentimiento por escrito de la otra parte o sin una orden de la corte, excepto en el curso normal de los negocios o para atender a las necesidades de la vida.*

Ustedes deben notificarse entre sí sobre cualquier gasto extraordinario propuesto, por lo menos con cinco días de antelación a la fecha en que se van a incurrir dichos gastos extraordinarios y responder ante la corte por todo gasto extraordinario hecho después de que estas prohibiciones judiciales entren en vigor. Sin embargo, nada de lo contenido en las prohibiciones judiciales le impedirá que use bienes de la sociedad conyugal para pagar honorarios razonables de abogados con el fin de obtener representación legal durante el proceso.

MARRIAGE OF *(last name, first name of parties)*:	CASE NUMBER:

Serve a copy of the documents on the person to be served. Complete the proof of service. Attach it to the original documents. File them with the court.

PROOF OF SERVICE OF SUMMONS (Family Law)

1. I served the Summons with Standard Restraining Orders (Family Law), **blank Response**, and Petition (Family Law) on respondent *(name)*:

   a. with (1) ☐ blank Confidential Counseling Statement   (4) ☐ completed and blank Income and
         (2) ☐ Order to Show Cause and Application   Expense Declarations
         (3) ☐ blank Responsive Declaration   (5) ☐ completed and blank Property Declarations
                                            (6) ☐ Other *(specify)*:

   b. ☐ By leaving copies with *(name and title or relationship to person served)*:

   c. ☐ By delivery at ☐ home ☐ business
      (1) Date of: (3) Address:
      (2) Time of:

   d. ☐ By mailing (1) Date of: (2) Place of:

2. Manner of service: *(Check proper box)*
   a. ☐ **Personal service.** By personally delivering copies to the person served. (CCP 415.10)
   b. ☐ **Substituted service on natural person, minor, incompetent.** By leaving copies at the dwelling house, usual place of abode, or usual place of business of the person served in the presence of a competent member of the household or a person apparently in charge of the office or place of business, at least 18 years of age, who was informed of the general nature of the papers, and thereafter mailing (by first-class mail, postage prepaid) copies to the person served at the place where the copies were left. (CCP 415.20(b)) **(Attach separate declaration stating acts relied on to establish reasonable diligence in first attempting personal service.)**
   c. ☐ **Mail and acknowledge service.** By mailing (by first-class mail or airmail) copies to the person served, together with two copies of the form of notice and acknowledgment and a return envelope, postage prepaid, addressed to the sender. (CCP 415.30) **(Attach completed acknowledgment of receipt.)**
   d. ☐ **Certified or registered mail service.** By mailing to address outside California (by registered or certified airmail with return receipt requested) copies to the person served. (CCP 415.40) **(Attach signed return receipt or other evidence of actual delivery to the person served.)**
   e. ☐ Other *(specify code section)*:
       ☐ Additional page is attached.

3. The NOTICE TO THE PERSON SERVED on the summons was completed as follows (CCP 412.30, 415.10, and 474):
   a. ☐ as an individual
   b. ☐ on behalf of Respondent
      under ☐ CCP 416.90 (Individual)   ☐ CCP 416.70 (Ward or Conservatee)   ☐ CCP 416.60 (Minor)
            ☐ Other *(specify)*:
   c. ☐ by personal delivery on *(date)*:

4. At the time of service I was at least 18 years of age and not a party to this action.

5. Fee for service: $

6. Person serving:
   a. ☐ Not a registered California process server.   e. ☐ California sheriff, marshal, or constable.
   b. ☐ Registered California process server.   f. Name, address, and telephone number and, if
   c. ☐ Employee or independent contractor of a   applicable, county of registration and number:
       registered California process server.
   d. ☐ Exempt from registration under Bus. & Prof.
       Code section 22350(b).

I declare under penalty of perjury under the laws of the State of California that the foregoing is true and correct.
Date:

▶

─────────────────────────
         (SIGNATURE)

(For California sheriff, marshal, or constable use only)
I certify that the foregoing is true and correct.
Date:

▶

─────────────────────────
         (SIGNATURE)

Form Adopted by Rule 1283.5
Judicial Council of California
1283.5 [New January 1, 1991]

PROOF OF SERVICE OF SUMMONS
(Family Law)

ATTORNEY OR PARTY WITHOUT ATTORNEY(Name, state bar number, and address)	FOR COURT USE ONLY
TELEPHONE NO.: FAX NO.:	
ATTORNEY FOR (Name):	

SUPERIOR COURT OF CALIFORNIA, COUNTY OF	
STREET ADDRESS:	
MAILING ADDRESS:	
CITY AND ZIP CODE:	
BRANCH NAME:	

MARRIAGE OF

PETITIONER:

RESPONDENT:

PETITION FOR	CASE NUMBER:
☐ **Dissolution of Marriage** ☐ **Legal Separation** ☐ **Nullity of Marriage** ☐ **AMENDED**	

1. RESIDENCE (Dissolution only) ☐ Petitioner ☐ Respondent has been a resident of this state for at least six months and of this county for at least three months immediately preceding the filing of this *Petition for Dissolution of Marriage*.

2. STATISTICAL FACTS
   a. Date of marriage:
   b. Date of separation:
   c. Period between marriage and separation
       Years: Months:

3. DECLARATION REGARDING MINOR CHILDREN *(include children of this relationship born prior to or during the marriage or adopted during the marriage)*:
   a. ☐ There are no minor children.
   b. ☐ The minor children are:

Child's name	Birth date	Age	Sex

   ☐ Continued on Attachment 3b.
   c. If there are minor children of the Petitioner and Respondent, a completed *Declaration Under the Uniform Child Custody Jurisdiction Act (UCCJA)* (form MC-150) must be attached.
   d. ☐ A completed voluntary declaration of paternity regarding minor children born to the Petitioner and Respondent prior to the marriage is attached.

4. ☐ **Petitioner requests** confirmation as separate property assets and debts the items listed
   ☐ in Attachment 4   ☐ below:

Item	Confirm to

NOTICE: Any party required to pay child support must pay interest on overdue amounts at the "legal" rate, which is currently 10 percent.

(Continued on reverse)

Form Adopted for Mandatory Use
Judicial Council of California
Rule 1281 [Rev. July 1, 1999]

PETITION
(Family Law)

Family Code, §§ 2330, 3409;
Cal. Rules of Court, rule 1215

183

MARRIAGE OF (last name, first name of parties):	CASE NUMBER:

5. DECLARATION REGARDING COMMUNITY AND QUASI-COMMUNITY ASSETS AND DEBTS AS CURRENTLY KNOWN

a. ☐ There are no such assets or debts subject to disposition by the court in this proceeding.

b. ☐ All such assets and debts have been disposed of by written agreement.

c. ☐ All such assets and debts are listed ☐ in Attachment 5c ☐ below (specify):

6. Petitioner requests

a. ☐ Dissolution of the marriage based on
    (1) ☐ irreconcilable differences. Fam. Code, § 2310(a)
    (2) ☐ incurable insanity. Fam. Code, § 2310(b)

b. ☐ Legal separation of the parties based on
    (1) ☐ irreconcilable differences. Fam. Code, § 2310(a)
    (2) ☐ incurable insanity. Fam. Code, § 2310(b)

c. ☐ Nullity of void marriage based on
    (1) ☐ incestuous marriage. Fam. Code, § 2200
    (2) ☐ bigamous marriage. Fam. Code, § 2201

d. ☐ Nullity of voidable marriage based on
    (1) ☐ petitioner's age at time of marriage. Fam. Code, § 2210(a)
    (2) ☐ prior existing marriage. Fam. Code, § 2210(b)
    (3) ☐ unsound mind. Fam. Code, § 2210(c)
    (4) ☐ fraud. Fam. Code, § 2210(d)
    (5) ☐ force. Fam. Code, § 2210(e)
    (6) ☐ physical incapacity. Fam. Code, § 2210(f)

7. Petitioner requests that the court grant the above relief and make injunctive (including restraining) and other orders as follows:

	Petitioner	Respondent	Joint	Other
a. Legal custody of children to	☐	☐	☐	☐
b. Physical custody of children to	☐	☐	☐	☐
c. Child visitation be granted to	☐	☐		☐
(1) ☐ Supervised for	☐	☐		
(2) ☐ No visitation for	☐	☐		
(3) ☐ Continued on Attachment 7c(3).				

d. ☐ Determination of parentage of any children born to the Petitioner and Respondent prior to the marriage.

	Petitioner	Respondent
e. Spousal support payable to (wage assignment will be issued)	☐	☐
f. Attorney fees and costs payable by	☐	☐

g. ☐ Terminate the court's jurisdiction (ability) to award spousal support to respondent.

h. ☐ Property rights be determined.

i. ☐ Petitioner's former name be restored (specify):

j. ☐ Other (specify):
    ☐ Continued on Attachment 7j.

8. If there are minor children born to or adopted by the Petitioner and Respondent before or during this marriage, the court will make orders for the support of the children. A wage assignment will be issued without further notice.

9. I HAVE READ THE RESTRAINING ORDERS ON THE BACK OF THE SUMMONS, AND I UNDERSTAND THAT THEY APPLY TO ME WHEN THIS PETITION IS FILED.

I declare under penalty of perjury under the laws of the State of California that the foregoing is true and correct.

Date:

_____ ▶ _____
(TYPE OR PRINT NAME)   (SIGNATURE OF PETITIONER)

Date:

_____ ▶ _____
(TYPE OR PRINT NAME)   (SIGNATURE OF ATTORNEY FOR PETITIONER)

NOTICE: Please review your will, insurance policies, retirement benefit plans, credit cards, other credit accounts and credit reports, and other matters you may want to change in view of the dissolution or annulment of your marriage, or your legal separation. However, some changes may require the agreement of your spouse or a court order (see Fam. Code, §§ 231-235). Dissolution or annulment of your marriage may automatically change a disposition made by your will to your former spouse.

ATTORNEY OR PARTY WITHOUT ATTORNEY *(Name and Mailing Address)*:	TELEPHONE NO.:	FOR COURT USE ONLY
ATTORNEY FOR *(Name)*:		

SUPERIOR COURT OF CALIFORNIA, COUNTY OF

STREET ADDRESS:

MAILING ADDRESS:

CITY AND ZIP CODE:

BRANCH NAME:

CASE NAME:

DECLARATION UNDER **UNIFORM CHILD CUSTODY JURISDICTION ACT (UCCJA)**	CASE NUMBER:

1. **I am a party** to this proceeding to determine custody of a child.

2. ☐ Declarant's present address is not disclosed. It is confidential under Family Code section 3409. The address of children presently residing with declarant is identified on this declaration as confidential.

3. *(Number):* _____ minor children are subject to this proceeding as follows:

   (Insert the information requested below. The residence information must be given for the last FIVE years.)

a. Child's name		Place of birth	Date of birth	Sex

Period of residence	Address	Person child lived with *(name and present address)*	Relationship
to present	☐ Confidential		
to			
to			
to			

b. Child's name		Place of birth	Date of birth	Sex

☐ Residence information is the same as given above for child **a.**
(If NOT the same, provide the information below.)

Period of residence	Address	Person child lived with *(name and present address)*	Relationship
to present	☐ Confidential		
to			
to			

c. ☐ Additional children are listed on Attachment 3c. *(Provide requested information for additional children on an attachment.)*

(Continued on reverse)

Form Approved by the
Judicial Council of California
MC-150 [Rev. January 1, 1997]

DECLARATION UNDER
UNIFORM CHILD CUSTODY JURISDICTION ACT (UCCJA)

Family Code, § 3409
Probate Code, §§ 1510(f), 1512

185

SHORT TITLE:	CASE NUMBER:

4. Have you participated as a party or a witness or in some other capacity in another litigation or custody proceeding, in California or elsewhere, concerning custody of a child subject to this proceeding?

☐ No ☐ Yes *(If yes, provide the following information:)*

a. Name of each child:

b. Capacity of declarant: ☐ party ☐ witness ☐ other *(specify):*

c. Court *(specify name, state, location):*

d. Court order or judgment *(date):*

5. Do you have information about a custody proceeding pending in a California court or any other court concerning a child subject to this proceeding, other than that stated in item 4?

☐ No ☐ Yes *(If yes, provide the following information:)*

a. Name of each child:

b. Nature of proceeding: ☐ dissolution or divorce ☐ guardianship ☐ adoption ☐ other *(specify):*

c. Court *(specify name, state, location):*

d. Status of proceeding:

6. Do you know of any person who is not a party to this proceeding who has physical custody or claims to have custody of or visitation rights with any child subject to this proceeding?

☐ No ☐ Yes *(If yes, provide the following information:)*

a. Name and address of person	b. Name and address of person	c. Name and address of person
☐ Has physical custody ☐ Claims custody rights ☐ Claims visitation rights	☐ Has physical custody ☐ Claims custody rights ☐ Claims visitation rights	☐ Has physical custody ☐ Claims custody rights ☐ Claims visitation rights
Name of each child	Name of each child	Name of each child

I declare under penalty of perjury under the laws of the State of California that the foregoing is true and correct.
Date:

▶

_____
(TYPE OR PRINT NAME)

_____
(SIGNATURE OF DECLARANT)

7. ☐ Number of pages attached after this page:

NOTICE TO DECLARANT: You have a continuing duty to inform this court if you obtain any information about a custody proceeding in a California court or any other court concerning a child subject to this proceeding.

**DECLARATION UNDER
UNIFORM CHILD CUSTODY JURISDICTION ACT (UCCJA)**

Name, Address and Telephone No. of Attorney(s)

Space Below for Use of Court Clerk Only

Attorney(s) for . . . .

SUPERIOR COURT OF CALIFORNIA, COUNTY OF . . . .

In re the marriage of

Petitioner:

and

Respondent:

CASE NUMBER

☐ **Petitioner's** ☐ **Respondent's**

CONFIDENTIAL COUNSELING STATEMENT (MARRIAGE)

I understand that conciliation services are available to me through the court in this county.

☐ I would like marriage counseling.

☐ I would like to talk with a trained person about my present family situation.

☐ I do not desire counseling at this time.

Mailing address of requesting party:

Name:

Street:

City/State/Zip

Mailing address of other party:

Name:

Street:

City/State/Zip

Date:

_____
(Signature)

Form Adopted by Rule 1284 of
The Judicial Council of California
Effective January 1, 1975

CONFIDENTIAL COUNSELING STATEMENT (MARRIAGE)

NAME AND ADDRESS OF SENDER:	TELEPHONE NO.:	For Court Use Only:
Insert name of court, judicial district or branch court, if any, and Post Office and Street Address:		

PLAINTIFF:

DEFENDANT:

NOTICE AND ACKNOWLEDGMENT OF RECEIPT	Case Number:

TO: . . . .

(Insert name of individual being served)

This summons and other document(s) indicated below are being served pursuant to Section 415.30 of the California Code of Civil Procedure. Your failure to complete this form and return it to me within 20 days may subject you (or the party on whose behalf you are being served) to liability for the payment of any expenses incurred in serving a summons on you in any other manner permitted by law.

If you are being served on behalf of a corporation, unincorporated association (including a partnership), or other entity, this form must be signed by you in the name of such entity or by a person authorized to receive service of process on behalf of such entity. In all other cases, this form must be signed by you personally or by a person authorized by you to acknowledge receipt of summons. Section 415.30 provides that this summons and other document(s) are deemed served on the date you sign the Acknowledgment of Receipt below, if you return this form to me.

Dated: . . . . _____

(Signature of sender)

ACKNOWLEDGMENT OF RECEIPT

This acknowledges receipt of: (To be completed by sender before mailing)

1. ☐ A copy of the summons and of the complaint.
2. ☐ A copy of the summons and of the Petition (Marriage) and:
   ☐ Blank Confidential Counseling Statement (Marriage)
   ☐ Order to Show Cause (Marriage)
   ☐ Blank Responsive Declaration
   ☐ Blank Financial Declaration
   ☐ Other: (Specify)

(To be completed by recipient)

Date of receipt: . . . . _____

(Signature of person acknowledging receipt, with title if acknowledgment is made on behalf of another person)

Date this form is signed: . . . . _____

(Type or print your name and name of entity, if any, on whose behalf this form is signed)

Form Approved by the
Judicial Council of California
Revised Effective January 1, 1975

NOTICE AND ACKNOWLEDGMENT OF RECEIPT

CCP 415.30, 417.10
Cal. Rules of Court,
Rule 1216

189

ATTORNEY OR PARTY WITHOUT ATTORNEY *(Name and Address)*:	TELEPHONE NO.:	*FOR COURT USE ONLY*

ATTORNEY FOR *(Name)*:

SUPERIOR COURT OF CALIFORNIA, COUNTY OF

STREET ADDRESS:

MAILING ADDRESS:

CITY AND ZIP CODE:

BRANCH NAME:

PETITIONER:

RESPONDENT:

DECLARATION OF DISCLOSURE	CASE NUMBER:
☐ **Petitioner's** ☐ **Preliminary** ☐ **Respondent's** ☐ **Final**	

DO NOT FILE WITH THE COURT

Both the preliminary and the final declaration of disclosure must be served on the other party with certain exceptions. Neither disclosure is filed with the court. A declaration stating service was made of the final declaration of disclosure must be filed with the court (see form 1292.05).

A preliminary declaration of disclosure but not a final declaration of disclosure is required in the case of a summary dissolution (see Family Code section 2109) or in a default judgment (see Family Code section 2110) provided the default is not a stipulated judgment or a judgment pursuant to a marriage settlement agreement.

A declaration of disclosure is required in a nullity or legal separation action as well as in a dissolution action.

Attached are the following:

1. ☐ A completed Schedule of Assets and Debts *(form 1292.11).*

2. ☐ A completed Income and Expense Declaration *(forms 1285.50, 1285.50a, 1285.50b, and 1285.50c (as applicable)).*

3. ☐ A statement of all material facts and information regarding valuation of all assets that are community property or in which the community has an interest *(not a form).*

4. ☐ A statement of all material facts and information regarding obligations for which the community is liable *(not a form).*

5. ☐ An accurate and complete written disclosure of any investment opportunity presented since the date of separation *(not a form).*

I declare under penalty of perjury under the laws of the State of California that the foregoing is true and correct.

Date:

. . . .

(TYPE OR PRINT NAME)   ▶   (SIGNATURE)

Form Adopted by Rule 1292 Judicial Council of California 1292 [Rev. January 1, 1994]	**DECLARATION OF DISCLOSURE** **(Family Law)**	Family Code, §§ 2104, 2105, 2106, 2112

ATTORNEY OR PARTY WITHOUT ATTORNEY *(Name and Address)*:	TELEPHONE NO.:

ATTORNEY FOR *(Name)*:

SUPERIOR COURT OF CALIFORNIA, COUNTY OF

MARRIAGE OF
  PETITIONER:

RESPONDENT:

SCHEDULE OF ASSETS AND DEBTS ☐ **Petitioner's** ☐ **Respondent's**	CASE NUMBER:

— INSTRUCTIONS —

List all your known community and separate assets or debts. Include assets even if they are in the possession of another person, including your spouse. If you contend an asset or debt is separate, put H or W in the first column (separate property) to indicate to whom you contend it belongs.

All values should be as of the date of signing the declaration unless you specify a different valuation date with the description.

For additional space, use a continuation sheet numbered to show what item is being continued.

ITEM NO.	ASSETS—DESCRIPTION	SEP. PROP.	DATE ACQUIRED	CURRENT GROSS FAIR MARKET VALUE	AMOUNT OF MONEY OWED OR ENCUMBRANCE
1.	REAL ESTATE *(Give street addresses and attach copies of deeds with legal descriptions and latest lender's statement.)*			$	$
2.	HOUSEHOLD FURNITURE, FURNISHINGS, APPLIANCES *(Identify)*				
3.	JEWELRY, ANTIQUES, ART, COIN COLLECTIONS, etc. *(Identify)*				

(Continued on reverse)

Page one of four

Form Approved by Rule 1292.11
Judicial Council of California
1292.11 [New July 1, 1990]

SCHEDULE OF ASSETS AND DEBTS
(Family Law)

Code of Civil Procedure, §§ 2030(c), 2033.5

193

ITEM NO.	ASSETS—DESCRIPTION	SEP. PROP.	DATE ACQUIRED	CURRENT GROSS FAIR MARKET VALUE	AMOUNT OF MONEY OWED OR ENCUMBRANCE
				$	$
4.	VEHICLES, BOATS, TRAILERS *(Describe and attach copy of title document.)*				
5.	SAVINGS ACCOUNTS *(Account name, account number, bank, and branch. Attach copy of latest statement.)*				
6.	CHECKING ACCOUNTS *(Account name and number, bank, and branch. Attach copy of latest statement.)*				
7.	CREDIT UNION, OTHER DEPOSIT ACCOUNTS *(Account name and number, bank, and branch. Attach copy of latest statement.)*				
8.	CASH *(Give location.)*				
9.	TAX REFUND				
10.	LIFE INSURANCE WITH CASH SURRENDER OR LOAN VALUE *(Attach copy of declaration page for each policy.)*				

(Continued on next page)

ITEM NO.	ASSETS—DESCRIPTION	SEP. PROP.	DATE ACQUIRED	CURRENT GROSS FAIR MARKET VALUE	AMOUNT OF MONEY OWED OR ENCUMBRANCE
				$	$
11.	STOCKS, BONDS, SECURED NOTES, MUTUAL FUNDS *(Give certificate number and attach copy of the certificate or copy of latest statement.)*				
12.	RETIREMENT AND PENSIONS *(Attach copy of latest summary plan documents and latest benefit statement.)*				
13.	PROFIT-SHARING, ANNUITIES, IRAS, DEFERRED COMPENSATION *(Attach copy of latest statement.)*				
14.	ACCOUNTS RECEIVABLE AND UNSECURED NOTES *(Attach copy of each.)*				
15.	PARTNERSHIPS AND OTHER BUSINESS INTERESTS *(Attach copy of most current K–1 form and schedule C.)*				
16.	OTHER ASSETS				
17.	TOTAL ASSETS FROM CONTINUATION SHEET				
18.	TOTAL ASSETS			$	$

(Continued on reverse)

1292.11 [New July 1, 1990]

SCHEDULE OF ASSETS AND DEBTS
(Family Law)

Page three of four

ITEM NO.	DEBTS—SHOW TO WHOM OWED	SEP. PROP	TOTAL OWING	DATE INCURRED
19. STUDENT LOANS *(Give details.)*			$	
20. TAXES *(Give details.)*				
21. SUPPORT ARREARAGES *(Attach copies of orders and statements.)*				
22. LOANS—UNSECURED *(Give bank name and loan No. and attach copy of latest statement.)*				
23. CREDIT CARDS *(Give creditor's name and address and the account number. Attach copy of latest statement.)*				
24. OTHER DEBTS *(specify):*				
25. TOTAL DEBTS FROM CONTINUATION SHEET				
26. TOTAL DEBTS			$	

27. ☐ _____ pages are attached as continuation sheets.

I declare under penalty of perjury under the laws of the State of California that the foregoing is true and correct.

Date:

....
(TYPE OR PRINT NAME)

▶ _____

(SIGNATURE OF DECLARANT)

SCHEDULE OF ASSETS AND DEBTS
(Family Law)

Page four of four

ATTORNEY OR PARTY WITHOUT ATTORNEY *(Name and Address)*:	TELEPHONE NO.:	**FOR COURT USE ONLY**

ATTORNEY FOR *(Name)*:

SUPERIOR COURT OF CALIFORNIA, COUNTY OF

STREET ADDRESS:

MAILING ADDRESS:

CITY AND ZIP CODE:

BRANCH NAME:

PETITIONER/PLAINTIFF:

RESPONDENT/DEFENDANT:

INCOME AND EXPENSE DECLARATION	CASE NUMBER:

Step 1
Attachments to this summary

I have completed ☐ Income ☐ Expense ☐ Child Support Information forms.
(If child support is not an issue, do not complete the Child Support Information Form. If your only income is AFDC, do not complete the Income Information Form.)

Step 2
Answer all questions that apply to you

1. Are you receiving or have you applied for or do you intend to apply for welfare or AFDC?
☐ Receiving ☐ Applied for ☐ Intend to apply for ☐ No
2. What is your date of birth *(month/day/year)*? . . . . ─────
3. What is your occupation? ─────
4. Highest year of education completed: ─────
5. Are you currently employed? ☐ Yes ☐ No
   a. If yes: (1) Where do you work? *(name and address)*: ─────

           (2) When did you start work there *(month/year)*? . . . . ─────
   b. If no: (1) When did you last work *(month/year)*? . . . . ─────
           (2) What were your gross monthly earnings? . . . . ─────
6. What is the total number of minor children you are legally obligated to support? . . . . ─────

Step 3
Monthly income information

7. Net monthly disposable income *(from line 16a of Income Information)*: . . . . $ _____

8. Current net monthly disposable income *(if different from line 7, explain below or on Attachment 8)*: . . . . $ _____

Step 4
Expense information

9. Total monthly expenses from line 2q of Expense Information: . . . . $ _____
10. Amount of these expenses paid by others: . . . . $ _____

Step 5 Other party's income

11. My estimate of the other party's gross monthly income is: . . . . $ _____

Step 6
Date and sign this form

I declare under penalty of perjury under the laws of the State of California that the foregoing and the attached information forms are true and correct.

Date:

▶

....
         (TYPE OR PRINT NAME)

_____
(SIGNATURE OF DECLARANT)
☐ Petitioner ☐ Respondent

Page one of _____

Form Adopted by Rule 1285.50
Judicial Council of California
1285.50 [Rev. January 1, 1995]

INCOME AND EXPENSE DECLARATION
(Family Law)

PETITIONER/PLAINTIFF:	CASE NUMBER:
RESPONDENT/DEFENDANT:	
INCOME INFORMATION OF *(name):*	

1. Total gross salary or wages, including commissions, bonuses, and overtime paid during the last 12 months: 1. $ _____

2. All other money received during the last 12 months **except welfare, AFDC,** *Specify sources below:*
   SSI, spousal support from this marriage, or any child support.
   Include pensions, social security, disability, unemployment, military _____ 2a. $ _____
   basic allowance for quarters (BAQ), spousal support from a different
   marriage, dividends, interest or royalty, trust income, and annuities. _____ 2b. $ _____
   Include income from a business, rental properties, and reimbursement
   of job-related expenses _____ 2c. $ _____

   → *Prepare and attach a schedule showing gross receipts less cash* _____ 2d. $ _____
      expenses for each business or rental property

3. Add lines 1 through 2d .... 3. _____
   Divide line 3 by 12 and place result on line 4a. $

	Average last 12 months:	Last month:
4. Gross income	4a. $ _____	4b. $ _____
5. State income tax	5a. $ _____	5b. $ _____
6. Federal income tax	6a. $ _____	6b. $ _____
7. Social Security and Hospital Tax ("FICA" and "MEDI") or self-employment tax, or the amount used to secure retirement or disability benefits	7a. $ _____	7b. $ _____
8. Health insurance for you and any children you are required to support	8a. $ _____	8b. $ _____
9. State disability insurance	9a. $ _____	9b. $ _____
10. Mandatory union dues	10a. $ _____	10b. $ _____
11. Mandatory retirement and pension fund contributions .... *Do not include any deduction claimed in item 7.*	11a. $ _____	11b. $ _____
12. Court-ordered child support, court-ordered spousal support, and voluntarily paid child support in an amount not more than the guideline amount, **actually being paid for a relationship *other* than that involved in this proceeding:**	12a. $ _____	12b. $ _____
13. Necessary job-related expenses *(attach explanation)*	13a. $ _____	13b. $ _____
14. Hardship deduction (Line 4d on Child Support Information Form)	14a. $ _____	14b. $ _____
15. Add lines 5 through 14. .... Total monthly deductions:	15a. $	15b. $
16. Subtract line 15 from line 4. .... Net monthly disposable income:	16a. $	16b. $

17. AFDC, welfare, spousal support from this marriage, and child support from other relationships received
    each month: .... 17. $ _____
18. Cash and checking accounts: .... 18. $ _____
19. Savings, credit union, certificates of deposit, and money market accounts: .... 19. $ _____
20. Stocks, bonds, and other liquid assets: .... 20. $ _____
21. All other property, real or personal *(specify below):* .... 21. $ _____

→ **Attach a copy of your three most recent pay stubs.** Page _____ of _____

Form Adopted by Rule 1285.50a
Judicial Council of California
1285.50a [Rev. January 1, 1995]

INCOME INFORMATION
(Family Law)

PETITIONER/PLAINTIFF:	CASE NUMBER:
RESPONDENT/DEFENDANT:	
EXPENSE INFORMATION OF *(name)*:	

1.

		name	age	relationship	gross monthly income
a. List all persons living in your home **whose expenses are included below** and their income: ☐ Continued on Attachment 1a.	1. 2. 3. 4.				
b. List all other persons living in your home and their income: ☐ Continued on Attachment 1b.	1. 2. 3.				

2. MONTHLY EXPENSES

a. Residence payments

   (1) ☐ Rent or ☐ mortgage . . . . $_____

   (2) If mortgage, include:
     Average principal . . . . $_____

     Average interest . . . . $_____
     Impound for real
       property taxes . . . . $_____
     Impound for home-
       owner's insurance . . . . . $_____

   (3) Real property taxes *(if not included in (item (2))* . . . . $_____

   (4) Homeowner's or renter's insurance *(if not included in item (2))* . . . . $_____

   (5) Maintenance . . . . $_____

b. Unreimbursed medical and dental expenses . . . . $_____

c. Child care . . . . $_____

d. Children's education . . . . $_____

e. Food at home and household supplies . . $_____

f. Food eating out . . . . $_____

g. Utilities . . . . $_____

h. Telephone . . . . $_____

i. Laundry and cleaning . . . . $_____

j. Clothing . . . . $_____

k. Insurance *(life, accident, etc. Do not include auto, home, or health insurance)* $_____

l. Education *(specify):* . . . . $_____

m. Entertainment . . . . $_____

n. Transportation and auto expenses *(insurance, gas, oil, repair)* . . . . $_____

o. Installment payments *(insert total and itemize below in item 3)* . . . . $_____

p. Other *(specify):* . . . . $_____

q. TOTAL EXPENSES (a-p) . . . . $_____   *(do not include amounts in a(2))*

3. ITEMIZATION OF INSTALLMENT PAYMENTS OR OTHER DEBTS ☐ Continued on Attachment 3.

CREDITOR'S NAME	PAYMENT FOR	MONTHLY PAYMENT	BALANCE	DATE LAST PAYMENT MADE

4. ATTORNEY FEES

  a. To date I have paid my attorney for fees and costs: $ [_____] The source of this money was:

  b. I owe to date the following fees and costs over the amount paid:

  c. My arrangement for attorney fees and costs is:

     I confirm this information and fee arrangement.

      ▶ _____
                  (SIGNATURE OF ATTORNEY)

      . . . .
                  (TYPE OR PRINT NAME OF ATTORNEY)

Page _____ of _____

Form Adopted by Rule 1285.50b
Judicial Council of California
1285.50b [Rev. January 1, 1995]

EXPENSE INFORMATION
(Family Law)

PETITIONER/PLAINTIFF:	CASE NUMBER:
RESPONDENT/DEFENDANT:	
CHILD SUPPORT INFORMATION OF *(name)*:	

THIS PAGE MUST BE COMPLETED IF CHILD SUPPORT IS AN ISSUE.

1. Health insurance for my children ☐ is ☐ is not available through my employer.

    a. Monthly cost paid by me or on my behalf for the children *only* is: $ _____
    Do not include the amount paid or payable by your employer.

    b. Name of carrier:

    c. Address of carrier:

    d. Policy or group policy number:

2. Approximate percentage of time each parent has primary physical responsibility for the children:

    Mother ____ % Father ____ %

3. ☐ The court is requested to order the following as additional child support:

    a. ☐ Child care costs related to employment or to reasonably necessary education or training for employment skills

        (1) Monthly amount currently paid by mother: $

        (2) Monthly amount currently paid by father: $

    b. ☐ Uninsured health care costs for the children *(for each cost state the purpose for which the cost was incurred and the estimated monthly, yearly, or lump sum amount paid by each parent):*

    c. ☐ Educational or other special needs of the children *(for each cost state the purpose for which the cost was incurred and the estimated monthly, yearly, or lump sum amount paid by each parent):*

    d. ☐ Travel expense for visitation

        (1) Monthly amount currently paid by mother: $

        (2) Monthly amount currently paid by father: $

4. ☐ The court is requested to allow the deductions identified below, which are justifiable expenses that have caused an extreme financial hardship.

	Amount paid per month	How many months will you need to make these payments
a. ☐ Extraordinary health care expenses *(specify and attach any supporting documents):*	$ _____	_____
b. ☐ Uninsured catastrophic losses *(specify and attach supportingdocuments):*	$ _____	_____
c. ☐ Minimum basic living expenses of dependent minor children from other marriages or relationships who live with you *(specify names and ages of these children):*	$ _____	_____
d. Total hardship deductions requested *(add lines a-c):*	$ _____	

Form Adopted by Rule 1285.50c
Judicial Council of California
1285.50c [Rev. January 1, 1995]

CHILD SUPPORT INFORMATION
(Family Law)

ATTORNEY OR PARTY WITHOUT ATTORNEY *(Name, state bar number, and address)*	FOR COURT USE ONLY
TELEPHONE NO.: FAX NO.:	
ATTORNEY FOR *(Name)*:	

SUPERIOR COURT OF CALIFORNIA, COUNTY OF

STREET ADDRESS:

MAILING ADDRESS:

CITY AND ZIP CODE:

BRANCH NAME:

PETITIONER:

RESPONDENT:

DECLARATION REGARDING SERVICE OF DECLARATION OF DISCLOSURE AND INCOME AND EXPENSE DECLARATION	CASE NUMBER:
☐ Petitioner's ☐ Preliminary ☐ Respondent's ☐ Final	

1. I am the ☐ Petitioner ☐ Respondent in this matter.

2. ☐ My *Preliminary Declaration of Disclosure* and *Income and Expense Declaration* was served on:
   ☐ Petitioner ☐ Respondent by: ☐ personal service ☐ mail ☐ other *(specify)*:

   on *(date)*:

3. ☐ My *Final Declaration of Disclosure* and *Income and Expense Declaration* was served on:
   ☐ Petitioner ☐ Respondent by: ☐ personal service ☐ mail ☐ other *(specify)*:

   on *(date)*:

4. ☐ Service of the *Final Declaration of Disclosure* has been waived pursuant to Family Code section 2105, subdivision (c).

I declare under penalty of perjury under the laws of the State of California that the foregoing is true and correct.

Date:

. . . .
(TYPE OR PRINT NAME)   ▶   (SIGNATURE)

> **Note:**
> File this document with the court.
> Do not file a copy of either the *Preliminary* or *Final Declaration of Disclosure* with this document.

**DECLARATION REGARDING SERVICE OF
DECLARATION OF DISCLOSURE
(Family Law)**

Family Code, §§ 2106, 2112

201

Your name and address or attorney's name and address:	TELEPHONE NO.:	FOR COURT USE ONLY

ATTORNEY FOR *(Name)*:

SUPERIOR COURT OF CALIFORNIA, COUNTY OF

STREET ADDRESS:

MAILING ADDRESS:

CITY AND ZIP CODE:

BRANCH NAME:

PETITIONER/PLAINTIFF:

RESPONDENT/DEFENDANT:

FINANCIAL STATEMENT (SIMPLIFIED)	CASE NUMBER:

NOTICE: See reverse for instructions and eligibility.

1. a. ☐ My only source of income is AFDC, SSI, or GA/GR. *(If you check this box, skip to item 8.)*

   b. ☐ I have applied for AFDC, SSI, or GA/GR.

2. I am the parent of the following number of natural or adopted children from this relationship: . . . . ._____

3. a. The children from this relationship are with me this amount of time: . . . . ._____ %

   b. The children from this relationship are with the other parent this amount of time: . . . . ._____ %

   c. Our arrangement for custody and visitation is *(specify, using extra sheet if necessary)*:

4. My tax filing status is: ☐ single ☐ married filing jointly ☐ head of household ☐ married filing separately.

5. My current gross income (before taxes) per month is *(specify amount)*: . . . .$_____

   This income comes from the following:

   ☐ Salary (wages): Amount before taxes per month *(specify amount)*: . . . .$_____

   ☐ Retirement: Amount before taxes per month *(specify amount)*: . . . .$_____

   ☐ Unemployment compensation: Amount per month *(specify amount)*: . . . .$_____

   ☐ Worker's compensation: Amount per month *(specify amount)*: . . . .$_____

   ☐ Social Security ☐ SSI ☐ Other Amount per month *(specify amount)*: . . . .$_____

   ☐ Disability: Amount per month *(specify amount)*: . . . .$_____

   I have no income other than as stated in this paragraph.

6. I pay the following monthly expenses for the children in this case:

   a. ☐ Day care or preschool to allow me to work or go to school *(specify amount)*: . . . .$_____

   b. ☐ Health care not paid for by insurance *(specify amount)*: . . . .$_____

   c. ☐ School, education, tuition, or other special needs of the child *(specify amount)*: . . . .$_____

   d. ☐ Travel expenses for visitation *(specify amount)*: . . . .$_____

7. ☐ There are *(specify number)* _____ other minor children of mine living with me. Their monthly expenses

   which I pay are *(specify amount)*: . . . .$_____

8. I spend the following average monthly amounts *(please attach proof)*:

   a. ☐ Job-related expenses that are not paid by my employer *(specify on separate sheet for what expenses are

   paid)*: . . . .$_____

   b. ☐ Required union dues *(specify amount)*: . . . .$_____

   c. ☐ Required retirement payments (not Social Security or FICA) *(specify amount)*: . . . .$_____

   d. ☐ Health insurance costs *(specify amount)*: . . . .$_____

   e. ☐ Child support I am paying for other minor children of mine who are not living with me *(specify amount)*: $_____

   f. ☐ Spousal support I am paying because of a court order for another relationship *(specify amount)*: . . . . . .$_____

   g. ☐ Monthly housing costs: ☐ rent or ☐ mortgage *(specify amount)*: . . . .$_____

9. Information concerning ☐ my current employment ☐ my most recent employment:

   Employer:

   Address:

   Telephone number:

   Occupation:

   Date work started:

(Continued on reverse)

Form Approved by the
Judicial Council of California
1285.52 [New July 1, 1995]

FINANCIAL STATEMENT (SIMPLIFIED)
(Family Law)

Family Code, § 4068(b)

MARRIAGE OF *(last name, first name of parties)*:	CASE NUMBER:

10. My estimate of the other party's gross monthly income (before taxes) is *(specify amount)*: . . . .$ _____

11. Other information I want the court to know concerning child support in my case *(attach extra sheet with the information)*.
I declare under penalty of perjury under the laws of the State of California that the foregoing is true and correct.

Date:

. . . . _____

(TYPE OR PRINT NAME) (SIGNATURE OF DECLARANT)

▶

☐ PETITIONER/PLAINTIFF   ☐ RESPONDENT/DEFENDANT

INSTRUCTIONS

Step 1: Are you eligible to use this form? *If your answer is YES to any of the following questions, you may NOT use this form:*

- Are you asking for spousal support (alimony) or a change in spousal support?
- Is your spouse or former spouse asking for spousal support (alimony) or a change in spousal support?
- Are you asking the other party to pay your attorney fees?
- Is the other party asking you to pay that party's attorney fees?
- Do you receive money (income) from any source other than the following?
    - Welfare (such as AFDC, GR, or GA)
    - Salary or Wages
    - Worker's Compensation
    - Disability
    - Social Security
    - Unemployment
    - Retirement
- Are you self-employed?

If you are eligible to use this form and choose to do so, you do not need to complete the Income and Expense Declaration (Form 1285.50). Even if you are eligible to use this form, you may choose instead to use the Income and Expense Declaration (Form 1285.50).

Step 2: Make 2 copies of each of your 3 most recent pay stubs. If you received money from other than wages of salary, include copies of the payment notice received with that money.

Privacy notice: If you wish, you may cross out your Social Security Number if it appears on the wage stub or other payment notice.

Step 3: Make 2 copies of your most recent federal income tax form.

Step 4: Complete this form with the required information. Type the form if possible or complete it neatly and clearly in black ink. If you need additional room, please use plain or lined paper, 8½" x 11", and staple to this form.

Step 5: Make 2 copies of each side of this completed form and any attached pages.

Step 6: Serve a copy on the other party. Have someone other than yourself mail to the attorney for the other party, the other party, or the District Attorney one copy of this form, one copy of each of your three most recent pay stubs, and one copy of your most recent federal income tax return.

Step 7: File the original with the court. Staple this form with one copy of each of your three most recent pay stubs. Take this document and give it to the clerk of the court.

Step 8: Keep the remaining copies of the documents for your file.

Step 9: Bring the copy of your latest federal income tax return to the court hearing.

It is very important that you attend the hearings scheduled for this case. If you do not attend a hearing, the court may make an order without considering the information you want the court to consider. This may result in an order that is not what you want.

ATTORNEY OR PARTY WITHOUT ATTORNEY *(Name, state bar number, and address)*:	FOR COURT USE ONLY
TELEPHONE NO.: FAX NO.:	
ATTORNEY FOR *(Name)*:	

SUPERIOR COURT OF CALIFORNIA, COUNTY OF
STREET ADDRESS:
MAILING ADDRESS:
CITY AND ZIP CODE:
BRANCH NAME:

PETITIONER:

RESPONDENT:

APPEARANCE, STIPULATIONS, AND WAIVERS	CASE NUMBER:

1. ☐ Respondent makes a general appearance.
2. ☐ Respondent has previously made a general appearance.
3. ☐ Respondent is a member of the military services of the United States of America and waives all rights under the Soldiers and Sailors Civil Relief Act of 1940, as amended, and does not contest this proceeding.
4. ☐ The parties stipulate that this cause may be tried as an uncontested matter.
5. ☐ The parties waive their rights to notice of trial, findings of fact and conclusions of law, motion for new trial, and the right to appeal.
6. ☐ This matter may be tried by a commissioner sitting as a temporary judge.
7. ☐ A written settlement agreement has been entered into between the parties.
8. ☐ A stipulation for judgment will be submitted to the court at the uncontested proceeding.
9. ☐ None of these stipulations or waivers shall apply unless the court approves the written settlement agreement or stipulation for judgment.
10. ☐ Both parties have executed an *Advisement and Waiver of Rights Re: Establishment of Parental Relationship* (form 1296.72).
11. ☐ Other *(specify)*:

12. Total number of boxes checked: _____

Date:

. . . .   ▶ _____
(TYPE OR PRINT NAME)   (SIGNATURE OF PETITIONER)

Date:

. . . .   ▶ _____
(TYPE OR PRINT NAME)   (SIGNATURE OF RESPONDENT)

Date:

. . . .   ▶ _____
(TYPE OR PRINT NAME)   (SIGNATURE OF ATTORNEY FOR PETITIONER)

Date:

. . . .   ▶ _____
(TYPE OR PRINT NAME)   (SIGNATURE OF ATTORNEY FOR RESPONDENT)

Form Approved by Rule 1282.50.
Judicial Council of California
1282.50 [Rev. January 1. ____]

APPEARANCE, STIPULATIONS, AND WAIVERS
(Family Law—Uniform Parentage)

ATTORNEY OR PARTY WITHOUT ATTORNEY *(Name, state bar number, and address)*:	FOR COURT USE ONLY
TELEPHONE NO.: FAX NO.:	
ATTORNEY FOR *(Name)*:	

SUPERIOR COURT OF CALIFORNIA, COUNTY OF
STREET ADDRESS:
MAILING ADDRESS:
CITY AND ZIP CODE:
BRANCH NAME:

PETITIONER:

RESPONDENT:

REQUEST TO ENTER DEFAULT	CASE NUMBER:

1. TO THE CLERK: Please enter the default of the respondent who has failed to respond to the petition.
2. A completed *Income and Expense Declaration* or *Financial Statement (Simplified)* ☐ is attached ☐ is not attached
   A completed *Property Declaration* ☐ is attached ☐ is not attached
   because *(check at least one of the following)*:
   (1) ☐ There have been no changes since the previous filing.
   (2) ☐ The issues subject to disposition by the court in this proceeding are the subject of a written agreement.
   (3) ☐ There are no issues of child or spousal support, or attorney fees and costs subject to determination by the court.
   (4) ☐ The petition does not request money, property, costs, or attorney fees. (Fam. Code, § 2330.5.)
   (5) ☐ There are no issues of division of community property.
   (6) ☐ This is an action to establish parental relationship.

Date:

. . . . ▶ _____
(TYPE OR PRINT NAME)   (SIGNATURE OF [ATTORNEY FOR] PETITIONER)

3. DECLARATION
   a. ☐ No mailing is required because service was by publication and the address of respondent remains unknown.
   b. ☐ A copy of this *Request to Enter Default* including any attachments and an envelope with sufficient postage was provided to the court clerk addressed as follows *(address of respondent's attorney or, if none, respondent's last known address)*:

   c. I declare under penalty of perjury under the laws of the State of California that the foregoing is true and correct.

Date:

. . . . ▶ _____
(TYPE OR PRINT NAME)   (SIGNATURE OF DECLARANT)

FOR COURT USE ONLY
☐ *Request to Enter Default* mailed to respondent or respondent's attorney on *(date)*:
☐ Default entered as requested on *(date)*:
☐ Default NOT entered. Reason:

                                        Clerk, by _____, Deputy

---

(See reverse for Memorandum of Costs and Declaration of Nonmilitary Status)

Form Adopted by Rule 1286 Judicial Council of California 1286 [Rev. January 1, 1999] Mandatory Form	**REQUEST TO ENTER DEFAULT** (Family Law—Uniform Parentage)	Code of Civil Procedure, §§ 585, 587; Family Code, § 2335.5

207

208

CASE NAME:	CASE NUMBER:

4. MEMORANDUM OF COSTS

a. ☐ Costs and disbursements are waived.

b. Costs and disbursements are listed as follows:
   (1) ☐ Clerk's fees . . . . $ . . . .

   (2) ☐ Process server's fees . . . . $ . . . .

   (3) ☐ Other (specify): . . . . $ . . . .

   . . . . $ . . . .

   . . . . $ . . . .

   . . . . $_____

   TOTAL . . . . $ . . . .

c. I am the attorney, agent, or party who claims these costs. To the best of my knowledge and belief the foregoing items of cost are correct and have been necessarily incurred in this cause or proceeding.

d. I declare under penalty of perjury under the laws of the State of California that the foregoing is true and correct.

Date:

. . . .
(TYPE OR PRINT NAME)

▶ _____
(SIGNATURE OF DECLARANT)

5. DECLARATION OF NONMILITARY STATUS

a. Respondent is not in the military service or in the military service of the United States as defined in section 101 of the Soldiers' and Sailors' Relief Act of 1940, as amended (50 U.S.C. appen. § 501 et seq.), and not entitled to the benefits of such act.

b. I declare under penalty of perjury under the laws of the State of California that the foregoing is true and correct.

Date:

. . . .
(TYPE OR PRINT NAME)

▶ _____
(SIGNATURE OF DECLARANT)

ATTORNEY OR PARTY WITHOUT ATTORNEY *(Name, state bar number, and address)*:	FOR COURT USE ONLY
TELEPHONE NO.: FAX NO.:	
ATTORNEY FOR *(Name)*:	

SUPERIOR COURT OF CALIFORNIA, COUNTY OF	
STREET ADDRESS:	
MAILING ADDRESS:	
CITY AND ZIP CODE:	
BRANCH NAME:	

MARRIAGE OF
PETITIONER:

RESPONDENT:

DECLARATION FOR DEFAULT OR UNCONTESTED ☐ **DISSOLUTION** or ☐ **LEGAL SEPARATION**	CASE NUMBER:

(NOTE: Items 1 through 16 apply to both dissolution and legal separation proceedings.)

1. I declare that if I appeared in court and were sworn, I would testify to the truth of the facts in this declaration.

2. I agree that my case will be proven by this declaration and that I will not appear before the court unless I am ordered by the court to do so.

3. All the information in the ☐ Petition ☐ Response is true and correct.

4. DEFAULT OR UNCONTESTED *(Check a or b)*
   a. ☐ The default of the respondent was entered or is being requested, and I am not seeking any relief not requested in the petition. **OR**
   b. ☐ The parties have agreed that the matter may proceed as an uncontested matter without notice, and the agreement is attached or it is incorporated in the attached marital settlement agreement or stipulated judgment.

5. MARITAL SETTLEMENT AGREEMENT *(Check a or b)*
   a. ☐ The parties have entered into an ☐ AGREEMENT or ☐ STIPULATED JUDGMENT regarding their property and marital rights, including support, the original of which is or has been submitted to the court. I request the court to approve the agreement. **OR**
   b. ☐ There is NO AGREEMENT or STIPULATED JUDGMENT, and the following statements are true *(check at least one, including item (2) if a community estate exists)*:
      (1) ☐ There are no community or quasi-community assets or community debts to be disposed of by the court.
      (2) ☐ The community and quasi-community assets and debts are listed on the attached **completed** current *Property Declaration* (form 1292), which includes an estimate of the value of the assets and debts that I propose to be distributed to each party. The division in the proposed *Judgment (Family Law)* is a fair and equal division of the property and debts, or if there is a negative estate, the debts are assigned fairly and equitably.

6. DECLARATION OF DISCLOSURE *(Check a, b, or c)*
   a. ☐ Both the petitioner and respondent have filed, or are filing concurrently, a *Declaration Regarding Service of the Preliminary and Final Declaration of Disclosure* and *Income and Expense Declaration*.
   b. ☐ This matter is proceeding by default. I am the Petitioner in this action and have filed a proof of service of the *Preliminary Declaration of Disclosure* with the court. I hereby waive receipt of the *Final Declaration of Disclosure* from the respondent.
   c. ☐ This matter is proceeding as an uncontested action. Service of the *Final Declaration of Disclosure* is mutually waived by both parties. A waiver provision is contained in the marital settlement agreement or proposed judgment.

7. ☐ CHILD CUSTODY should be ordered as set forth in the proposed *Judgment (Family Law)*.

8. ☐ CHILD VISITATION should be ordered as set forth in the proposed *Judgment (Family Law)*.

9. SPOUSAL AND FAMILY SUPPORT *If a support order or attorney fees are requested, submit a completed* Income and Expense Declaration *(form 1285.50), unless a current form is on file. Include your best estimate of the other party's income.*
   (Check at least one of the following)
   a. ☐ I knowingly give up forever any right to receive spousal support.
   b. ☐ I ask the court to reserve jurisdiction to award spousal support in the future to *(name)*:
   c. ☐ Spousal support should be ordered as set forth in the proposed *Judgment (Family Law)*.
   d. ☐ Family support should be ordered as set forth in the proposed *Judgment (Family Law)*.

(Continued on reverse)

Form Adopted for Mandatory Use Judicial Council of California Rule 1286.50 [Rev. July 1, 1999]	**DECLARATION FOR DEFAULT OR UNCONTESTED DISSOLUTION OR LEGAL SEPARATION** *(Family Law)*	Family Code, § 2336; Cal. Rules of Court, rule 1241

PETITIONER:	CASE NUMBER:
RESPONDENT:	

10. ☐ CHILD SUPPORT should be ordered as set forth in the proposed *Judgment (Family Law)*.

11. a. I ☐ am receiving ☐ am not receiving ☐ intend to apply for public assistance for the child or children listed in the proposed order.

    b. To the best of my knowledge the other party ☐ is ☐ is not receiving public assistance.

12. ☐ Petitioner ☐ Respondent is presently receiving public assistance and all support should be made payable to the Family Support Division of the District Attorney's Office at the address set forth in the proposed judgment. A representative of the District Attorney's Family Support Division has signed the proposed judgment.

13. If there are minor children, check and complete item a and item b or c:

    a. My gross (before taxes) monthly income is as follows: $

    b. ☐ The estimated gross monthly income of the other party is as follows: $

    c. ☐ I have no knowledge of the estimated monthly income of the other party for the following reasons *(specify)*:

    d. ☐ I request that this order be based on ☐ Petitioner's ☐ Respondent's earning ability. The facts in support of my estimate of earning ability are *(specify)*:

        ☐ Continued in Attachment 13d.

14. ☐ PARENTAGE of the children of the Petitioner and Respondent born prior to their marriage should be ordered as set forth in the proposed *Judgment (Family Law)*. A declaration regarding parentage is attached.

15. ☐ ATTORNEY FEES should be ordered as set forth in the proposed *Judgment (Family Law)*.

16. There are irreconcilable differences that have led to the irremediable breakdown of the marriage and there is no possibility of saving the marriage through counseling or other means.

17. This declaration may be reviewed by a commissioner sitting as a temporary judge who may determine whether to grant this request or require my appearance under Family Code section 2336.

STATEMENTS IN THIS BOX APPLY ONLY TO DISSOLUTIONS - items 18 through 21

18. Petitioner and/or the Respondent has been a resident of this county for at least three months and of the State of California for at least six months continuously and immediately preceding the date of the filing of the petition.

19. I ask that the court grant the request for a judgment for dissolution of marriage based upon irreconcilable differences and that the court make the orders set forth in the proposed *Judgment (Family Law)* submitted with this declaration.

20. ☐ This declaration is for the termination of **marital status only**. I ask the court to reserve jurisdiction over all issues whose determination is not requested in this declaration.

21. ☐ Petitioner ☐ Respondent requests restoration of his/her former name as set forth in the proposed *Judgment (Family Law)*.

THIS STATEMENT APPLIES ONLY TO LEGAL SEPARATIONS

22. I ask that the court grant the request for a judgment for legal separation based upon irreconcilable differences and that the court make the orders set forth in the proposed *Judgment (Family Law)* submitted with this declaration.

I UNDERSTAND THAT A JUDGMENT OF LEGAL SEPARATION DOES NOT TERMINATE A MARRIAGE AND I AM STILL MARRIED.

---

23. ☐ Other *(specify)*:

I declare under penalty of perjury under the laws of the State of California that the foregoing is true and correct.

Date:

. . . . ▶ _____

       (TYPE OR PRINT NAME)   (SIGNATURE OF DECLARANT)

DECLARATION FOR DEFAULT OR UNCONTESTED DISSOLUTION OR LEGAL SEPARATION
(Family Law)

ATTORNEY OR PARTY WITHOUT ATTORNEY (NAME AND ADDRESS):	TELEPHONE NO.:	FOR COURT USE ONLY
ATTORNEY FOR (NAME):		

SUPERIOR COURT OF CALIFORNIA, COUNTY OF
STREET ADDRESS:
MAILING ADDRESS:
CITY AND ZIP CODE:
BRANCH NAME:

MARRIAGE OF
PETITIONER:

RESPONDENT:

☐ **PETITIONER'S** ☐ **RESPONDENT'S**
   ☐ **COMMUNITY & QUASI-COMMUNITY PROPERTY DECLARATION**
   ☐ **SEPARATE PROPERTY DECLARATION**

CASE NUMBER:

INSTRUCTIONS

When this form is attached to Petition or Response, values and your proposal regarding division need not be completed. Do not list community, including quasi-community, property with separate property on the same form. Quasi-community property must be so identified. For additional space, use the form ''Continuation of Property Declaration.''

ITEM NO.	BRIEF DESCRIPTION	GROSS FAIR MARKET VALUE	AMOUNT OF DEBT	NET FAIR MARKET VALUE	PROPOSAL FOR DIVISION AWARD TO	
					PETITIONER	RESPONDENT
		$	$	$	$	$
1.	REAL ESTATE					
2.	HOUSEHOLD FURNITURE, FURNISHINGS, APPLIANCES					
3.	JEWELRY, ANTIQUES, ART, COIN COLLECTIONS, etc.					
4.	VEHICLES, BOATS, TRAILERS					
5.	SAVINGS, CHECKING, CREDIT UNION, CASH					

(Continued on reverse)

The declaration under penalty of perjury must be signed in California or in a state that authorizes use of a declaration in place of an affidavit; otherwise an affidavit is required.

Form Adopted by Rule 1285.55
Judicial Council of California
Effective January 1, 1980

**PROPERTY DECLARATION
(FAMILY LAW)**

ITEM NO.	BRIEF DESCRIPTION	GROSS FAIR MARKET VALUE	AMOUNT OF DEBT	NET FAIR MARKET VALUE	PROPOSAL FOR DIVISION AWARD TO	
					PETITIONER	RESPONDENT
		$	$	$	$	$
6.	LIFE INSURANCE (CASH VALUE)					
7.	EQUIPMENT, MACHINERY, LIVESTOCK					
8.	STOCKS, BONDS, SECURED NOTES					
9.	RETIREMENT, PENSION, PROFIT-SHARING, ANNUITIES					
10.	ACCOUNTS RECEIVABLE, UNSECURED NOTES, TAX REFUNDS					
11.	PARTNERSHIPS, OTHER BUSINESS INTERESTS					
12.	OTHER ASSETS AND DEBTS					
13.	TOTAL FROM CONTINUATION SHEET					
14.	TOTALS					

15. ☐ A Continuation of Property Declaration is attached and incorporated by reference.

. . . . _____
(Type or print name of attorney)   (Signature of attorney)

I declare under penalty of perjury that, to the best of my knowledge, the foregoing is a true and correct listing of assets and obligations and that the amounts shown are correct; and that this declaration was executed on (date): . . . . at (place): . . . ., California.

. . . . _____
(Type or print name)   (Signature)

[1285.55]

MARRIAGE OF (Last name—first names of parties)				CASE NUMBER	

☐ **PETITIONER'S** ☐ **RESPONDENT'S**
 ☐ **COMMUNITY & QUASI-COMMUNITY PROPERTY DECLARATION**
 ☐ **SEPARATE PROPERTY DECLARATION**

ITEM NO.	BRIEF DESCRIPTION	GROSS FAIR MARKET VALUE	AMOUNT OF DEBT	NET FAIR MARKET VALUE	PROPOSAL FOR DIVISION AWARD TO	
					PETITIONER	RESPONDENT
		$	$	$	$	$

(Continued on reverse)

Form Adopted by Rule 1285.56
Judicial Council of California
Effective January 1, 1980

**CONTINUATION OF PROPERTY DECLARATION
(FAMILY LAW)**

213

ITEM NO.	BRIEF DESCRIPTION	GROSS FAIR MARKET VALUE	AMOUNT OF DEBT	NET FAIR MARKET VALUE	PROPOSAL FOR DIVISION AWARD TO	
					PETITIONER	RESPONDENT
		$	$	$	$	$

[1285.56]

ATTORNEY OR PARTY WITHOUT ATTORNEY *(Name and Address)*:	TELEPHONE NO.:	*FOR COURT USE ONLY*

ATTORNEY FOR *(Name)*:

SUPERIOR COURT OF CALIFORNIA, COUNTY OF

STREET ADDRESS:

MAILING ADDRESS:

CITY AND ZIP CODE:

BRANCH NAME:

PETITIONER/PLAINTIFF:

RESPONDENT/DEFENDANT:

STIPULATION TO ESTABLISH OR MODIFY CHILD SUPPORT AND ORDER	CASE NUMBER:

1. a. ☐ Mother's net monthly disposable income: $
   Father's net monthly disposable income: $
   —OR—
   b. ☐ A printout of a computer calculation of the parents' financial circumstances is attached.
2. ☐ Percentage of time each parent has primary responsibility for the children: Mother ____ % Father ____ %
3. a. ☐ A nardship is being experienced by the mother for: $ ____ per month because of *(specify)*:

   The hardship will last until *(date)*:
   b. ☐ A hardship is being experienced by the father for: $ ____ per month because of *(specify)*:

   The hardship will last until *(date)*:
4. The amount of child support payable by *(name)*: ____ referred to as the "obligor" below,
   as calculated under the guideline is: $ ____ per month.
5. ☐ We agree to guideline support.
6. ☐ The guideline amount should be rebutted because of the following:
   a. ☐ We agree to child support in the amount of: $ ____ per month; the agreement is in the best interest of
      the children; the needs of the children will be adequately met by the agreed amount; and application of the guideline
      would be unjust or inappropriate in this case.
   b. ☐ Other rebutting factors *(specify)*:
7. Obligor shall pay child support as follows beginning *(date)*:
   a. **BASIC CHILD SUPPORT**

Child's name	Monthly amount	Payable to *(name)*

   Total: $ ____ payable ☐ on the first of the month ☐ other *(specify)*:
   b. ☐ In addition obligor shall pay the following:
       ☐ $ ____ per month for child care costs to *(name)*: ____ on *(date)*:
       ☐ $ ____ per month for health care costs not deducted from gross income
       to *(name)*: ____ on *(date)*:
       ☐ $ ____ per month for special educational or other needs of the children
       to *(name)*: ____ on *(date)*:
       ☐ other *(specify)*:

   c. **Total monthly child support** payable by obligor shall be: $ ____
   payable ☐ on the first of the month ☐ other *(specify)*:

(Continued on reverse)

Form Adopted by Rule 1285.27
Judicial Council of California
1285.27 [Rev. January 1, 1995]
**STIPULATION TO ESTABLISH OR MODIFY
CHILD SUPPORT AND ORDER**
(Family Law—Domestic Violence Prevention—Uniform Parentage)
Family Code, § 4065

PETITIONER/PLAINTIFF:	CASE NUMBER:
RESPONDENT/DEFENDANT:	

8. a. Health insurance shall be maintained by *(specify name)*:

   b. ☐ A health insurance coverage assignment shall issue if available through employment or other group plan or otherwise available at reasonable cost. Both parents are ordered to cooperate in the presentation, collection, and reimbursement of any medical claims.

   c. Any health expenses not paid by insurance shall be shared: Mother   %   Father   %

9. a. A Wage and Earnings Assignment Order shall issue.

   b. ☐ We agree that service of the wage assignment be stayed because we have made the following alternative arrangements to ensure payment *(specify)*:

10. ☐ Travel expenses for visitation shall be shared: Mother   %   Father   %

11. ☐ We agree that we shall promptly inform each other of any change of residence or employment, including the employer's name, address, and telephone number.

12. ☐ Other *(specify)*:

13. We agree that we are fully informed of our rights under the California child support guidelines.

14. We make this agreement freely without coercion or duress.

15. The right to support

   a. ☐ has not been assigned to any county and no application for public assistance is pending.

   b. ☐ has been assigned or an application for public assistance is pending in *(county name)*:

   If you checked b., a district attorney of the county named must sign below, joining in this agreement.

   Date:

   . . . .   ▶   _____
   (TYPE OR PRINT NAME)   (SIGNATURE OF DISTRICT ATTORNEY)

Notice: If the amount agreed to is less than the guideline amount, no change of circumstances need be shown to obtain a change in the support order to a higher amount.

Date:

. . . .   ▶   _____
(TYPE OR PRINT NAME)   (SIGNATURE OF PETITIONER)

Date:

. . . .   ▶   _____
(TYPE OR PRINT NAME)   (SIGNATURE OF RESPONDENT)

Date:

. . . .   ▶   _____
(TYPE OR PRINT NAME)   (SIGNATURE OF ATTORNEY FOR PETITIONER)

. . . .   _____
(TYPE OR PRINT NAME)   (SIGNATURE OF ATTORNEY FOR RESPONDENT)

THE COURT ORDERS

16. a. ☐ The guideline child support amount in item 4 is rebutted by the factors stated in item 6.

   b. Items 7 through 12 are ordered. All child support payments shall continue until further order of the court, or until the child marries, dies, is emancipated, or reaches age 18. The duty of support continues as to an unmarried child who has attained the age of 18 years, is a full-time high school student, and resides with a parent, until the time the child completes the 12th grade or attains the age of 19 years, whichever first occurs. Except as modified by this stipulation, all provisions of any previous orders made in this action shall remain in effect.

Date:

                                             _____
                                             JUDGE OF THE SUPERIOR COURT

> **NOTICE:** Any party required to pay child support must pay interest on overdue amounts at the "legal" rate, which is currently 10 percent. This can be a large added amount.

**STIPULATION TO ESTABLISH OR MODIFY
CHILD SUPPORT AND ORDER**
(Family Law—Domestic Violence Prevention—Uniform Parentage)

MARITAL SETTLEMENT AGREEMENT (MSA)

THIS AGREEMENT is made on _____ by _____ (Wife) and _____ (Husband).
This agreement shall become effective on the date it is approved by the court in the pending dissolution proceeding;or on the date a final judgment is entered.

Purpose. The purpose of this agreement is to settle the parties' rights and obligations as to their property, debts, and support.

RECITALS

This agreement is made in light of the facts stated below.

1. Marriage. The parties were married to each other on _____, and ever since have been, and are now, husband and wife.

2. Separation. Irreconcilable differences have arisen between the parties which have led to the irremediable breakdown of their marriage. The parties agree that no further waiting period, marriage counseling, or conciliation efforts would save the marriage, and the parties have filed for dissolution of their marriage. They have lived separate and apart since _____. They now intend to live apart permanently.

3. Legal Proceedings. An action for dissolution of marriage has been filed by ☐ Wife ☐ Husband and is now pending in the Superior Court of the State of California, County of _____ Case No. _____.

4. Children of the Marriage.

☐ No children have been born to, or adopted by, the parties during their marriage, and the wife is not now pregnant.

☐ The minor children of the parties are as follows (name and birthdate of child(ren) under 18 years:

The surname of the child(ren) shall not be changed.

5. Social Security Identification. The Social Security numbers of the parties are as follows:

Husband: _____

Wife: _____

6. Health of Parties.

☐ The parties are both in good health and neither has any known illness, disability, or physical condition which renders either incapable of gainful employment or makes either subject to extraordinary medical or dental expenditures in the near future.

☐ Husband ☐ Wife is not in good health because _____
_____
_____.

7. <u>Employment</u>. Husband is presently employed by _____
_____ and his sole gross monthly earnings are $_____,
as shown on his wage stub attached as part of this document. Wife is presently employed by
_____ and her sole gross monthly earnings are
$_____, as shown on her pay stub attached as part of this document.

8. <u>Voluntariness</u>. The parties acknowledge and agree that they enter into this agreement voluntarily, free from duress, fraud, undue influence, coercion, or misrepresentation of any kind.

For valuable consideration, the parties agree as follows:

WARRANTIES

9. <u>Full Disclosure</u>. Each party expressly promises that he or she has fully disclosed all of the real and personal property belonging to each of them and all debts.

10. <u>Warranty of Values of Property</u>. The parties intend the transfers of property in this agreement to be a substantially equal division of their community property. Husband and Wife each agree that they have had sufficient opportunity to investigate the values of the property and that each warrants to the other that each has no knowledge of any fact which would affect the distribution of any property listed in this agreement.

11. <u>After Discovered Property</u>. The parties agree that any property discovered after the date of this agreement which would have been their community or quasi-community property as of the effective date of this agreement shall be divided equally between them. If one party wilfully concealed such property, that party shall be obligated to pay any costs and attorneys fees incurred by the other party to collect such after-discovered community property.

12. <u>Transfers for Adequate Consideration</u>. Each party promises that he or she has not gifted or transferred any community property without the other's knowledge and consent. Each party signs this agreement relying on these representations.

DIVISION OF PROPERTY

13. <u>Wife's Share of Community Property</u>. Husband hereby transmutes and transfers to Wife as her sole and separate property the following property (list all community property going to Wife, including family residence and other real property, attach additional page if needed and make sure you include the legal description):

14. <u>Confirmation of Wife's Separate Property</u>. Husband hereby confirms that the following property owned by Wife prior to this marriage or received by Wife by gift of inheritance during the marriage shall remain the sole and separate property of Wife (List any separate property that Wife had before her marriage and property received by gift or inheritance during her marriage):

15. <u>Husband's Share of Community Property</u>. Wife hereby transmutes and transfers to Husband as his sole and separate property the following property (list all community property going to Husband, attach additional page if needed):

16. <u>Confirmation of Husband's Separate Property</u>. Wife hereby confirms that the following property owned by Husband prior to this marriage or received by him by gift of inheritance shall remain the sole and separate property of Husband (list any separate property that Husband had before the marriage and property received by gift or inheritance during his marriage):

The division shall be effected when necessary by a transfer of title. All property is transferred subject to any debt attached to it.

FAMILY RESIDENCE

17. Family Residence. The family residence is commonly known as _____
_____,
and its legal description is as follows:

□ The family residence is to be sold promptly and the proceeds after all debt, taxes, selling and other related expenses are deducted are to be divided evenly between the parties.

OR

□ The □ Wife □ Husband shall remain living in the family residence until _____
_____, at which time the home shall be sold and the proceeds after all debt, taxes, selling and other related expenses are deducted are to be divided evenly between the parties. During the time the □ Wife □ Husband remains in the home, he/she will be responsible for all mortgage payments, taxes, insurance, and general maintenance. Capital improvements if needed will be shared equally between the parties.

OR

□ The family residence is to be disposed of as follows: _____
_____
_____.

OBLIGATIONS TO THIRD PARTIES & DIVISION OF DEBTS

18. The parties agree not to incur any further debts or obligations for which the other may be liable. The parties agree that any debt incurred by either after the effective date of this agreement shall be the sole responsibility of that party, and each agrees to hold the other harmless against any such debt and agrees to indemnify the other against any liability in connection with it, including court costs and attorney's fees. The court shall retain jurisdiction over this issue.

19. Distribution of Debt to Wife. The Wife agrees to assume, to make payment on, and to hold the Husband harmless from the following obligations, with each debt described as "community" or "separate":

a. Any loans acquired by Wife where Wife is on the account as the sole debtor, as follows (list them):

b. Any credit cards where Wife is on the account as the sole debtor, as follows (list them):

c. Other debts as follows(list them):

d. If a creditor makes an attempt to obtain satisfaction from the Husband for any obligation listed above, the Wife shall defend and fully indemnify the Husband with regard to such attempt.

20. Distribution of Debt to Husband. The Husband agrees to assume, to make payment on, and to hold the Wife harmless from the following obligations, with each debt described as "community" or "separate":

a. Any loans acquired by Husband where Husband is on the account as the sole debtor, as follows (list them):

b. Any credit cards where Husband is on the account as the sole debtor, as follows (list them):

c. Other debts as follows (list them):

d. If a creditor makes an attempt to obtain satisfaction from the Wife for any obligation listed above, the Husband shall defend and fully indemnify the Wife with regard to such attempt.

WAIVER

21. Waiver of Rights and Respective Estates: Husband and Wife agree that each party waives all right, title, claim, lien or interest in the other's separate property, separate property income, and separate property estate, by reason of their marriage, including the following:

1. All community property, quasi-community property, and quasi-marital property rights.
2. The right to a probate family allowance.
3. The right to a probate homestead.
4. The right or claims of dower, curtesy, or any statutory substitute now or hereafter provided under the laws of the state of California. The court shall retain jurisdiction over this issue indefinitely.
5. The right to inherit separate property from the other by intestate succession.
6. The right to receive separate property which would pass from the decedent party by testamentary disposition in a Will executed before this agreement.
7. The right of election to take against the Will of the other.
8. The right to take the statutory share of an omitted spouse.

9. The right to be appointed as administrator of the deceased party's estate, or as executor of the deceased party's Will, unless appointed pursuant to a Will executed after the date of this agreement.

10. The right to have exempt property set aside in probate.

11. Any right created under federal law, including without limitation, the Retirement Equity Act of 1984.

12. Any right, title, claim or interest in or to the separate property, separate income or separate estate of the other by reason of the party's marriage.

22. <u>Confirmation of Personal Belongings</u>. Certain items of personal wearing apparel, jewelry, furniture, furnishings, and other miscellaneous items have previously been divided between the parties, and the parties agree that the distribution was an equal division of such property and each confirms to the other all such property now in that party's possession.

EMPLOYEE RETIREMENT BENEFITS

23. <u>Employee Retirement Benefits</u>. We understand that retirement and pension plans are community property to the extent either party received such benefits during the time of the marriage to the date of separation. The plans are valued at _____, and we are disposing of the asset(s) as follows: _____
_____
_____.

SPOUSAL SUPPORT, CHILD SUPPORT, CUSTODY

24. <u>Spousal Support</u>.

☐ We are aware that it is mandated that the Court reserve spousal support for long-term marriages of more than ten years, when requested by either party. We waive the right to receive spousal support now or at anytime in the future. This waiver shall not be modifiable by the parties or the court for any reason whatsoever. By executing this agreement, we each agree and acknowledge that we understand that by waiving spousal support we will be forever barred from seeking spousal support at any time in the future regardless of the circumstances.

OR

☐ We waive spousal support as to each other at this time. However, the Court shall retain jurisdiction over this issue until _____(date), so that during such time either of us may petition the court for spousal support if circumstances warrant.

OR

☐ _____ shall pay to _____ for support and maintenance the sum of $_____ per month payable on the _____ of each month beginning _____. This payment shall continue until _____, or the death of either spouse, or the remarriage of the payee spouse, or further order of court, or when payee spouse receives a gross income of $_____ monthly for _____ consecutive months, or _____, whichever occurs first. This support shall be paid pursuant to a Wage and Earnings Assignment Order to be served on payor's employer immediately upon receipt of the judgment.

25. <u>Child Custody</u>. The parenting plan is as follows(pick one):

☐ The legal and physical custody of our minor children during minority is jointly awarded to both Husband and Wife; the ☐ Husband's ☐ Wife's home shall be considered the child's primary residence for purposes of school registration, insurance, and other purposes.

OR

☐ The legal custody of our minor children during minority is jointly awarded to both Husband and Wife. Physical custody is awarded to ☐ Husband ☐ Wife subject to reasonable visitation by ☐ Husband ☐ Wife.

The parent who has the physical care of the children at any given time shall have the routine decision-making rights and responsibilities during such times. However, all major decisions as to health, education, and daycare shall be a joint decision, unless in an emergency. Each parent shall have the right of reasonable private telephone communication with the children. The estimated time which each parent will spend with the children is _____% with Husband and _____% with Wife. If one parent wishes to travel outside California with the child(ren), he or she must obtain the written consent of the other parent. The parties must keep each other informed as to the name, address, and phone number of their respective employers. Additionally, each parent shall keep the other apprised of the child(ren)'s health care provider's name, address, phone number, and identification number, as well as his or her own personal address and phone number. Each shall also keep the other informed during visitations of any medication the child(ren) may be taking and provide such medication to the visitation parent. A Wage and Earnings Assignment Order shall be submitted to the court at the time of judgment and served on the employer of the spouse obligated to pay child support.

If a disagreement arises as to reasonable visitation, "reasonable visitation" shall mean:

(a) Regular Visitation:

1. On (the first and third) (the second and fourth) weekends of each month from six (6:00) P.M. Friday to six (6:00) P.M. Sunday, commencing Friday, _____, _____.

2. The entire month of July, _____, the entire month of August the following year, and alternating July and August in subsequent years.

(b) Holidays and Special Days:

1. Lincoln's Birthday, _____, from seven (7:00) P.M. the day before the holiday to seven (7:00) P.M. the day of said holiday and thereafter on alternate years.

2. Washington's Birthday, _____, from seven (7:00) P.M. the day before said holiday to seven (7:00) P.M. the day of said holiday and thereafter on alternate years.

3. Memorial Day, _____, from seven (7:00) P.M. the day before said holiday to seven (7:00) P.M. the day of said holiday and thereafter on alternate years.

4. Independence Day, _____, from seven (7:00) P.M. the day before said holiday to seven (7:00) P.M. the day of said holiday and thereafter on alternate years.

5. Labor Day, _____, from seven (7:00) P.M. the day before said holiday to seven (7:00) P.M. the day of said holiday, and thereafter on alternate years.

6. Thanksgiving Day, _____, from six (6:00) P.M. the Wednesday before said holiday to six (6:00) P.M. the Sunday after said holiday and thereafter on alternate years.

7. Christmas, _____, the first week of the Christmas school vacation, commencing seven (7:00) P.M. the last day of school before the vacation and ending at ten (10:00) A.M. Christmas Day, and thereafter on alternate years.

8. Christmas, _____, the second week of the Christmas school vacation, commencing ten (10:00) A.M. Christmas Day to five (5:00) P.M. New Year's Day, and thereafter on alternate years.

9. One-half Easter school vacation defined as four (4) days, to include Easter Sunday in ☐ even ☐ odd numbered years.

10. On the children's birthdays in the year _____, and thereafter on alternate years.
11. Every (Father's Day)(Mother's Day).
12. On (Father's)(Mother's) birthday.

26. <u>Child Support</u>. ☐ Husband ☐ Wife shall pay ☐ Husband ☐ Wife child support beginning _____ in the amount of $_____ monthly. This support shall be paid pursuant to a Wage and Earnings Assignment Order to be served on payor's employer immediately upon receipt of the judgment. This support is based on ☐ Wife ☐ Husband having physical custody of the children _____ percent of the time. Payment shall be for the benefit of the following minor children (use the computer guideline for the distribution of child support among the children if more than one):

NAME OF CHILD	DATE OF BIRTH	AMOUNT OF CHILD SUPPORT

These payments shall continue at the rates until the child marries, dies, is emancipated, reaches 19, or reaches 18 and is not a full-time high school student residing with a parent, or further order of court, whichever first occurs.

Medical, dental, orthodontia, and hospital insurance for the children is provided for by ☐ Wife ☐ Husband ☐ both through employment. Wife and Husband shall cooperate in the presentation, collection, and reimbursement of any claims, and any medical, dental, orthodontic, optometric, psychiatric, psychological, or other related expense not otherwise covered by insurance shall be shared equally by the parties. In the event such insurance terminates for whatever reason, either or both parents shall immediately replace it and share the costs.

As additional support, child care costs to enable the custody parent to work shall be shared between the parents equally until the child is at an age where child care is unnecessary.

☐ Costs for special needs or travel expenses for visitation shall be paid as follows:
_____
_____.

☐ Wife ☐ Husband shall be entitled to claim the following child(ren) as dependents for income tax purposes: _____.

☐ We are aware that the child support is less than the guideline amount of approximately $_____. We therefore state:
1. We agree that we are fully informed of our rights concerning child support;
2. We make this agreement freely without coercion or duress;
3. This agreement is in the best interests of the children involved;
4. The needs of the children will be adequately met by the stipulated amount;
5. The right to support has not been assigned to the county pursuant to Section 11477 of the Welfare and Institutions Code and no public assistance application is pending.

INCOME TAX RETURNS

27. <u>Tax Refunds or Deficiencies</u>. If at any time after the effective date of this agreement any federal or state income tax deficiency is assessed against either of us for any year in which we filed joint returns, the liability shall be shared equally. If any refund shall become due for any federal or state income tax previously paid by us for any year in which we filed a joint return, the refund shall be divided between us. Any refund from overpayment of estimated taxes is not a "refund" for the purposes of this paragraph, and shall be the separate property of the party paying the overage.

28. <u>Tax Deficiencies</u>. Each party shall bear one-half of all liabilities for income tax, including interest and penalties, assessed on all joint income tax returns previously filed by the parties or resulting from a failure to file returns for prior years.

29. <u>Notices</u>. Each party, or the representative of the party's estate, will immediately send the other party a copy of any communication or notice he or she receives from the state or federal taxing authorities which relates to a joint return formerly filed by the parties.

PROPERTY TRANSFER PROVISIONS

30. The parties agree that neither know of any transfer of property which should result in any income tax consequences to either party other than as stated in this agreement.

GENERAL PROVISIONS

31. <u>Freedom From Interference</u>. Each party may lawfully continue to live apart from the other as though he or she were unmarried and free from the other's direct and indirect control. Each party may engage in any employment or business of his/her choosing, entirely free of the other party's interference.

32. <u>Freedom From Harassment</u>. Each party agrees not to annoy, harass, embarrass, or interfere with the other in any way and agrees not to interfere with property that the other now owns or will later acquire.

33. <u>Further Acts to Implement Agreement</u>. On the demand of the other party, each party will promptly execute any document or perform any other act reasonably necessary to implement the terms of this agreement. A party who fails to comply with this provision will pay all attorney's fees and other expenses resulting from noncompliance.

34. <u>Release of All Claims</u>. Except as provided in this agreement, each party releases the other from all claims, liabilities, debts, obligations, actions, and causes of action that have been or will be asserted or incurred. This release does not apply to any obligation incurred under this agreement, under any document executed pursuant to the agreement, or under any order issued incident to the agreement. The release is binding on each party's heirs, executors, administrators, and assigns.

35. <u>Effect of Reconciliation</u>. Any reconciliation between the parties after they execute this agreement will have no effect on the agreement unless the parties modify or cancel it in a writing signed by both parties.

36. <u>Breach</u>. If any provision of this agreement is breached, the non-breaching party has a right to remedy the breach. If the breach involves an amount of money that is due, the non-breaching party has the right to collect the money as well as legal interest on it. Should an action for breach be brought and proved, the breaching party will pay all reasonable attorney's fees and other expenses that the non-breaching party has incurred in bringing the action. Either party's failure to insist upon the strict performance of any provision of this agreement will not be construed as a waiver of the provision, which will continue in full force. No breach or claimed breach will impair any rights or obligations that the parties have under the agreement.

37. <u>Waiver of Final Declaration of Disclosure and Declaration as to Preliminary Declaration of Disclosure</u>. Each of us waives the final Declaration of Disclosure, and we have complied with Family Code section 2104, and the preliminary Declarations of Disclosure have been completed and exchanged. We have completed and exchanged a current income and expense statement. This waiver is knowingly, intelligently, and voluntarily entered into by each of us and we understand that by signing below we may be affecting the ability to have the judgment set aside as provided by law.

38. <u>Governing Law</u>. This agreement shall be interpreted according to the laws of the State of California.

39. <u>Parties and Persons Bound</u>. This agreement shall bind the parties to the agreement and their respective heirs, assigns, representatives, executors and administrators and any other successors in interest.

40. <u>Costs of Enforcement</u>. If either party be required to bring any action to enforce this agreement or any court order made after merger of any provision of this agreement in the judgment, the prevailing party shall be entitled to recover costs and reasonable attorney fees.

41. <u>Execution of Instruments</u>. The parties agree that each will execute and deliver to the other upon request any legal instrument or title document which may be necessary to carry out this agreement including, but not limited to, the division of property or confirmation of property set forth in this agreement.

42. <u>Execution Formalities</u>. The parties agree that upon their signing of this agreement, their signatures shall be acknowledged by a notary public. This agreement, or final judgment of dissolution into which this agreement has been merged, may be recorded at any time by either party in any place.

43. <u>Modification, Revocation or Termination</u>. This agreement may be amended or revoked only by a writing expressly referring to this agreement and signed by both Husband and Wife. Each of the parties waives the right to claim in the future that this agreement was modified, canceled, or superseded by oral agreement or conduct.

44. <u>Invalidity; Severability</u>. If any provision or condition of this agreement is held by a court as invalid, void or unenforceable, the remainder of the provisions shall remain in full force and effect.

45. <u>Entire Agreement</u>. The parties intend this agreement to be a final and complete settlement of all of their rights and obligations arising out of their marriage.

46. <u>Merger of Agreement</u>. If either party obtains a judgment of dissolution of marriage, this agreement shall be incorporated into the judgment and be a part of it, or otherwise filed with court pursuant to local court procedure. The parties shall ask the court to approve the agreement as fair and to order each of them to comply with all of its provisions.

DATE:_____   _____
                                  Husband

DATE:_____   _____
                                  Wife

State of California   )
) s.s.
County of _____   )

On _____, before me, _____, Notary Public,
personally appeared _____, ☐ personally known
to me or ☐ proved to me on the basis of satisfactory evidence to be the person whose name is
subscribed to the within instrument and acknowledged to me that he executed the same in his
authorized capacity, and that by his signature on the instrument the person or the entity upon
behalf of which the person acted, executed the instrument.

WITNESS my hand and official seal.

_____

Notary Public

State of California   )
) s.s.
County of _____   )

On _____, before me, _____, Notary Public,
personally appeared _____, ☐ personally known
to me or ☐ proved to me on the basis of satisfactory evidence to be the person whose name is
subscribed to the within instrument and acknowledged to me that she executed the same in her
authorized capacity, and that by her signature on the instrument the person or the entity upon
behalf of which the person acted, executed the instrument.

WITNESS my hand and official seal.

_____

Notary Public

ATTORNEY OR PARTY WITHOUT ATTORNEY *(Name, state bar number, and address)*:	FOR COURT USE ONLY
TELEPHONE NO.: FAX NO.: ATTORNEY FOR *(Name)*:	

SUPERIOR COURT OF CALIFORNIA, COUNTY OF

STREET ADDRESS:

MAILING ADDRESS:

CITY AND ZIP CODE:

BRANCH NAME:

MARRIAGE OF

PETITIONER:

RESPONDENT:

JUDGMENT	CASE NUMBER:

☐ **Dissolution**   ☐ **Legal separation**   ☐ **Nullity**
    ☐ **Status only**
    ☐ **Reserving jurisdiction over termination of marital status**
    ☐ **Judgment on reserved issues**
Date marital status ends:	

1. ☐ This judgment ☐ contains personal conduct restraining orders ☐ modifies existing restraining orders.
   The restraining orders are contained on page(s)   of the attachment. They expire on *(date)*:

2. This proceeding was heard as follows: ☐ default or uncontested ☐ by declaration under Fam. Code, § 2336
   ☐ contested
   a. Date: Dept.:   Rm.:
   b. Judicial officer *(name)*:   ☐ Temporary judge
   c. ☐ Petitioner present in court   ☐ Attorney present in court *(name)*:
   d. ☐ Respondent present in court   ☐ Attorney present in court *(name)*:
   e. ☐ Claimant present in court *(name)*:   ☐ Attorney present in court *(name)*:
   f. ☐ Other *(specify name)*:

3. The court acquired jurisdiction of the respondent on *(date)*:
   ☐ Respondent was served with process   ☐ Respondent appeared

4. THE COURT ORDERS, GOOD CAUSE APPEARING:
   a. ☐ Judgment of dissolution be entered. Marital status is terminated and the parties are restored to the status of unmarried persons
       (1) ☐ on the following date *(specify)*:
       (2) ☐ on a date to be determined on noticed motion of either party or on stipulation.
   b. ☐ Judgment of legal separation be entered.
   c. ☐ Judgment of nullity be entered. The parties are declared to be unmarried persons on the ground of *(specify)*:

   d. ☐ This judgment shall be entered nunc pro tunc as of *(date)*:
   e. ☐ Judgment on reserved issues.
   f. ☐ Wife's ☐ Husband's former name be restored *(specify)*:
   g. ☐ Jurisdiction is reserved over all other issues and all present orders remain in effect except as provided below.
   h. ☐ This judgment contains provisions for child support or family support. Both parties shall complete and file with the court a *Child Support Case Registry Form* (form 1285.92) within 10 days of the date of this judgment. The parents shall notify the court of any change in the information submitted within 10 days of the change by filing an updated form. The forms *Notice of Rights and Responsibilities* (form 1285.78) and *Information Sheet on Changing a Child Support Order* (form 1285.79) are attached.

(Continued on reverse)

Form Adopted for Mandatory Use Judicial Council of California Rule 1287 [Rev. July 1, 1999]	**JUDGMENT** **(Family Law)**	Family Code, §§ 2340, 2343, 2346

229

MARRIAGE OF (last name, first name of parties):	CASE NUMBER:

4. i. ☐ A marital settlement agreement between the parties is attached.
   j. ☐ A written stipulation for judgment between the parties is attached.
   k. ☐ Child custody and visitation is ordered as
   set forth in the attached

        ☐ Marital settlement agreement, stipulation for judgment, or other written agreement.

        ☐ *Child Custody and Visitation Order Attachment* (form 1296.31A)

        ☐ Other *(specify):*

    l. ☐ Child support is ordered as set forth in
the attached

        ☐ Marital settlement agreement, stipulation for judgment, or other written agreement.

        ☐ *Child Support Information and Order Attachment* (form 1296.31B)

        ☐ *Non-Guideline Child Support Findings Attachment* (form 1296.31B(1))

        ☐ *Stipulation to Establish or Modify Child Support Order* (form 1285.27)

        ☐ Other *(specify):*

    m. ☐ Spousal support is ordered as set forth
in the attached

        ☐ Marital settlement agreement, stipulation for judgment, or other written agreement.

        ☐ *Spousal or Family Support Order Attachment* (form 1296.31C)

        ☐ Other *(specify):*

    ☐ NOTICE: It is the goal of this state that each party shall make reasonable good faith efforts to become self-supporting as provided for in Family Code section 4320. The failure to make reasonable good faith efforts may be one of the factors considered by the court as a basis for modifying or terminating spousal support.

    n. ☐ Parentage is established for children of this relationship born prior to the marriage.
    o. ☐ Other *(specify):*

Each attachment to this judgment is incorporated into this judgment, and the parties are ordered to comply with each attachment's provisions.

Jurisdiction is reserved to make other orders necessary to carry out this judgment.

Date:

                               JUDGE OF THE SUPERIOR COURT

5. Number of pages attached: _____   ☐ SIGNATURE FOLLOWS LAST ATTACHMENT

NOTICE

Please review your will, insurance policies, retirement benefit plans, credit cards, other credit accounts and credit reports, and other matters that you may want to change in view of the dissolution or annulment of your marriage, or your legal separation. Dissolution or annulment of your marriage may automatically change a disposition made by your will to your former spouse. A debt or obligation may be assigned to one party as part of the division of property and debts, but if that party does not pay the debt or obligation, the creditor may be able to collect from the other party.

An earnings assignment will automatically be issued if child support, family support, or spousal support is ordered.

Any party required to pay support must pay interest on overdue amounts at the "legal rate," which is currently 10 percent.

JUDGMENT
(Family Law)

NOTICE OF RIGHTS AND RESPONSIBILITIES
Health Care Costs and Reimbursement Procedures

IF YOU HAVE A CHILD SUPPORT ORDER THAT INCLUDES A PROVISION FOR THE REIMBURSEMENT OF A PORTION OF THE CHILD'S OR CHILDREN'S HEALTH CARE COSTS AND THOSE COSTS ARE NOT PAID FOR BY INSURANCE, THE LAW SAYS:

1. NOTICE. You must give the other parent an itemized statement of the charges that have been billed for any health care costs that are not paid for by insurance. You must give this statement to the other parent within a reasonable time, but no longer than 30 days after those costs were given to you.

2. PROOF OF FULL PAYMENT. If you have already paid all of the uninsured costs, you must (1) provide the other parent with proof that you have paid those costs, and (2) ask for reimbursement for the other parent's court-ordered share of those costs.

3. PROOF OF PARTIAL PAYMENT. If you have only paid your share of the uninsured costs, you must (1) provide the other parent with proof that you have paid your share, (2) ask that the other parent pay his or her share of the costs directly to the health care provider, and (3) provide the other parent with the information necessary for that parent to be able to pay the bill.

4. PAYMENT BY NOTIFIED PARENT. If you receive notice from a parent that an uninsured health care cost has been incurred, you must pay your share of that cost within the time the court orders, or if the court has not specified a period of time, you must make payment either (1) within 30 days from the time you were given notice of the amount due, (2) according to any payment schedule set by the health care provider, (3) according to a schedule agreed to in writing by yourself and the other parent, or (4) according to a schedule adopted by the court.

5. DISPUTED CHARGES. If you dispute a charge, you may file a motion in court to resolve the dispute, but only if you pay that charge before filing your motion. If you claim that the other party has failed to reimburse you for a payment, or the other party has failed to make a payment to the provider after proper notice has been given, you may file a motion in court to resolve the dispute. The court will presume that if uninsured costs have been paid, those costs were reasonable. The court may award attorney fees against a party who has been unreasonable.

6. COURT-ORDERED INSURANCE COVERAGE. If a parent provides health care insurance pursuant to a court order, that insurance shall be used at all times to the extent that it is available for health care costs.

a. **Burden to prove.** The burden to prove to the court that the coverage is inadequate to meet the child(ren)'s needs is upon the party claiming that inadequacy.

b. **Cost of additional coverage.** If a parent purchases health care insurance in addition to that being ordered, the purchasing parent shall pay for all the costs of the additional coverage. In addition, if the parent uses the alternative coverage, that parent shall pay for all costs that exceed what would have been incurred under the coverage provided by court order.

7. PREFERRED HEALTH PROVIDERS. If the court ordered coverage designates a preferred health care provider, that provider shall be used at all times consistent with the terms of the health insurance policy. When any party uses a health care provider other than the preferred provider, any health care costs that would have been paid by the preferred health provider had that provider been used shall be the sole responsibility of the party incurring those costs.

Form Approved by Rule 1285.78
Judicial Council of California
1285.78 [New January 1, 1995]

NOTICE OF RIGHTS AND RESPONSIBILITIES
Health Care Costs and Reimbursement Procedures

Family Code, §§ 4062, 4063

ATTORNEY OR PARTY WITHOUT ATTORNEY *(Name, state bar number, and address)*:	FOR COURT USE ONLY
TELEPHONE NO.: FAX NO.: ATTORNEY FOR *(Name)*:	

SUPERIOR COURT OF CALIFORNIA, COUNTY OF
STREET ADDRESS:
MAILING ADDRESS:
CITY AND ZIP CODE:
BRANCH NAME:

PETITIONER:

RESPONDENT:

NOTICE OF ENTRY OF JUDGMENT	CASE NUMBER:

You are notified that the following judgment was entered on *(date)*:

1. ☐ Dissolution of Marriage
2. ☐ Dissolution of Marriage — Status Only
3. ☐ Dissolution of Marriage — Reserving Jurisdiction over Termination of Marital Status
4. ☐ Legal Separation
5. ☐ Nullity
6. ☐ Parent-Child Relationship
7. ☐ Judgment on Reserved Issues
8. ☐ Other *(specify)*:

Date:

Clerk, by _____, Deputy

— NOTICE TO ATTORNEY OF RECORD OR PARTY WITHOUT ATTORNEY —

Pursuant to the provisions of Code of Civil Procedure section 1952, if no appeal is filed the court may order the exhibits destroyed or otherwise disposed of after 60 days from the expiration of the appeal time.

STATEMENTS IN THIS BOX APPLY ONLY TO JUDGMENTS OF DISSOLUTION
Effective date of termination of marital status *(specify)*:
WARNING: NEITHER PARTY MAY REMARRY UNTIL THE EFFECTIVE DATE OF THE TERMINATION OF MARITAL STATUS AS SHOWN IN THIS BOX.

CLERK'S CERTIFICATE OF MAILING

I certify that I am not a party to this cause and that a true copy of the Notice of Entry of Judgment was mailed first class, postage fully prepaid, in a sealed envelope addressed as shown below, and that the notice was mailed
at *(place)*: , California,
on *(date)*:

Date:

Clerk, by _____, Deputy

Form Adopted by Rule 1290
Judicial Council of California
1290 [Rev. January 1, 1999]
Mandatory Form

NOTICE OF ENTRY OF JUDGMENT
(Family Law—Uniform Parentage)

Family Code, §§ 2338, 7636, 7637

233

ATTORNEY OR PARTY WITHOUT ATTORNEY *(Name, state bar number, and address)*:	FOR COURT USE ONLY
TELEPHONE NO.:　　　　　　　FAX NO.:	
ATTORNEY FOR *(Name)*:	

SUPERIOR COURT OF CALIFORNIA, COUNTY OF

STREET ADDRESS:

MAILING ADDRESS:

CITY AND ZIP CODE:

BRANCH NAME:

PETITIONER/PLAINTIFF:

RESPONDENT/DEFENDANT:

OTHER PARENT:

WAGE AND EARNINGS ASSIGNMENT ORDER FOR SPOUSAL SUPPORT ☐ Modification	CASE NUMBER:

TO THE PAYOR: This is a court order. You must withhold a portion of the earnings of *(Obligor's name and date of birth)*:

and pay as directed below. *(An explanation of this order is printed on the reverse.)*

THE COURT ORDERS YOU TO

1. Pay part of the earnings of the employee or other person ordered to pay support as follows:

   a. ☐ $ _____　per month current **spousal support**　　b. ☐ $ _____　per month **spousal support arrearages**

   c. TOTAL DEDUCTIONS PER MONTH: $ _____

2. ☐ The payments ordered under item 1a shall be paid to *(name, address)*:

3. ☐ The payments ordered under item 1b shall be paid to *(name, address)*:

4. The payments ordered under item 1 shall continue until further written notice from the payee or the court.

5. ☐ This order modifies an existing order. **The amount you must withhold may have changed.** The existing order continues in effect until this modification is effective.

6. This order affects all earnings payable beginning as soon as possible but not later than 10 days after you receive it.

7. Give the Obligor a copy of this order and the blank *Request for Hearing Regarding Wage and Earnings Assignment* (form 1299.28) within 10 days.

8. ☐ Other *(specify)*:

9. For the purposes of this order, spousal support arrearages are set at: $ _____　as of *(date)*: _____

Date: _____

_____
JUDICIAL OFFICER

(Instructions and information on reverse)

Form Adopted for Mandatory Use
Judicial Council of California
1285.70 [Rev. January 1, 2000]

**WAGE AND EARNINGS ASSIGNMENT ORDER
FOR SPOUSAL SUPPORT
(Family Law)**

Family Code, § 5208;
Code of Civil Procedure, § 706.031;
15 U.S.C. §§ 1672–1673

235

INSTRUCTIONS FOR THE WAGE AND EARNINGS ASSIGNMENT ORDER

1. **DEFINITIONS OF IMPORTANT WORDS IN THE WAGE AND EARNINGS ASSIGNMENT ORDER:**

   a. **Earnings:**

      (1) wages, salary, bonuses, vacation pay, retirement pay, and commissions paid by an employer;

      (2) payments for services of independent contractors;

      (3) dividends, interest, rents, royalties, and residuals;

      (4) patent rights and mineral or other natural resource rights;

      (5) any payments due as a result of written or oral contracts for services or sales, regardless of title;

      (6) payments due for workers' compensation temporary benefits, or payments from a disability or health insurance policy or program; and

      (7) any other payments or credits due regardless of source.

   b. **Wage and Earnings Assignment Order:** a court order issued in every court case where one person is ordered to pay for the support of another person. This order has top priority over any other orders such as garnishments or earnings withholding orders.

      Earnings should not be withheld for any other order until the amounts necessary to satisfy this order have been withheld in full. However, an *Order/Notice to Withhold Income for Child Support* for child support or family support has top priority over this order for spousal support.

   c. **Obligor:** any person ordered by a court to pay support. The Obligor is named before item 1 in the Order.

   d. **Obligee:** the person to whom the support is to be paid or a governmental agency in some cases.

   e. **Payor:** the person or entity, including an employer, that pays earnings to an Obligor.

2. **INFORMATION FOR ALL PAYORS:** Withhold money from the earnings payable to the Obligor as soon as possible but no later than 10 days after you receive the *Wage and Earnings Assignment Order for Spousal Support.* Send the money withheld to the payee(s) named in items 2 and 3 in the Order within 10 days of the pay date. You may deduct $1 from the Obligor's earnings for each payment you make.

   When sending the withheld earnings to the payee, state the date that the earnings were withheld. You may combine amounts withheld for more than one Obligor in a single payment to each payee, and identify what portion of that payment is for each Obligor.

   You will be liable for any amount you fail to withhold and can be cited for contempt of court.

3. **SPECIAL INSTRUCTIONS FOR PAYORS WHO ARE EMPLOYERS:**

   a. State and federal laws limit the amount that you can withhold and pay as directed by this Order. This limitation applies only to earnings defined above in item 1a(1) and are usually half the Obligor's disposable earnings.

      Disposable earnings are different from gross pay or take-home pay. Disposable earnings are earnings left after subtracting the money that state or federal law requires an employer to withhold. Generally these required deductions are (1) federal income tax, (2) social security, (3) state income tax, (4) state disability insurance, and (5) payments to public employees' retirement systems.

      After the Obligor's disposable earnings are known, withhold the amount required by the Order, **but never withhold more than 50 percent of the disposable earnings unless the court order specifies a higher percentage.** Federal law prohibits withholding more than 65 percent of disposable earnings of an employee in any case.

      If the Obligor has more than one assignment for support, add together the amount of support due for each assignment. If 50 percent of the Obligor's net disposable earnings will not pay in full all of the assignments for support, prorate it first among all of the current support assignments in the same proportion that each assignment bears to the total current support owed. Apply any remainder to the assignments for arrearage support in the same proportion that each assignment bears to the total arrearage owed. If you have any questions, please contact the office or person that sent this form to you. This office or person's name appears in the upper left-hand corner of the Order.

   b. If the employee is paid by a different time period from that specified in the Order, prorate the amount ordered to be withheld so part of it is withheld from each of the Obligor's paychecks.

   c. If the Obligor stops working for you, notify the office that sent you this form no later than the date of the next payment, by first-class mail. Give the Obligor's last known address and, if known, the name and address of any new employer.

   d. California law prohibits you from firing, refusing to hire, or taking any disciplinary action against any employee ordered to pay support through a wage and earnings assignment. Such action can lead to a $500 civil penalty per employee.

4. **INFORMATION FOR ALL OBLIGORS:** You should have received a *Request for Hearing Regarding Wage and Earnings Assignment* (form 1299.28) with the *Wage and Earnings Assignment Order for Spousal Support.* If not, you may get one from either the court clerk or the family law facilitator. If you want the court to stop or modify your wage assignment you must file (hand-deliver or mail) an original copy of the form with the court clerk within 10 days of the date you received this Order. Keep a copy of the form for your records.

   If you think your support order is wrong, you can ask for a modification of the order, or in some cases, you can have the order set aside and have a new order issued. You can talk to an attorney or get information from the family law facilitator about this.

5. **SPECIAL INFORMATION FOR THE OBLIGOR WHO IS AN EMPLOYEE:** State law requires you to notify the payees named in items 2 and 3 in the Order if you change your employment. You must provide the name and address of your new employer.

**WAGE AND EARNINGS ASSIGNMENT ORDER
FOR SPOUSAL SUPPORT**
(Family Law)

ATTORNEY OR PARTY WITHOUT ATTORNEY *(Name, state bar number, and address)*	FOR COURT USE ONLY
TELEPHONE NO.: FAX NO.:	
ATTORNEY FOR *(Name)*:	

SUPERIOR COURT OF CALIFORNIA, COUNTY OF
STREET ADDRESS:
MAILING ADDRESS:
CITY AND ZIP CODE:
BRANCH NAME:

MARRIAGE OF
PETITIONER:

RESPONDENT:

RESPONSE ☐ **and REQUEST FOR**	CASE NUMBER:
☐ **Dissolution of Marriage**	
☐ **Legal Separation**	
☐ **Nullity of Marriage** ☐ **AMENDED**	

1. RESIDENCE (Dissolution only) ☐ Petitioner ☐ Respondent has been a resident of this state for at least six months and of this county for at least three months immediately preceding the filing of the *Petition for Dissolution of Marriage.*

2. STATISTICAL FACTS
   a. Date of marriage:
   b. Date of separation:
   c. Period between marriage and separation
        Years: Months:

3. DECLARATION REGARDING MINOR CHILDREN *(include children of this relationship born prior to or during the marriage or adopted during the marriage)*:
   a. ☐ There are no minor children.
   b. ☐ The minor children are:

Child's name	Birth date	Age	Sex

   ☐ Continued on Attachment 3b.
   c. If there are minor children of the petitioner and respondent, a completed *Declaration Under the Uniform Child Custody Jurisdiction Act (UCCJA)* (form MC-150) must be attached.
   d. ☐ A completed voluntary declaration of paternity regarding minor children born to the Petitioner and Respondent prior to the marriage is attached.

4. ☐ **Respondent requests** confirmation as separate property assets and debts the items listed
   ☐ in Attachment 4   ☐ below:
   Item   Confirm to

NOTICE: Any party required to pay child support must pay interest on overdue amounts at the "legal" rate, which is currently 10 percent.

(Continued on reverse)

Form Adopted for Mandatory Use
Judicial Council of California
Rule 1282 [Rev. July 1, 1999]

RESPONSE
(Family Law)

Family Code, § 2020;
Cal. Rules of Court, rule 1215

237

MARRIAGE OF *(last name, first name of parties)*:	CASE NUMBER:

5. DECLARATION REGARDING COMMUNITY AND QUASI-COMMUNITY ASSETS AND DEBTS AS CURRENTLY KNOWN
   a. ☐ There are no such assets or debts subject to disposition by the court in this proceeding.
   b. ☐ All such assets and debts have been disposed of by written agreement.
   c. ☐ All such assets and debts are listed ☐ in Attachment 5c ☐ below *(specify)*:

6. ☐ **Respondent contends** that there is a reasonable possibility of reconciliation.

7. ☐ **Respondent denies** the grounds set forth in item 6 of the petition.

8. **Respondent requests**
   a. ☐ Dissolution of the marriage based on
      (1) ☐ irreconcilable differences. Fam. Code, § 2310(a)
      (2) ☐ incurable insanity. Fam. Code, § 2310(b)
   b. ☐ Legal separation of the parties based on
      (1) ☐ irreconcilable differences. Fam. Code, § 2310(a)
      (2) ☐ incurable insanity. Fam. Code, § 2310(b)
   c. ☐ Nullity of void marriage based on
      (1) ☐ incestuous marriage. Fam. Code, § 2200
      (2) ☐ bigamous marriage. Fam. Code, § 2201

   d. ☐ Nullity of voidable marriage based on
      (1) ☐ respondent's age at time of marriage. Fam. Code, § 2210(a)
      (2) ☐ prior existing marriage. Fam. Code. § 2210(b)
      (3) ☐ unsound mind. Fam. Code, § 2210(c)
      (4) ☐ fraud. Fam. Code, § 2210(d)
      (5) ☐ force. Fam. Code, § 2210(e)
      (6) ☐ physical incapacity. Fam. Code, § 2210(f)

9. **Respondent requests** that the court grant the above relief and make injunctive (including restraining) and other orders as follows:

	Petitioner	Respondent	Joint	Other
a. Legal custody of children to	☐	☐	☐	☐
b. Physical custody of children to	☐	☐	☐	☐
c. Child visitation be granted to	☐	☐		☐
(1) ☐ Supervised for:	☐	☐		
(2) ☐ No visitation for:	☐	☐		

      (3) ☐ Continued on Attachment 9c(3).
   d. ☐ Determination of parentage of any children born to the Petitioner and Respondent prior to the marriage.
   e. Spousal support payable to (wage assignment will be issued) . . . . ☐ ☐
   f. Attorney fees and costs payable by . . . . ☐ ☐
   g. ☐ Terminate the court's jurisdiction (ability) to award spousal support to petitioner.
   h ☐ Property rights be determined.
   i. ☐ Respondent's former name be restored *(specify)*:
   j. ☐ Other *(specify)*:

      ☐ Continued on Attachment 9j.

10. If there are minor children born to or adopted by the Petitioner and Respondent before or during this marriage. the court will make orders for the support of the children. A wage assignment will be issued without further notice.

I declare under penalty of perjury under the laws of the State of California that the foregoing is true and correct.
Date:

▶
_____
(TYPE OR PRINT NAME)   (SIGNATURE OF RESPONDENT)

Date:

▶
_____
(TYPE OR PRINT NAME)   (SIGNATURE OF ATTORNEY FOR RESPONDENT)

> **The original response must be filed in the court with proof of service of a copy on petitioner.**

       RESPONSE
(Family Law)

ATTORNEY OR PARTY WITHOUT ATTORNEY *(Name and Address)*:	TELEPHONE NO.:	*FOR COURT USE ONLY*
ATTORNEY FOR *(Name)*:		

SUPERIOR COURT OF CALIFORNIA, COUNTY OF
STREET ADDRESS:
MAILING ADDRESS:
CITY AND ZIP CODE:
BRANCH NAME:

MARRIAGE OF
HUSBAND:

WIFE:

JOINT PETITION FOR SUMMARY DISSOLUTION OF MARRIAGE	CASE NUMBER:

WE PETITION FOR A SUMMARY DISSOLUTION OF MARRIAGE and declare that all the following conditions exist on the date this petition is filed with the court:

1. We have read and understand the Summary Dissolution Information booklet.

2. We were married on *(date)*:
[A SUMMARY DISSOLUTION OF YOUR MARRIAGE WILL NOT BE GRANTED IF YOU FILE THIS PETITION MORE THAN FIVE YEARS AFTER THE DATE OF YOUR MARRIAGE.]

3. One of us has lived in California for at least six months and in the county of filing for at least three months preceding the date of filing.

4. There are no minor children born of our relationship before or during our marriage or adopted by us during our marriage and the wife, to her knowledge, is not pregnant.

5. Neither of us has an interest in any real property anywhere. *(You may have a lease for a residence in which one of you lives. It must terminate within a year from the date of filing this petition. The lease must not include an option to purchase.)*

6. Except for obligations with respect to automobiles, on obligations either or both of us incurred during our marriage, we owe no more than $5,000.

7. The total fair market value of community property assets, excluding all encumbrances and automobiles, is less than $25,000.

8. Neither of us has separate property assets, excluding all encumbrances and automobiles, in excess of $25,000.

9. We also attach completed copies of the worksheets on pages 9, 11, and 13 of the Information Booklet used in determining the value and division of our property.

10. *(Check whichever statement is true)*
    a. ☐ We have no community assets or liabilities.

    b. ☐ We have signed an agreement listing and dividing all our community assets and liabilities and have signed all papers necessary to carry out our agreement. A copy of our agreement is attached to this petition.

11. Irreconcilable differences have caused the irremediable breakdown of our marriage and each of us wishes to have the court dissolve our marriage without our appearing before a judge.

12. ☐ Wife desires to have her former name restored. Her former name is *(specify name)*:

(Continued on reverse)

Form Adopted by Rule 1295.10
Judicial Council of California
1295.10 [Rev. January 1, 1995]

**JOINT PETITION FOR SUMMARY
DISSOLUTION OF MARRIAGE**
(Family Law—Summary Dissolution)

Family Code, §§ 2400–2406

239

HUSBAND:	CASE NUMBER:
WIFE:	

13 Upon entry of judgment of summary dissolution of marriage, we each give up our rights as follows:
  - a. to appeal, and
  - b. to move for a new trial.

14. EACH OF US FOREVER GIVES UP ANY RIGHT TO SPOUSAL SUPPORT FROM THE OTHER.

15. We stipulate that this matter may be determined by a commissioner sitting as a temporary judge.

16. **Mailing Address of Husband**
Name:
Address:

City
State:
Zip
Code:

16. **Mailing Address of Wife**
Name:
Address:

City
State:
Zip
Code:

I declare under penalty of perjury under the laws of the State of California that the foregoing is true and correct.

I declare under penalty of perjury under the laws of the State of California that the foregoing is true and correct.

Date:

Date:

▶ _____
(SIGNATURE OF HUSBAND)

▶ _____
(SIGNATURE OF WIFE)

YOU HAVE A RIGHT TO REVOKE THIS PETITION ANY TIME BEFORE A REQUEST FOR JUDGMENT IS FILED. YOU WILL REMAIN MARRIED UNTIL ONE OF YOU FILES FOR AND OBTAINS A JUDGMENT OF DISSOLUTION. YOU MAY NOT REQUEST A JUDGMENT OF DISSOLUTION SOONER THAN SIX MONTHS FROM THE DATE THIS PETITION IS FILED.

NOTICE: Please review your will, insurance policies, retirement benefit plans, credit cards, other credit accounts and credit reports, and other matters you may want to change in view of the dissolution or annulment of your marriage, or your legal separation.

ATTORNEY OR PARTY WITHOUT ATTORNEY *(Name and Address)*:	TELEPHONE NO.:	*FOR COURT USE ONLY*
ATTORNEY FOR *(Name)*:		

SUPERIOR COURT OF CALIFORNIA, COUNTY OF

STREET ADDRESS:

MAILING ADDRESS:

CITY AND ZIP CODE:

BRANCH NAME:

MARRIAGE OF PETITIONERS

HUSBAND:

WIFE:

REQUEST FOR JUDGMENT, JUDGMENT OF DISSOLUTION OF MARRIAGE, AND NOTICE OF ENTRY OF JUDGMENT	CASE NUMBER:

1. The Joint Petition for Summary Dissolution of Marriage was filed on *(date)*:
2. No notice of revocation has been filed and the parties have not become reconciled.
3. I request that judgment of dissolution of marriage be
   a. ☐ entered to be effective now.
   b. ☐ entered to be effective (nunc pro tunc) as of *(date)*:
      for the following reason:

I declare under penalty of perjury under the laws of the State of California that the foregoing is true and correct.
Date:

▶

....
(TYPE OR PRINT NAME)

_____
(SIGNATURE OF HUSBAND OR WIFE)

4. ☐ Wife, who did **not** request her former name be restored when she signed the joint petition, now requests that it be restored *(type former name)*:

▶

....
(TYPE OR PRINT NAME)

_____
(SIGNATURE OF WIFE)

(For Court Use Only)
JUDGMENT OF DISSOLUTION OF MARRIAGE

5. THE COURT ORDERS
   a. A judgment of dissolution of marriage shall be entered, and the parties are restored to the status of unmarried persons.
   b. ☐ The judgment of dissolution of marriage shall be entered nunc pro tunc as of *(date)*:
   c. ☐ Wife's former name is restored *(specify)*:
   d. Husband and wife shall comply with any agreement attached to the petition.

Date: _____
JUDGE OF THE SUPERIOR COURT

NOTICE
Please review your will, insurance policies, retirement benefit plans, credit cards, other credit accounts and credit reports, and other matters you may wish to change in view of the dissolution of your marriage. Ending your marriage may automatically change a disposition made by your will to your former spouse.

(See reverse for Notice of Entry of Judgment)

Form Adopted by Rule 1295.20
Judicial Council of California
1295.20 [Rev. January 1, 1995]

**REQUEST FOR JUDGMENT, JUDGMENT OF DISSOLUTION
OF MARRIAGE, AND NOTICE OF ENTRY OF JUDGMENT**
(Family Law—Summary Dissolution)

Family Code, § 2403

HUSBAND:	CASE NUMBER:
WIFE:	

NOTICE OF ENTRY OF JUDGMENT

6. You are notified that a judgment of dissolution of marriage was entered on *(date)*:

Date: _____   Clerk, by _____ , Deputy

CLERK'S CERTIFICATE OF MAILING

I certify that I am not a party to this cause and that a true copy of the Notice of Entry of Judgment was mailed first class, postage fully prepaid, in a sealed envelope addressed as shown below, and that the notice was mailed
at *(place)*:   , California,
on *(date)*:

Date: _____   Clerk, by _____ , Deputy

HUSBAND'S ADDRESS   WIFE'S ADDRESS

ATTORNEY OR PARTY WITHOUT ATTORNEY *(Name and Address)*:	TELEPHONE NO.:	FOR COURT USE ONLY

ATTORNEY FOR *(Name)*:

SUPERIOR COURT OF CALIFORNIA, COUNTY OF

STREET ADDRESS:

MAILING ADDRESS:

CITY AND ZIP CODE:

BRANCH NAME:

MARRIAGE OF

PETITIONER:

RESPONDENT:

NOTICE OF REVOCATION OF PETITION FOR SUMMARY DISSOLUTION	CASE NUMBER:

Notice is given that the undersigned terminates the summary dissolution proceedings and revokes the Joint Petition for Summary Dissolution of Marriage filed on *(date)*:

I declare under penalty of perjury under the laws of the State of California that the foregoing is true and correct.

Date:

....
(TYPE OR PRINT NAME)

▶ _____
(SIGNATURE OF DECLARANT)

COMPLETE THIS NOTICE, EXCEPT FOR THE PLACE AND DATE OF MAILING AND CLERK'S NAME. SUBMIT THE ORIGINAL AND TWO COPIES TO THE COUNTY CLERK'S OFFICE. IF NO REQUEST FOR JUDGMENT HAS BEEN FILED, THE CLERK WILL NOTIFY YOU THAT THIS NOTICE OF REVOCATION HAS BEEN FILED BY COMPLETING THE CERTIFICATE BELOW.

CLERK'S CERTIFICATE OF MAILING

I certify that I am not a party to this cause and that a copy of the foregoing was mailed first class postage prepaid, in a sealed envelope as shown below, and that the mailing of the foregoing and execution of this certificate occurred at
(place):
                                                        California, on

(Date):

Clerk, by _____, Deputy

Name and address of husband   Name and address of wife:

NOTICE

IF THE CLERK'S CERTIFICATE OF MAILING ABOVE HAS BEEN DATED AND SIGNED BY THE CLERK, THIS SUMMARY DISSOLUTION PROCEEDING IS ENDED. YOU ARE STILL MARRIED.

The declaration under penalty of perjury must be signed in California, or in a state that authorizes use of a declaration in place of an affidavit; otherwise an affidavit is required.

Form Adopted by Rule 1295.30
Judicial Council of California
1295.30 [Rev. January 1, 1995]

**NOTICE OF REVOCATION OF PETITION
FOR SUMMARY DISSOLUTION**
(Family Law—Summary Dissolution)

Family Code, § 2402
Calif. Rules of Court, rule 1241

_____
(name)

_____
(street address)

_____
(city   state   zip)

_____
(phone number)

_____
(date)

MEMORANDUM OF REQUEST FOR MILITARY SERVICE STATUS

TO: U.S. Coast Guard Commander, GPIM-2, Locators
      2100 2nd St., S.W.,
      Washington, DC 20593

      AFMPC/RMIQL, Attn: Air Force Locator
      Randolph AFB, TX 78150-6001

      Department of Navy, Bureau of Navy Personnel
      2 Navy Annex
      Washington, DC 20370-5000

      CMC MMSB-10, HQ USMC, Bldg. 2008
      Quantico, VA 22134-5002

      Surgeon General, U.S. Public Health Service, Div. of Comm., Off. Personnel
      5600 Fishers Land
      Rockville, MD 20857

      Army World Wide Locator, U.S. Army Enlisted Records Center
      Fort Benjamin Harrison, IN 46249-5601

      Commander, U.S. Army Personnel Center, Officer Locator Branch, Attn: Locators
      200 Stovall Street
      Alexandria, VA 22332

RE: _____   _____
              [Party]   [Soc. Sec. #]

This case involves a family matter. It is imperative that a determination be made whether the above named individual, who has an interest in these proceedings, is presently in the military service of the United States, and the date of induction and discharge, if any. This information is necessary to comply with §581 of the Soldier's and Sailor's Civil Relief Act of 1940, as amended. Please supply a certification of verification as soon as possible. My check in enclosed for your search fees. Self-addressed, stamped envelopes are enclosed.

Very truly yours,

_____
(signature)

ATTORNEY OR PARTY WITHOUT ATTORNEY *(Name and Address)*:	TELEPHONE NO.:	*FOR COURT USE ONLY*
ATTORNEY FOR *(Name)*:		

NAME OF COURT:

STREET ADDRESS:

MAILING ADDRESS:

CITY AND ZIP CODE:

BRANCH NAME:

PLAINTIFF/PETITIONER:

DEFENDANT/RESPONDENT:

DECLARATION	CASE NUMBER:

I declare under penalty of perjury under the laws of the State of California that the foregoing is true and correct.

Date:

. . . .
(TYPE OR PRINT NAME)

▶ _____
(SIGNATURE OF DECLARANT)

☐ Petitioner/Plaintiff ☐ Respondent/Defendant ☐ Attorney
☐ Other *(specify)*:

SHORT TITLE:	CASE NUMBER:

1
2
3
4
5
6
7
8
9
10
11
12
13
14
15
16
17
18
19
20
21
22
23
24
25
26 *(Required for verified pleading)* The items on this page stated on information and belief are *(specify item numbers, **not** line numbers)*:
27

This page may be used with any Judicial Council form or any other paper filed with the court.　Page _____

Form Approved by the
Judicial Council of California
MC-020 [New January 1, 1987]

ADDITIONAL PAGE
Attach to Judicial Council Form or Other Court Paper

CRC 201, 501

249

ATTORNEY OR PARTY WITHOUT ATTORNEY OR GOVERNMENTAL AGENCY (pursuant to Welf. & Inst. Code, §§ 11475.1, 11478.2) (Name, state bar number, and address):	FOR COURT USE ONLY
TELEPHONE NO.: FAX NO.:	
ATTORNEY FOR (Name):	
SUPERIOR COURT OF CALIFORNIA, COUNTY OF	
STREET ADDRESS:	
MAILING ADDRESS:	
CITY AND ZIP CODE:	
BRANCH NAME:	
PETITIONER/PLAINTIFF:	
RESPONDENT/DEFENDANT:	
OTHER PARENT:	
PROOF OF SERVICE BY MAIL	CASE NUMBER:

NOTICE: To serve temporary restraining orders you must use personal service (see form 1285.84).

1. I am over the age of 18, not a party to this cause, and not a protected person listed in any of the orders. I am a resident of or employed in the county where the mailing took place.

2. My residence or business address is:

3. I served a copy of the following documents *(specify)*:

by enclosing them in an envelope AND
   a. ☐ **depositing** the sealed envelope with the United States Postal Service with the postage fully prepaid.
   b. ☐ **placing** the envelope for collection and mailing on the date and at the place shown in item 4 following our ordinary business practices. I am readily familiar with this business's practice for collecting and processing correspondence for mailing. On the same day that correspondence is placed for collection and mailing, it is deposited in the ordinary course of business with the United States Postal Service in a sealed envelope with postage fully prepaid.

4. The envelope was addressed and mailed as follows:
   a. Name of person served:
   b. Address:

   c. Date mailed:
   d. Place of mailing *(city and state)*:

5. I declare under penalty of perjury under the laws of the State of California that the foregoing is true and correct.

Date:

. . . .
(TYPE OR PRINT NAME)   ▶   (SIGNATURE OF PERSON COMPLETING THIS FORM)

(See instructions on reverse)

Form Approved by Rule 1285.85 Judicial Council of California 1285.85 [New July 1, 1998]	PROOF OF SERVICE BY MAIL (Family Law)	Code of Civil Procedure, §§ 1013, 1013a

INFORMATION SHEET FOR PROOF OF SERVICE BY MAIL
(California Rules of Court, rule 1285.85)

Use these instructions to complete the *Proof of Service by Mail* (form 1285.85).

A person 18 years of age or older must serve the documents. There are two ways to serve documents: (1) personal delivery and (2) by mail. See the *Proof of Personal Service* (form 1285.84) if the documents are being personally served. The person who serves the documents must complete a proof of service form for the documents being served. **You cannot serve documents if you are a party to the action.**

INSTRUCTIONS FOR THE PERSON WHO SERVES THE DOCUMENTS (TYPE OR PRINT IN BLACK INK)

You must complete a proof of service for each package of documents you serve. For example, if you serve the Respondent and the Other Parent, you must complete two proofs of service, one for the Respondent and one for the Other Parent.

Complete the top section of the proof of service forms as follows:
First box, left side: In this box print the name, address, and phone number of the person for whom you are serving the documents.
Second box, left side: Print the name of the county in which the legal action is filed and the court's address in this box. Use the same address for the court that is on the documents you are serving.
Third box, left side: Print the names of the Petitioner/Plaintiff, Respondent/Defendant, and Other Parent in this box. Use the same names listed on the documents you are serving.
First box, top of form, right side: Leave this box blank for the court's use.
Second box, right side: Print the case number in this box. This number is also stated on the documents you are serving.

You cannot serve a temporary restraining order by mail. You must serve those documents by personal service.

1. You are stating that you are over the age of 18 and that you are neither a party to this action nor a protected person listed in any of the orders. You are also stating that you either live in or are employed in the county where the mailing took place.
2. Print your home or business address.
3. List the name of each document that you mailed (the exact names are listed on the bottoms of the forms).
   a. Check this box if you put the documents in the regular U.S. mail.
   b. Check this box if you put the documents in the mail at your place of employment.
4. a. Print the name you put on the envelope containing the documents.
   b. Print the address you put on the envelope containing the documents.
   c. Write in the date that you put the envelope containing the documents in the mail.
   d. Write in the city and state you were in when you mailed the envelope containing the documents.
5. You are stating under penalty of perjury that the information you have provided is true and correct.

Print your name, fill in the date, and sign the form.

If you need additional assistance with this form, contact the Family Law Facilitator in your county.

— THIS FORM MUST BE KEPT CONFIDENTIAL —

ATTORNEY OR PARTY WITHOUT ATTORNEY *(Name, state bar number, and address)*:	FOR COURT USE ONLY
TELEPHONE NO.: FAX NO.:	
ATTORNEY FOR *(Name)*:	

NAME OF COURT:
STREET ADDRESS:
MAILING ADDRESS:
CITY AND ZIP CODE:
BRANCH NAME:

PLAINTIFF/ PETITIONER:	
DEFENDANT/ RESPONDENT:	
APPLICATION FOR WAIVER OF COURT FEES AND COSTS	CASE NUMBER:

I request a court order so that I do not have to pay court fees and costs.

1. a. ☐ I am *not* able to pay any of the court fees and costs.
   b. ☐ I am able to pay *only* the following court fees and costs *(specify)*:

2. My current street or mailing address is *(if applicable, include city or town, apartment no., if any, and zip code)* :

3. My date of birth is *(specify)*:

4. a. My occupation, employer, and employer's address are *(specify)*:

   b. My spouse's occupation, employer, and employer's address are *(specify)*:

5. ☐ I am receiving financial assistance under one or more of the following programs:
   a. ☐ **SSI and SSP:** Supplemental Security Income and State Supplemental Payments Programs
   b. ☐ **CalWORKs:** California Work Opportunity and Responsibility to Kids Act, implementing TANF, Temporary Assistance for Needy Families (formerly AFDC)
   c. ☐ **Food Stamps:** The Food Stamps Program
   d. ☐ **County Relief, General Relief (G.R.) or General Assistance (G.A.)**

6. *If you checked box 5 above, you must check and complete* **one or the other box, except if you are a defendant in an unlawful detainer action. Do not check both boxes.**
   a. ☐ (Optional) My social security number is *(specify)*: ☐☐☐ – ☐☐ – ☐☐☐☐
      [Federal law does not require that you give your social security number. However, if you don't give your social security number, you must check box b and attach documents to verify the benefits checked in item 4.]
   b. ☐ I am attaching documents to verify receipt of the benefits checked in item 5, above.
      [See the Information Sheet on Waiver of Court Fees and Costs, available from the clerk's office, for a list of acceptable documents.]

[If you checked box 5 above, skip items 7 and 8, and sign at the bottom of this side.]

7. ☐ My total gross monthly household income is less than the amount shown on the *Information Sheet on Waiver of Court Fees and Costs* available from the clerk's office.

[If you checked box 7 above, skip item 8, complete items 9, 10a, 10d, 10f, and 10g on the back of this form, and sign at the bottom of this side.]

8. ☐ My income is not enough to pay for the common necessaries of life for me and the people in my family I support and also pay court fees and costs. *[If you checked this box you must complete the back of this form.]*

WARNING: You must immediately tell the court if you become able to pay court fees or costs during this action. You may be ordered to appear in court and answer questions about your ability to pay court fees or costs.

I declare under penalty of perjury under the laws of the State of California that the information on both sides of this form and all attachments are complete, true, and correct.

Date:

▶

....
(TYPE OR PRINT NAME)   (Financial information on reverse)   (SIGNATURE)

Form Adopted by the
Judicial Council of California
982(a)(17) [Rev. January 1, 1999]
APPLICATION FOR WAIVER OF COURT FEES AND COSTS
(In Forma Pauperis)
Government Code,
§ 68511.3
Mandatory Form

PLAINTIFF/PETITIONER:	CASE NUMBER:
DEFENDANT/RESPONDENT:	

FINANCIAL INFORMATION

9. ☐ My pay changes considerably from month to month. **[If you check this box, each of the amounts reported in item 10 should be your average for the past 12 months.]**

10. **MY MONTHLY INCOME**

a. My gross monthly pay is: . . . . $ _____

b. **My payroll deductions are** *(specify purpose and amount)*:

(1) _____ $ _____
(2) _____ $ _____
(3) _____ $ _____
(4) _____ $ _____

My TOTAL payroll deduction amount is: $ _____

c. My monthly take-home pay is *(a. minus b.)*: . . . . $ _____

d. Other money I get each month is *(specify **source** and **amount**; include spousal support, child support, parental support, support from outside the home, scholarships, retirement or pensions, social security, disability, unemployment, military basic allowance for quarters (BAQ), veterans payments, dividends, interest or royalty, trust income, annuities, net business income, net rental income, reimbursement of job-related expenses, and net gambling or lottery winnings)*:

(1) _____ $ _____
(2) _____ $ _____
(3) _____ $ _____
(4) _____ $ _____

The TOTAL amount of other money is: $ _____
(If more space is needed, attach page labeled Attachment 10d.)

e. **MY TOTAL MONTHLY INCOME IS** *(c. plus d.)*: . . . . $ _____

f. Number of persons living in my home: _____
Below list all the persons living in your home, including your spouse, who depend in whole or in part on you for support, **or** on whom you depend in whole or in part for support:

	Name	Age	Relationship	Gross Monthly Income
(1)	_____	_____	_____	$ _____
(2)	_____	_____	_____	$ _____
(3)	_____	_____	_____	$ _____
(4)	_____	_____	_____	$ _____
(5)	_____	_____	_____	$ _____

The TOTAL amount of other money is: $ _____
(If more space is needed, attach page labeled Attachment 10f.)

g. **MY TOTAL GROSS MONTHLY HOUSEHOLD INCOME IS** *(a. plus d. plus f.)*: . . . . $ _____

11. **I own or have an interest in the following property:**

a. Cash . . . . $ _____

b. Checking, savings and credit union accounts *(list banks)*:

(1) _____ $ _____
(2) _____ $ _____
(3) _____ $ _____
(4) _____ $ _____

11. c. Cars, other vehicles, and boats *(list make, year, fair market value (FMV), and loan balance of each)*:

	Property	FMV	Loan Balance
(1)	_____	$ _____	$ _____
(2)	_____	$ _____	$ _____
(3)	_____	$ _____	$ _____

d. Real estate *(list address, estimated fair market value (FMV), and loan balance of each property)*:

	Property	FMV	Loan Balance
(1)	_____	$ _____	$ _____
(2)	_____	$ _____	$ _____
(3)	_____	$ _____	$ _____

e. Other personal property — jewelry, furniture, furs, stocks, bonds, etc. *(list separately)*:

$ _____

12. **My monthly expenses not already listed in item 10b above are the following:**

a. Rent or house payment & maintenance $ _____
b. Food and household supplies . . . . $ _____
c. Utilities and telephone . . . . $ _____
d. Clothing . . . . $ _____
e. Laundry and cleaning . . . . $ _____
f. Medical and dental payments . . . . $ _____
g. Insurance (life, health, accident, etc.) . . . $ _____
h. School, child care . . . . $ _____
i. Child, spousal support (prior marriage) . . . $ _____
j. Transportation and auto expenses (insurance, gas, repair) . . . . $ _____
k. Installment payments *(specify **purpose** and **amount**)*:

(1) _____ $ _____
(2) _____ $ _____
(3) _____ $ _____

The TOTAL amount of monthly installment payments is: . . . . $ _____

l. Amounts deducted due to wage assignments and earnings withholding orders: $ _____

m. Other expenses *(specify)*:

(1) _____ $ _____
(2) _____ $ _____
(3) _____ $ _____
(4) _____ $ _____
(5) _____ $ _____

The TOTAL amount of other monthly expenses is: . . . . $ _____

n. **MY TOTAL MONTHLY EXPENSES ARE** *(add a. through m.)*: . . . . $ _____

13. Other facts which support this application are *(describe unusual medical needs, expenses for recent family emergencies, or other unusual circumstances or expenses to help the court understand your budget; if more space is needed, attach page labeled Attachment 13)*:

WARNING: You must immediately tell the court if you become able to pay court fees or costs during this action. You may be ordered to appear in court and answer questions about your ability to pay court fees or costs.

982(a)(17) [Rev. January 1, 1999]   **APPLICATION FOR WAIVER OF COURT FEES AND COSTS**   Page two
(In Forma Pauperis)

ATTORNEY OR PARTY WITHOUT ATTORNEY *(Name, state bar number, and address)*	FOR COURT USE ONLY

TELEPHONE NO.:   FAX NO.:

ATTORNEY FOR *(Name)*:

SUPERIOR COURT OF CALIFORNIA, COUNTY OF

    STREET ADDRESS:

    MAILING ADDRESS:

    CITY AND ZIP CODE:

    BRANCH NAME:

PETITIONER/PLAINTIFF:

RESPONDENT/DEFENDANT:

ORDER TO SHOW CAUSE FOR ☐ **MODIFICATION**	CASE NUMBER:
☐ **Child Custody** ☐ **Visitation** ☐ **Injunctive Order**	
☐ **Child Support** ☐ **Spousal Support** ☐ **Other** *(specify)*:	
☐ **Attorney Fees and Costs**	

1. TO *(name)*:
2. YOU ARE ORDERED TO APPEAR IN THIS COURT AS FOLLOWS TO GIVE ANY LEGAL REASON WHY THE RELIEF SOUGHT IN THE ATTACHED APPLICATION SHOULD NOT BE GRANTED. *If child custody or visitation is an issue in this proceeding, Family Code section 3170 requires mediation before or concurrently with the hearing listed below.*

     a. Date: Time: ☐ Dept.:   ☐ Rm.:

     b. Address of court   ☐ same as noted above   ☐ other *(specify)*:

     c. ☐ The parties are ordered to attend custody mediation services as follows:

3. IT IS FURTHER ORDERED that a completed *Application for Order and Supporting Declaration*, a **blank** *Responsive Declaration*, and the following documents shall be served with this order:

     a. (1) ☐ Completed *Income and Expense Declaration* and a **blank** *Income and Expense Declaration*

        (2) ☐ Completed *Financial Statement (Simplified)* and a **blank** *Financial Statement (Simplified)*

        (3) ☐ Completed *Property Declaration* and a **blank** *Property Declaration*

        (4) ☐ Points and authorities

        (5) ☐ Other *(specify)*:

     b. ☐ Time for ☐ service ☐ hearing   is shortened. Service shall be on or before *(date)*:

        Any responsive declaration shall be served on or before *(date)*:

     c. ☐ You are ordered to comply with the temporary orders attached.

     d. ☐ Other *(specify)*:

Date: _____

_____
JUDGE OF THE SUPERIOR COURT

NOTICE: If you have children from this relationship, the court is required to order payment of child support based on the income of both parents. The amount of child support can be large. It normally continues until the child is 18. You should supply the court with information about your finances. Otherwise, the child support order will be based on the information supplied by the other parent.

You do not have to pay any fee to file responsive declarations in response to this order to show cause (including a completed *Income and Expense Declaration* (form 1285.50) or *Financial Statement (Simplified)* (form 1285.52) that will show your finances). In the absence of an order shortening time, the original of the responsive declaration must be filed with the court and a copy served on the other party at least five court days before the hearing date.

Form Adopted by Rule 1285
Judicial Council of California
1285 [Rev. January 1, 1999]
Mandatory Form

ORDER TO SHOW CAUSE
(Family Law—Uniform Parentage)

Family Code, §§ 215, 271–272, 2030–2034,
2045, 2254, 4330–4339, 4359, 4370,
4455, 4801, 4809; Government Code, § 26826

PETITIONER/PLAINTIFF:	CASE NUMBER:
RESPONDENT/DEFENDANT:	

(THIS IS NOT AN ORDER)

☐ **Petitioner** ☐ **Respondent** ☐ **Claimant**   requests the following orders be made:

1. ☐ CHILD CUSTODY   ☐ **To be ordered pending the hearing**
   a. Child *(name and age)*   b. Request custody to *(name)*   c. ☐ Modify existing order
                                                            (1) filed on *(date)*:
                                                            (2) ordering *(specify)*:

2. ☐ CHILD VISITATION   ☐ **To be ordered pending the hearing**
   a. ☐ Reasonable   d. ☐ Modify existing order
   b. ☐ Other *(specify)*:   (1) filed on *(date)*:
   c. ☐ Petitioner ☐ Respondent shall not remove   (2) ordering *(specify)*:
       the minor child or children of the parties
       (1) ☐ from the State of California   (2) ☐ other *(specify)*:

3. ☐ CHILD SUPPORT *(A Wage and Earnings Assignment Order will be issued.)*
   a. Child *(name and age)*   b. Monthly amount   c. ☐ Modify existing order
                                      (if not by guideline)   (1) filed on *(date)*:
                                              $ (2) ordering *(specify)*:

4. ☐ SPOUSAL SUPPORT *(A Wage and Earnings Assignment Order will be issued.)*
   a. ☐ Amount requested *(monthly)*: $ c. ☐ Modify existing order
   b. ☐ Terminate existing order   (1) filed on *(date)*:
       (1) filed on *(date)*:   (2) ordering *(specify)*:
       (2) ordering *(specify)*:

5. ☐ ATTORNEY FEES AND COSTS   a. ☐ Fees: $ b. ☐ Costs: $

6. ☐ PROPERTY RESTRAINT   ☐ **To be ordered pending the hearing**
   a. The ☐ petitioner ☐ respondent ☐ claimant   are restrained from transferring, encumbering, hypothecating, concealing, or in any way disposing of any property, real or personal, whether community, quasi-community, or separate, except in the usual course of business or for the necessities of life.
       ☐ and applicant will be notified at least five business days before any proposed extraordinary expenditures and an accounting of such will be made to the court.
   b. ☐ Both parties are restrained and enjoined from cashing, borrowing against, canceling, transferring, disposing of, or changing the beneficiaries of any insurance or other coverage including life, health, automobile, and disability held for the benefit of the parties or their minor children.
   c. ☐ Neither party shall incur any debts or liabilities for which the other may be held responsible, other than in the ordinary course of business or for the necessities of life.

NOTE: TO OBTAIN DOMESTIC VIOLENCE (PERSONAL CONDUCT AND HARASSMENT) RESTRAINING ORDERS, YOU MUST USE THE FORMS *APPLICATION AND DECLARATION FOR ORDER (DOMESTIC VIOLENCE PREVENTION)* (FORM DV-100) AND *ORDER TO SHOW CAUSE AND TEMPORARY RESTRAINING ORDER (CLETS) (DOMESTIC VIOLENCE PREVENTION)* (FORM DV-110).

(Continued on reverse)

Form Adopted by Rule 1285.20
Judicial Council of California
1285.20 [Rev. January 1, 1999]
Mandatory Form

APPLICATION FOR ORDER AND SUPPORTING DECLARATION
(Family Law—Uniform Parentage)

Family Code. §§ 2045. 6224. 6226.
6320–6326, 6380–6383

257

PETITIONER/PLAINTIFF:	CASE NUMBER:
RESPONDENT/DEFENDANT:	

7. ☐ PROPERTY CONTROL   ☐ **To be ordered pending the hearing**

    a. ☐ Petitioner ☐ Respondent   are given the exclusive temporary use, possession, and control of the following property we own or are buying (specify):

    b. ☐ Petitioner ☐ Respondent   are ordered to make the following payments on liens and encumbrances coming due while the order is in effect:

    <u>Debt</u>   <u>Amount of payment</u>   <u>Pay to</u>

8. ☐ **I request** that time for service of the Order to Show Cause and accompanying papers be shortened so that they may be served no less than (specify number):   days before the time set for the hearing. I need to have the order shortening time because of the facts specified in the attached declaration.

9. ☐ OTHER RELIEF (specify):

10. ☐ FACTS IN SUPPORT of relief requested and change of circumstances for any modification are (specify):
    ☐ contained in the attached declaration.

I declare under penalty of perjury under the laws of the State of California that the foregoing is true and correct.

Date:

. . . . ▶ _____

(TYPE OR PRINT NAME)   (SIGNATURE OF APPLICANT)

PETITIONER/PLAINTIFF:	CASE NUMBER:
RESPONDENT/DEFENDANT:	

TEMPORARY ORDERS
(Attachment to Order to Show Cause)

NOTE: TO OBTAIN DOMESTIC VIOLENCE (PERSONAL CONDUCT AND HARASSMENT) RESTRAINING ORDERS, YOU MUST USE FORMS *APPLICATION AND DECLARATION FOR ORDER (DOMESTIC VIOLENCE PREVENTION) (FORM DV-100)* **AND** *ORDER TO SHOW CAUSE AND TEMPORARY RESTRAINING ORDER (CLETS) (DOMESTIC VIOLENCE PREVENTION) (FORM DV-110).*

1. ☐ PROPERTY RESTRAINT
   a. ☐ Petitioner ☐ Respondent is restrained from transferring, encumbering, hypothecating, concealing, or in any way disposing of any property, real or personal, whether community, quasi-community, or separate, except in the usual course of business or for the necessities of life.
   ☐ The other party is to be notified of any proposed extraordinary expenditures and an accounting of such is to be made to the court.
   b. ☐ Both parties are restrained and enjoined from cashing, borrowing against, canceling, transferring, disposing of, or changing the beneficiaries of any insurance or other coverage including life, health, automobile, and disability held for the benefit of the parties or their minor child or children.
   c. ☐ Neither party shall incur any debts or liabilities for which the other may be held responsible, other than in the ordinary course of business or for the necessities of life.

2. ☐ PROPERTY CONTROL
   a. ☐ Petitioner ☐ Respondent is given the exclusive temporary use, possession, and control of the following property the parties own or are buying *(specify)*:

   b. ☐ Petitioner ☐ Respondent is ordered to make the following payments on liens and encumbrances coming due while the order is in effect:

Debt	Amount of payment	Pay to

3. ☐ MINOR CHILDREN
   a. ☐ Petitioner ☐ Respondent shall have the temporary physical custody, care, and control of the minor children of the parties, ☐ subject to the other party's rights of visitation as follows:

   b. ☐ Petitioner ☐ Respondent shall not remove the minor child or children of the parties
   (1) ☐ from the State of California.
   (2) ☐ from the following counties *(specify)*:
   (3) ☐ other *(specify)*:

4. ☐ OTHER ORDERS *(specify)*:

Date: _____

_____
JUDGE OF THE SUPERIOR COURT

5. **The date of the court hearing is** *(insert date when known)*: _____

CLERK'S CERTIFICATE
I certify that the foregoing is a true and correct copy of the original on file in my office.

[SEAL]

Date: _____ Clerk, by _____, Deputy

Form Adopted by Rule 1285.05
Judicial Council of California
1285.05 [Rev. January 1, 1999]
Mandatory Form

TEMPORARY ORDERS
(Family Law—Uniform Parentage)

Family Code, §§ 2045, 6224, 6226, 6302,
6320–6326, 6380–6383

ATTORNEY OR PARTY WITHOUT ATTORNEY OR GOVERNMENTAL AGENCY (pursuant to Welf. & Inst. Code, §§ 11475.1, 11478.2) *(Name, state bar number, and address)*:

FOR COURT USE ONLY

TELEPHONE NO.:   FAX NO.:

ATTORNEY FOR *(Name)*:

SUPERIOR COURT OF CALIFORNIA, COUNTY OF

STREET ADDRESS:

MAILING ADDRESS:

CITY AND ZIP CODE:

BRANCH NAME:

PETITIONER/PLAINTIFF:

RESPONDENT/DEFENDANT:

OTHER PARENT:

PROOF OF PERSONAL SERVICE	CASE NUMBER:

1. ☐ This is a proof of service of a temporary or permanent restraining order regarding personal conduct, stayaway, or residence exclusion. (This information is required for the Domestic Violence Restraining Order Registry.)

2. I am over the age of 18, not a party to this action, and not a protected person listed in any of the orders.

3. Person served *(name)*:

4. I served copies of the following documents *(specify)*:

by personally delivering copies to the person served, as follows:

a. Date: b. Time:

c. Address:

5. I am
   a. ☐ not a registered California process server.
   b. ☐ a registered California process server.
   c. ☐ an employee or independent contractor of a registered California process server.
   d. ☐ exempt from registration under Bus. & Prof. Code section 22350(b).
   e. ☐ a California sheriff or marshal.

6. My name, address, and telephone number, and, if applicable, county of registration and number *(specify)*:

7. ☐ I declare under penalty of perjury under the laws of the State of California that the foregoing is true and correct.

8. ☐ I am a California sheriff or marshal and I certify that the foregoing is true and correct.

Date:

▶

. . . .
(TYPE OR PRINT NAME OF PERSON WHO SERVED THE PAPERS)

_____
(SIGNATURE OF PERSON WHO SERVED THE PAPERS)

(See instructions on reverse)

Form Approved by Rule 1285.84 Judicial Council of California 1285.84 [New July 1, 1998] Optional Form	**PROOF OF PERSONAL SERVICE** (Family Law)	Code of Civil Procedure, § 1011

INFORMATION SHEET FOR PROOF OF PERSONAL SERVICE
(California Rules of Court, rule 1285.84)

Use these instructions to complete the *Proof of Personal Service* (form 1285.84).

A person 18 years of age or older must serve the documents. There are two ways to serve documents: (1) personal delivery and (2) by mail. See the *Proof of Service by Mail* (form 1285.85) if the documents are being served by mail. The person who serves the documents must complete a proof of service form for the documents being served. **You cannot serve documents if you are a party to the action.**

INSTRUCTIONS FOR THE PERSON WHO SERVES THE DOCUMENTS (TYPE OR PRINT IN BLACK INK)

You must complete a proof of service for each package of documents you serve. For example, if you serve the Respondent and the Other Parent, you must complete two proofs of service, one for the Respondent and one for the Other Parent.

Complete the top section of the proof of service forms as follows:
First box, left side: In this box print the name, address, and phone number of the person for whom you are serving the documents.
Second box, left side: Print the name of the county in which the legal action is filed and the court's address in this box. Use the same address for the court that is on the documents you are serving.
Third box, left side: Print the names of the Petitioner/Plaintiff, Respondent/Defendant, and Other Parent in this box. Use the same names listed on the documents you are serving.
First box, top of form, right side: Leave this box blank for the court's use.
Second box, right side: Print the case number in this box. This number is also stated on the documents you are serving.

1. Check this box if you are serving either a temporary or permanent restraining order.
2. You are stating that you are over the age of 18 and that you are neither a party of this action nor a protected person listed in any of the orders.
3. Print the name of the party to whom you handed the documents.
4. List the name of each document that you delivered to the party.
   a. Write in the date that you delivered the documents to the party.
   b. Write in the time of day that you delivered the documents to the party.
   c. Print the address where you delivered the documents.
5. Check the box that applies to you. If you are a private person serving the documents for a party, check box "a."
6. Print your name, address, and telephone number. If applicable, include the county in which you are registered as a process server and your registration number.
7. You must check this box if you are not a California sheriff or marshal. You are stating under penalty of perjury that the information you have provided is true and correct.
8. Do not check this box unless you are a California sheriff or marshal.

Print your name, fill in the date, and sign the form.

If you need additional assistance with this form, contact the Family Law Facilitator in your county.

ATTORNEY OR PARTY WITHOUT ATTORNEY *(Name and Address)*	TELEPHONE NO.:	*FOR COURT USE ONLY*

ATTORNEY FOR *(Name)*:

SUPERIOR COURT OF CALIFORNIA, COUNTY OF
STREET ADDRESS:
MAILING ADDRESS:
CITY AND ZIP CODE:
BRANCH NAME:

PETITIONER/PLAINTIFF:

RESPONDENT/DEFENDANT:

CLAIMANT:

FINDINGS AND ORDER AFTER HEARING **(Family Law—Domestic Violence Prevention—Uniform Parentage)**	CASE NUMBER:

1. This proceeding was heard
   on *(date)*:   at *(time)*:   in Dept.:   Room:
   by Judge *(name)*:   ☐ Temporary Judge

   ☐ Petitioner/plaintiff present   ☐ Attorney present *(name)*:
   ☐ Respondent/defendant present   ☐ Attorney present *(name)*:
   ☐ Claimant present   ☐ Attorney present *(name)*:
   On the order to show cause or motion filed *(date)*:   by *(name)*:

2. **THE COURT ORDERS**
3. Custody and visitation: ☐ As attached   ☐ Not applicable

4. Child support: ☐ As attached   ☐ Not applicable

5. Spousal-Family support: ☐ As attached   ☐ Not applicable

6. Property orders: ☐ As attached   ☐ Not applicable

7. Domestic Violence Miscellaneous Orders   ☐ As attached   ☐ Not applicable

8. Other orders: ☐ As attached   ☐ Not applicable

9. ☐ Attorney fees *(specify amount)*: $ ☐ payable as child support   ☐ payable as spousal support
   Payable to *(name and address)*:

   Payable ☐ forthwith   ☐ other *(specify)*:

10. All other issues are reserved until further order of court.

Date:

▶ _____
                    JUDGE OF THE SUPERIOR COURT

Approved as conforming to court order.

▶ _____

SIGNATURE OF ATTORNEY FOR ☐ PETITIONER / PLAINTIFF ☐ RESPONDENT / DEFENDANT

(Continued)   Page 1 of ____

Form Adopted by Rule 1296.31
Judicial Council of California
1296.31 [Rev. January 1, 1992]

FINDINGS AND ORDER AFTER HEARING
(Family Law—Domestic Violence Prevention—Uniform Parentage)

263

Name:
Address:
Phone:
Fax:

Attorney for _____
In Propria Persona

SUPERIOR COURT OF THE STATE OF CALIFORNIA

COUNTY OF _____

_____ DIVISION

Marriage of: ⟩	CASE NO. _____
⟩	
PETITIONER: _____ ⟩	EX PARTE APPLICATION FOR
⟩	PUBLICATION OF SUMMONS
⟩	ORDER; DECLARATION OF
RESPONDENT: _____ ⟩	PETITIONER IN SUPPORT
⟩	THEREOF; MEMORANDUM OF
⟩	POINTS AND AUTHORITIES
⟩	
⟩	DATE: _____
⟩	TIME: _____
_____ ⟩	DEPT: _____

    Application is hereby made by Petitioner _____
for an order directing the service of the Summons—Family Law on Respondent
_____ by publication in the _____
_____ newspaper, a newspaper of general circulation most
likely to give notice to Respondent, pursuant to California Code of Civil Procedure 415.50.

    A copy of the Summons—Family Law and the petition and other papers could not be
served on Respondent because after reasonable diligence Respondent could not be located
and served by any of the methods in California Code of Civil Procedure sections 415.10
through 415.40.

The petition for dissolution of marriage in this matter was filed on _____.

This application is supported by the declaration of Petitioner _____
_____immediately following at the top of the next page.

DATED: _____   _____
                                       (Petitioner's signature)

                                       _____
                                       (Petitioner's printed name)

DECLARATION OF _____
IN SUPPORT OF APPLICATION FOR ORDER
FOR PUBLICATION OF SUMMONS—FAMILY LAW

I, _____, am the Petitioner in this matter. I declare that I have personal knowledge of the facts herein and would and could testify competently to them if called upon to do so, except for those matters which are stated on information and belief, and as to those matters I believe them to be true.

I have tried to serve Respondent _____ ever since _____. I filed the petition for dissolution of marriage in this matter on _____.

The _____ newspaper is a newspaper of general circulation most likely to give notice to the Respondent because:

_____

_____

_____.

I have made the following unsuccessful attempts to serve Respondent with the Summons—Family Law, Petition, a blank Response, and completed and blank Confidential Counseling Statements:

_____

_____

_____

_____

_____

_____

_____

_____

_____

_____.

In addition, I have unsuccessfully tried to locate Respondent by the following methods (certified mail, return receipt requested; records; persons who may have information; any other method):

_____

_____

_____

_____

_____

_____

_____

_____

_____.

I am unaware of any other reasonable source of information or informant that would have facts leading me to locate Respondent.

I declare under penalty of perjury under the laws of the State of California that the above is true and correct. Signed at _____,

on _____, _____.

_____
Petitioner

SUPERIOR COURT OF THE STATE OF CALIFORNIA
COUNTY OF _____
_____ DIVISION

Marriage of:

PETITIONER: _____

RESPONDENT: _____

_____

CASE NO. _____

ORDER FOR PUBLICATION
OF SUMMONS—FAMILY LAW

After consideration of the application of Petitioner _____ and the other evidence submitted for an order for publication of Summons—Family Law for service on Respondent _____, and it satisfactorily appearing therefrom that the Respondent _____ cannot be served with reasonable diligence in any manner specified in California Code of Civil Procedure sections 415.10 through 415.40, and it also appearing that a good cause of action exists against Respondent, or that Respondent is a necessary party to this action, or that Respondent claims an interest in property subject to this action that is subject to the jurisdiction of this court;

IT IS HEREBY ORDERED THAT service of said Summons—Family Law in this action be made upon Respondent _____ by publication thereof in the _____, a newspaper of general circulation published in _____, hereby designated as the newspaper most likely to give notice to said Respondent and that publication be made at least once a week for four successive weeks;

IT IS FURTHER ORDERED THAT, a copy of the Summons—Family Law, Petition, Confidential Counseling Statement, and blank Response Response and Confidential Counseling Statement forms, and the Order for Publication be forthwith mailed to Respondent _____ in the event the address is ascertained before the time herein prescribed for publication of Summons—Family Law expires.

DATED: _____

_____
JUDGE OF THE SUPERIOR COURT

ATTORNEY OR PARTY WITHOUT ATTORNEY *(Name, state bar number, and address)*:	COURT PERSONNEL: STAMP DATE RECEIVED HERE

TELEPHONE NO.:   FAX NO.:

ATTORNEY FOR *(Name)*:

SUPERIOR COURT OF CALIFORNIA, COUNTY OF

STREET ADDRESS:

MAILING ADDRESS:

CITY AND ZIP CODE:

BRANCH NAME:

PETITIONER/PLAINTIFF:

RESPONDENT/DEFENDANT:

OTHER PARENT:

CHILD SUPPORT CASE REGISTRY FORM	CASE NUMBER:
☐ Mother ☐ First form completed	
☐ Father ☐ Change to previous information	

THIS FORM WILL NOT BE FILED IN THE COURT FILE. IT WILL BE MAINTAINED IN A CONFIDENTIAL FILE.

Notice: This form must be completed and delivered to the court along with the court order for support. If you did not file the court order, you must complete this form and deliver it to the court within 10 days of the date on which you received a copy of the support order. Any later change to the information on this form must be delivered to the court on another form within 10 days of the change. It is important that you keep the court informed in writing of any changes of your address and telephone number. HOWEVER, if the district attorney is involved in this case, you must deliver this form, and any updates to the form, to the district attorney instead of delivering it to the court.

1. Support order information *(this information is on the court order you are filing or have received)*.
   a. Date order filed: _____
   b. ☐ Initial child support order or family support order   ☐ Modification
   c. Total monthly base current child or family support amount ordered for children listed below *(do not include child care, special needs, uninsured medical expenses, travel for visitation, spousal support, or court-ordered payments on past due support)*:
      (1) ☐ child support: $ _____ ☐ reserved order ☐ $0 (zero) order
      (2) ☐ family support: $ _____ ☐ reserved order ☐ $0 (zero) order

2. a. Person required to pay child or family support *(name)*: _____
   b. Relationship to child *(specify)*: _____

3. a. Person or agency to receive child or family support payments *(name)*: _____
   b. Relationship to child *(if applicable)*: _____

4. The child support order is for the following children:

Child's name	Date of birth	Social security number
a. _____	/ /	— —
b. _____	/ /	— —
c. _____	/ /	— —
d. _____	/ /	— —
e. _____	/ /	— —

☐ Additional children are listed on a page attached to this document.

TYPE OR PRINT IN INK

(Continued on reverse)   **Page one of four**

Form Adopted for Mandatory Use
Judicial Council of California
Rule 1285.92 [Rev. January 1, 2000]

CHILD SUPPORT CASE REGISTRY FORM
(Family Law—Domestic Violence Prevention
Uniform Parentage—Governmental)

Family Code, § 4014

PETITIONER/PLAINTIFF:	CASE NUMBER:
RESPONDENT/DEFENDANT:	
OTHER PARENT:	

You are required to complete the following information about yourself. You are not required to provide information about the other person, but you are encouraged to provide as much as you can. This form is confidential and will not be filed in the court file. It will be maintained in a confidential file.

5. Father's name: _____

   a. Date of birth: _____ / _____ / _____

   b. Social security number: _____ – _____ – _____

   c. Street address: _____

       _____

       City, state, ZIP code: _____

   d. Mailing address: _____

       _____

       City, state, ZIP code: _____

   e. Driver's license number: _____

       State: _____

   f. Telephone number: ( ) _____

   g. ☐ Employed ☐ Not Employed ☐ Self-Employed

       Employer's name: _____

       _____

       Street address: _____

       City, state, ZIP code: _____

       Telephone number: ( ) _____

6. Mother's name: _____

   a. Date of birth: _____ / _____ / _____

   b. Social security number: _____ – _____ – _____

   c. Street address: _____

       _____

       City, state, ZIP code: _____

   d. Mailing address: _____

       _____

       City, state, ZIP code: _____

   e. Driver's license number: _____

       State: _____

   f. Telephone number: ( ) _____

   g. ☐ Employed ☐ Not Employed ☐ Self-Employed

       Employer's name: _____

       _____

       Street address: _____

       City, state, ZIP code: _____

       Telephone number: ( ) _____

7. ☐ A restraining order, protective order, or non-disclosure order due to domestic violence is in effect.

   a. The order protects ☐ Father ☐ Mother ☐ Children

   b. From ☐ Father ☐ Mother

   c. The restraining order expires (date): _____

I declare under penalty of perjury under the laws of the State of California that the foregoing is true and correct.

Date: _____

▶

. . . .

       (TYPE OR PRINT NAME)   (SIGNATURE OF PERSON COMPLETING THIS FORM)

(Continued on page three)

INFORMATION SHEET FOR CHILD SUPPORT CASE REGISTRY FORM
(Do NOT deliver this Information Sheet to the court clerk.)

Please follow these instructions to complete the *Child Support Case Registry Form* (form 1285.92) if you do not have an attorney to represent you. Your attorney, if you have one, should complete this form.

Both parents must complete a *Child Support Case Registry Form*. The information on this form will be included in a national database which, among other things, is used to locate absent parents. When you file a court order, you must deliver a completed form to the court clerk along with your court order. If you did not file a court order, you must deliver a completed form to the court clerk **WITHIN 10 DAYS** of the date you received a copy of your court order. If any of the information you provide on this form changes, you must complete a new form and deliver it to the court clerk within 10 days of the change. The address of the court clerk is the same as the one shown for the Superior Court on your order. This form is confidential and will not be filed in the court file. **HOWEVER,** if the district attorney is involved in this case, you must deliver this form and any updates to the form to the district attorney, instead of delivering it to the court. It is important to keep the court or the district attorney informed, in writing, of any changes in your address or phone number.

INSTRUCTIONS FOR COMPLETING THE *CHILD SUPPORT CASE REGISTRY FORM* (TYPE OR PRINT IN INK):

If the top section of the form has already been filled out, skip down to number 1 below. If the top section of the form is blank, you must provide this information.

Front page, first box, top of form, left side: Print your name, address, telephone number, and fax number, if any, in this box. Attorneys must include their state bar number.

Front page, second box, left side: Print the name of the county and the court's address in this box. Use the same address for the court that is on the court order you are filing or have received.

Front page, third box, left side: Print the names of Petitioner/Plaintiff, Respondent/Defendant, and Other Parent in this box. Use the same names listed on the court order you are filing or have received.

Front page, fourth box, left side: Check the box indicating whether you are the mother or the father, or the attorney for either. Also, if this is the first time you have filled out this form, check the box by "first form completed." If you have filled out a form like this before, and you are changing any of the information, check the box by "change to previous information."

Front page, first box, top of form, right side: Leave this box blank for the court's use.

Front page, second box, right side: Print the court case number in this box. This number is also shown on the court order.

Instructions for numbered paragraphs:

1. a. Enter the date the court order was filed. This date is shown in the "COURT PERSONNEL: STAMP DATE RECEIVED HERE" box on the front page at the top of the order on the right side. If the order has not been filed, leave this item blank for the court clerk to fill in.

   b. If the court order you filed or received is the first child or family support order for this case, check the box by "Initial child support order or family support order." If this is a change to your order, check the box by "Modification."

   c. Information regarding the amount and type of support ordered is on the court order you are filing or have received.

   (1) Check this box if your order says that child support is ordered. If there is an amount, put it in the blank provided. If the order says the amount is reserved, check the "reserved order" box. If the order says the amount is zero, check the "$0 (zero) order" box. Do not include child care, special needs, uninsured medical expenses, travel for visitation, spousal support, or court-ordered payments on past due support.

   (2) Check this box if your order says that family support is ordered. If there is an amount, put it in the blank provided. If the order says the amount is reserved, check the "reserved order" box. If the order says the amount

(Continued on reverse)

1285.92 [Rev. January 1, 2000] **CHILD SUPPORT CASE REGISTRY FORM** Page three of four
(Family Law—Domestic Violence Prevention
Uniform Parentage—Governmental)

273

is zero, check the "$0 (zero) order" box. Do not include child care, special needs, uninsured medical expenses, travel for visitation, spousal support, or court-ordered payments on past due support.

2. a. Write the name of the person who is supposed to pay child or family support.

   b. Write the relationship of that person to the children.

3. a. Write the name of the person or agency that is supposed to receive child or family support payments.

   b. Write the relationship of that person to the children.

4. List the full name, date of birth, and social security number for each child included in the support order. If there are more than five children included in the support order, check the box after item 4e and list the remaining children with dates of birth and social security numbers on another sheet of paper. Attach the other sheet to this form.

<u>Top of second page, box on left side</u>: Print the names of the Petitioner/Plaintiff, Respondent/Defendant, and Other Parent in this box. Use the same names listed on the front page.

<u>Top of second page, box on right side</u>: Print your court case number in this box. Use the same case number as on the front page, second box, right side.

You are required to complete information about yourself. If you know information about the other person, you may also fill in what you know about him or her.

5. If you are the father in this case, list your full name in this space. See instructions for a-g under number six below.

6. If you are the mother in this case, list your full name in this space.

   a. List your date of birth.

   b. Write in your social security number.

   c. List the street address, city, state, zip code, and country where you live.

   d. List the street address, city, state, zip code, and country where you want your mail to be sent, if different from the address where you live.

   e. Write in your driver's license number and the state where it was issued.

   f. List the telephone number where you live.

   g. Indicate whether you are employed, self-employed, or not employed by checking the appropriate box. If you are employed, write in the name, street address, city, state, zip code, country, and telephone number where you work.

7. a. If there is a restraining order, protective order, or non-disclosure order, check this box. Check the box beside each person who is being protected by the restraining order.

   b. Check the box beside the parent who is being restrained.

   c. Write in the date the restraining order expires. See the restraining order, protective order, or non-disclosure order for this date.

If you are in fear of domestic violence, you may want to ask the court for a restraining order, protective order, or non-disclosure order.

You must print your name, fill in the date, and sign the *Child Support Case Registry Form* under penalty of perjury. When you sign under penalty of perjury, you are stating that the information you have provided is true and correct.

1285.92 [Rev. January 1. 2000]   **CHILD SUPPORT CASE REGISTRY FORM**   Page four of four
(Family Law—Domestic Violence Prevention
Uniform Parentage—Governmental)

274

INFORMATION SHEET ON CHANGING A CHILD SUPPORT ORDER
(California Rules of Court, rule 1285.79)

General Information

The court has just made a child support order in your case. This order will remain the same unless a party to the action requests that the support be changed (modified). An order for child support can be modified only by filing a Notice of Motion (NOM) or an Order to Show Cause (OSC) and serving each party involved in your case. If both parents and the district attorney (if involved) agree on a new child support amount, you can complete, have all parties sign, and file with the court a *Stipulation to Establish or Modify Child Support Order* (form 1285.27).

When a Child Support Order May Be Modified

The court takes several things into account when ordering the payment of child support. First, the number of children is considered. Next, the net income of both parents is determined, along with the percentage of time each parent has physical custody of the child(ren). The court considers both parties' tax filing status and may consider hardships, such as a child of another relationship. An existing order for child support may be modified when there has been a significant change in one of the parent's net income or a significant change in the parenting schedule or when a new child is born.

Examples:
You have been ordered to pay $500 per month in child support. You lose your job. You will continue to owe $500 per month, plus 10% interest on any unpaid support, unless you file a NOM or OSC to modify your child support to a lower amount and the court orders a reduction.

You are currently receiving $300 per month for child support from the other parent, whose net income has just increased substantially. You will continue to receive $300 per month unless you file a NOM or OSC to modify your child support to a higher amount and the court orders an increase.

You are paying child support based upon having physical custody of your child(ren) 30% of the time. After several months it turns out that you actually have physical custody of the child(ren) 50% of the time. You may file a NOM or OSC to modify child support to a lower amount.

How to Modify an Existing Child Support Order

1. **Obtain and fill out the modification forms.**
   The forms are available from the court clerk, Family Law Facilitator, your local law library, and from various legal publishers. You will need to complete the following forms:
   - *Order to Show Cause* (form 1285) **or** *Notice of Motion* (form 1285.10) **and** *Application for Order and Supporting Declaration* (form 1285.20) **or** *Notice of Motion and Motion for Simplified Modification of Order for Child Support* (form 1285.30).
   - *Income and Expense Declaration* (forms 1285.50, 1285.50a, 1285.50b, 1285.50c) **or** *Financial Statement (Simplified)* (form 1285.52).

2. **File the forms and obtain a hearing date from the court clerk. Write the hearing date on the modification forms. You will have to pay a filing fee. If you cannot afford a filing fee you can request a waiver of the fee by filing an *Application for Waiver of Court Fees and Costs* (form 982(a)(17)).**

3. **"Serve" the modification forms on the other parent, and, if involved, on the district attorney.**
   "Service" means "legally" delivering a copy of the papers. The forms generally must be served no later than 20 days prior to the hearing. The delivery can normally be done by mail, but must be done by a person over the age of 18 **other than you.** This person must serve all papers you completed for the court as well as a blank *Responsive Declaration* (form 1285.40) and blank *Income and Expense Declaration* (forms 1285.50, 1285.50a, 1285.50b, 1285.50c) or *Financial Statement (Simplified)* (form 1285.52).

4. **File *Proof of Service* (form 1285.85 or 1285.84) with the court clerk that the court papers were served on the other parent and, if involved, the district attorney.**

5. **Attend the court hearing.**
   Bring your most recent two years of tax returns and three most recent pay stubs to the court hearing. The judge will review your modification forms and the other parent's response, listen to both of you, and make an order. You should then prepare a *Findings and Order After Hearing* (form 1296.31).

If you are unable to complete these forms by yourself, contact the Family Law Facilitator in your county or the Lawyer Referral Service of your local bar association or check the yellow pages of your telephone book under "Attorneys."

Form Approved by Rule 1285.79
Judicial Council of California
1285.79 [New January 1, 1999]
Optional Form

INFORMATION SHEET ON CHANGING A CHILD SUPPORT ORDER
(Family Law—Domestic Violence Prevention—Uniform Parentage—Governmental)

Family Code, § 4010

275

PETITIONER / PLAINTIFF:	CASE NUMBER:
RESPONDENT / DEFENDANT:	

CHILD CUSTODY AND VISITATION ORDER ATTACHMENT

Attachment to ☐ **Findings and Order After Hearing** ☐ **Judgment** ☐ **Restraining Order After Hearing (CLETS)**
☐ **Order to Show Cause and Temporary Restraining Order** ☐ **Other**

1. ☐ **CUSTODY** Custody of the minor children of the parties is awarded as follows:

Child's name	Child's birth date	Legal custody to *(name)*	Physical custody to *(name)*

2. ☐ **VISITATION**
   a. ☐ No visitation.
   b. ☐ Reasonable right of visitation to the party without physical custody. (Not appropriate in cases involving domestic violence.)
   c. ☐ As set forth in the attached custody and visitation agreement, recommendation, or schedule consisting of *(number)*: _____ pages, dated: _____
   d. ☐ The parties are referred to court-affiliated mandatory mediation forthwith. The address and telephone number are *(specify)*:
   e. ☐ Pending further order of the court, specific visitation as follows:

   (i) ☐ **WEEKENDS** *(specify starting date)*: _____
       ☐ Father ☐ Mother   shall have the children with him/her:

☐ First weekend of the month *(specify day(s) and time)*:	from _____ at _____	☐ a.m. ☐ p.m.	
	to _____ at _____	☐ a.m. ☐ p.m.	
☐ Second weekend of the month *(specify day(s) and time)*:	from _____ at _____	☐ a.m. ☐ p.m.	
	to _____ at _____	☐ a.m. ☐ p.m.	
☐ Third weekend of the month *(specify day(s) and time)*:	from _____ at _____	☐ a.m. ☐ p.m.	
	to _____ at _____	☐ a.m. ☐ p.m.	
☐ Fourth weekend of the month *(specify day(s) and time)*:	from _____ at _____	☐ a.m. ☐ p.m.	
	to _____ at _____	☐ a.m. ☐ p.m.	
☐ Fifth weekend of the month *(specify day(s) and time)*:	from _____ at _____	☐ a.m. ☐ p.m.	
	to _____ at _____	☐ a.m. ☐ p.m.	

   (ii) ☐ **ALTERNATE WEEKENDS** *(specify starting date)*: _____
       ☐ Father ☐ Mother   shall have the children with him/her *(specify day(s) and time)*:   from _____
       at _____ ☐ a.m. ☐ p.m.   to _____ at _____ ☐ a.m. ☐ p.m.

   (iii) ☐ **MID-WEEK**
       ☐ Father ☐ Mother   shall have the children with him/her *(specify day(s) and time)*:   from _____
       at _____ ☐ a.m. ☐ p.m.   to _____ at _____ ☐ a.m. ☐ p.m.

   (iv) ☐ **Other** *(specify day(s) and time(s) as well as any additional restrictions)*: ☐ See Attachment 2e(iv).

3. ☐ **SUPERVISED VISITATION** ☐ See Attachment 1296.31A(1)
   until ☐ further order of the court ☐ other
   ☐ Father ☐ Mother   shall have supervised visitation with the minor children according to the schedule
   set forth in item 2 above. The visits shall be supervised by *(name)*:
   The supervisor's phone number is:
   Costs for supervision shall be paid as follows: Father: _____%, Mother: _____%

4. ☐ **TRANSPORTATION FOR VISITATION AND PLACE OF EXCHANGE**
   a. ☐ Transportation to the visits shall be provided by ☐ Father ☐ Mother ☐ Other *(specify)*:
   b. ☐ Transportation from the visits shall be provided by ☐ Father ☐ Mother ☐ Other *(specify)*:

   c. ☐ The exchange of the children shall occur at *(specify location)*:
   d. ☐ Other *(specify)*:

5. ☐ **THE MINOR CHILDREN SHALL NOT BE REMOVED BY** ☐ Father ☐ Mother
   a. ☐ from the State of California
   b. ☐ from the following counties:
   c. ☐ other *(specify)*:
   without the written consent of the other parent or order of court, except as specified in this order.

Page ____ of ____

Form Adopted for Mandatory Use
Judicial Council of California
Rule 1296.31A [Rev. July 1, 1999]

CHILD CUSTODY AND VISITATION ORDER ATTACHMENT
(Family Law—Domestic Violence Prevention—Uniform Parentage)

Family Code, §§ 3020,
3022, 3040-3043,
3100, 6340, 7604

PETITIONER / PLAINTIFF:	CASE NUMBER:
RESPONDENT / DEFENDANT:	

SUPERVISED VISITATION ORDER
Attachment to *Child Custody and Visitation Order* (form 1296.31A)

1. Evidence has been presented in support of a request that the contact of ☐ Petitioner ☐ Respondent with the child(ren) be supervised based upon allegations of
   ☐ abduction of child(ren) ☐ physical abuse ☐ drug abuse ☐ neglect
   ☐ sexual abuse ☐ domestic violence ☐ alcohol abuse ☐ other *(specify)*:

   ☐ Petitioner ☐ Respondent disputes these allegations and the court reserves the findings on these issues pending further investigation and hearing or trial.

2. The court finds, pursuant to Family Code section 3100, that the best interest of the child(ren) requires that visitation by ☐ Petitioner ☐ Respondent shall, until further order of the court, be limited to contact supervised by the person(s) set forth in item 6 below pending further investigation and hearing or trial.

THE COURT MAKES THE FOLLOWING ORDERS

3. **CHILD(REN) TO BE SUPERVISED**

Child's name	Birth date	Age	Sex

4. **TYPE**
   a. ☐ Supervised visitation   b. ☐ Supervised exchange only   c. ☐ Therapeutic visitation

5. **SUPERVISED VISITATION PROVIDER**
   a. ☐ Professional (individual provider or supervised visitation center)   b. ☐ Nonprofessional

6. **AUTHORIZED PROVIDER**

Name	Address	Telephone

   ☐ Any other mutually agreed-upon third party as arranged.

7. **DURATION AND FREQUENCY OF VISITS** (see form 1296.31A for specifics of visitation):

8. **PAYMENT RESPONSIBILITY**   Petitioner: _____%   Respondent: _____%

9. ☐ Petitioner will contact professional provider or supervised visitation center no later than *(date)*:
   ☐ Respondent will contact professional provider or supervised visitation center no later than *(date)*:

10. **THE COURT FURTHER ORDERS**

Date: _____

_____
JUDICIAL OFFICER

Form Adopted by Rule 1296.31A(1)
Judicial Council of California
1296.31A(1) [New January 1, 1999]
Mandatory Form

SUPERVISED VISITATION ORDER
(Family Law—Domestic Violence Prevention—Uniform Parentage)

Family Code,
§§3100, 3031

PETITIONER / PLAINTIFF:	CASE NUMBER:
RESPONDENT DEFENDANT:	

CHILD SUPPORT INFORMATION AND ORDER ATTACHMENT

Attachment to ☐ Findings and Order After Hearing   ☐ Restraining Order After Hearing (CLETS)
☐ Judgment   ☐ Other

THE COURT USED THE FOLLOWING INFORMATION IN DETERMINING THE AMOUNT OF CHILD SUPPORT

1. ☐ A printout of a computer calculation and findings is attached and incorporated in this order for all required items not filled out below.

2. ☐ **INCOME**

	Gross monthly income	Net monthly income	Receiving TANF/CalWORKS
a. Each parent's monthly income is as follows:			
Mother:	$	$	☐
Father:	$	$	☐

   b. Imputation of Income. The court finds that the ☐ Mother ☐ Father has the capacity to earn: $ _____ per _____ and has based the support order upon this imputed income.

3. ☐ **CHILDREN OF THIS RELATIONSHIP**

   a. Number of children who are the subjects of the support order (specify):

   b. Approximate percentage of time spent with: Mother _____ %
   Father _____ %

4. ☐ **HARDSHIPS**

   a. ☐ Hardships for the following have been allowed in calculating child support:

		Mother	Father	Approximate ending time for the hardship
(1) ☐	Other minor children:	$	$	
(2) ☐	Extraordinary medical expenses:	$	$	
(3) ☐	Catastrophic losses:	$	$	

   b. ☐ Not available because the minor child who is the subject of the support order is receiving TANF/CalWORKS.

THE COURT ORDERS

5. ☐ **LOW INCOME ADJUSTMENT**

   The court finds that the net income of the parent who will pay support is less than $1,000 per month. Based on the facts presented to the court, the principles provided in Family Code section 4053, and the impact of the contemplated adjustment on the respective net incomes of the mother and father, the court makes the following determination:

   a. ☐ There shall be no low income adjustment.

   b. ☐ There shall be a low income adjustment of: $ _____ per month based upon (specify):

6. ☐ **CHILD SUPPORT**

   a. **Base child support**

   ☐ Mother ☐ Father shall pay child support beginning (date): _____
   and continuing until further order of the court, or until the child marries, dies, is emancipated, reaches age 19, or reaches age 18 and is not a full-time high school student, whichever occurs first, as follows:

Child's name	Monthly amount	Payable to (name)

   Payable ☐ on the 1st of the month   ☐ one-half on the 1st and one-half on the 15th of the month
   ☐ other (specify):

   b. ☐ **Mandatory additional child support**

   (1) ☐ Child care costs related to employment or reasonably necessary job training.
   ☐ Mother shall pay: _____ % of total or ☐ $ _____ per month child care costs.
   ☐ Father shall pay: _____ % of total or ☐ $ _____ per month child care costs.
   ☐ Costs to be paid as follows (specify):

Page _____ of _____

(Continued on reverse)

Form Adopted by Rule 1296.31B
Judicial Council of California
1296.31B [Rev. January 1, 1999]
Mandatory Form

CHILD SUPPORT INFORMATION AND ORDER ATTACHMENT
(Family Law—Domestic Violence Prevention
Uniform Parentage—Governmental)

Family Code, §§
4055–4069

PETITIONER / PLAINTIFF:	CASE NUMBER:
RESPONDENT / DEFENDANT:	

THE COURT FURTHER ORDERS

6. b. **Mandatory additional child support (continued)**

(2) ☐ Reasonable uninsured health care costs for the children
  ☐ Mother shall pay: _____ % of total   or ☐ $ _____   per month.
  ☐ Father shall pay: _____ % of total   or ☐ $ _____   per month.
  ☐ Costs to be paid as follows (specify):

c. ☐ **Additional child support**

(1) ☐ Costs related to the educational or other special needs of the children
  ☐ Mother shall pay: _____ % of total   or ☐ $ _____   per month.
  ☐ Father shall pay: _____ % of total   or ☐ $ _____   per month.
  ☐ Costs to be paid as follows (specify):

(2) ☐ Travel expenses for visitation
  ☐ Mother shall pay: _____ % of total   or ☐ $ _____   per month.
  ☐ Father shall pay: _____ % of total   or ☐ $ _____   per month.
  ☐ Costs to be paid as follows (specify):

Total child support per month: $

7. **HEALTH CARE EXPENSES**

a. Health insurance coverage for the minor children of the parties shall be maintained by both parties. if available at no or reasonable cost through their respective places of employment or self-employment. Both parties are ordered to cooperate in the presentation, collection, and reimbursement of any health care claims.

b. ☐ Health insurance is not available at a reasonable cost at this time.

c. ☐ The party providing coverage shall assign the right of reimbursement to the other party.

8. **WAGE AND EARNINGS ASSIGNMENT**

a. A *Wage and Earnings Assignment Order* for child support shall issue. Note: The payor of child support is responsible for the payment of support directly to the recipient until support payments are deducted from the payor's wages. and for any support not paid by the assignment.

b. ☐ A Health Insurance Coverage Assignment Order shall issue to ☐ Mother ☐ Father.

9. ☐ **NON-GUIDELINE ORDER**

This order does not meet the child support guidelines set forth in Family Code section 4055. A *Non-Guideline Child Support Findings Attachment* (form 1296.31B(1)) is attached.

10. ☐ **EMPLOYMENT SEARCH ORDER (Fam. Code, § 4505)**

☐ Mother ☐ Father   is ordered to seek employment with the following terms and conditions:

11. **REQUIRED ATTACHMENTS**

A *Notice of Rights and Responsibilities re: Health Care Costs and Reimbursement Procedures* (form 1285.78) and *Information Sheet Regarding Change of Child Support Orders* (form 1285.79) must be attached and are incorporated into this order.

12. **CHILD SUPPORT CASE REGISTRY FORM**

Both parties shall complete and file with the court a *Child Support Case Registry Form* (form 1285.92) within 10 days of the date of this order. Thereafter, the parties shall notify the court of any change in the information submitted within 10 days of the change by filing an updated form.

NOTICE: Any party required to pay child support must pay interest on overdue amounts at the "legal" rate, which is currently 10 percent.

CHILD SUPPORT INFORMATION AND ORDER ATTACHMENT
(Family Law—Domestic Violence Prevention
Uniform Parentage—Governmental)

PETITIONER/PLAINTIFF:	CASE NUMBER:
RESPONDENT/DEFENDANT:	

NON-GUIDELINE CHILD SUPPORT FINDINGS ATTACHMENT
Attachment to ☐ Child Support Information and Order Attachment (form 1296.31)
☐ Judgment (Governmental) ☐ Order (Governmental)

The court makes the following findings required by Family Code sections 4056, 4057, and 4065:

1. **STIPULATION TO NON-GUIDELINE ORDER**
   ☐ The child support agreed to by the parties is ☐ below or ☐ above the statewide child support guidelines. The amount of support that would have been ordered under the guideline formula is: $ _____ per month. The parties have been fully informed of their rights concerning child support. Neither party is acting out of duress or coercion. Neither party is receiving public assistance and no application for public assistance is pending. The needs of the children will be adequately met by this agreed upon amount of child support. No change of circumstances will be required to modify this order. The order is in the best interest of the children because *(specify)*:

OTHER REBUTTAL FACTORS

2. ☐ **Support calculation**

   a. The guideline amount of child support calculated is: $ _____ per month **payable** by ☐ mother ☐ father

   b. The court finds by a preponderance of the evidence that rebuttal factors exist. The rebuttal factors result in an ☐ increase ☐ decrease in child support. The revised amount of support is: $ _____ per month.

   c. The court finds the child support amount revised by these factors to be in the best interests of the child and that application of the formula would be unjust or inappropriate in this case.
   These changes remain in effect ☐ until *(date)*: _____
   ☐ until further order

   d. **The factors are:**
   (1) ☐ The sale of the family residence is deferred under Family Code section 3800, and the rental value of the family residence in which the children reside exceeds the mortgage payments, homeowners insurance, and property taxes by: $ _____ per month. (Fam. Code, § 4057(b)(2).)

   (2) ☐ The parent paying support has extraordinarily high income, and the amount determined under the guideline would exceed the needs of the child. (Fam. Code, § 4057(b)(3).)

   (3) ☐ The ☐ mother ☐ father is not contributing to the needs of the children at a level commensurate with that party's custodial time. (Fam. Code, § 4057(b)(4).)

   (4) ☐ Special circumstances exist in this case. The special circumstances are:
   (i) ☐ The parents have different timesharing arrangements for different children. (Fam. Code, § 4057(b)(5)(A).)
   (ii) ☐ The parents have substantially equal custody of the children and one parent has a much lower or high percentage of income used for housing than the other parent. (Fam. Code. § 4057(b)(5)(B).)
   (iii) ☐ The child has special medical or other needs that require support greater than the formula amount. These needs are (Fam. Code, § 4057(b)(5)(C)) *(specify)*:

   (iv) ☐ Other (Fam. Code, § 4057(b)(5)) *(specify)*:

Page ____ of ____

Form Adopted by Rule 1296.31B(1)
Judicial Council of California
1296.31B(1) [Rev. January 1, 1999]
Mandatory Form

NON-GUIDELINE CHILD SUPPORT FINDINGS ATTACHMENT
(Family Law—Domestic Violence Prevention—Uniform Parentage—Governmental)

Family Code, § 4056

283

PETITIONER / PLAINTIFF:	CASE NUMBER:
RESPONDENT / DEFENDANT:	

SPOUSAL OR FAMILY SUPPORT ORDER ATTACHMENT
Attachment to ☐ Findings and Order After Hearing   ☐ Judgment

THE COURT FINDS

1. A printout of a computer calculation of the parties' financial circumstances is attached for all required items not filled out below.

2. **NET INCOME** *(Check at least one)*:
   a. The parties' monthly income and deductions are as follows:

	Total gross monthly income	Net monthly disposable income

   Petitioner: ☐ receiving TANF/CalWORKS
   Respondent: ☐ receiving TANF/CalWORKS

3. **OTHER FACTORS** *(specify)*:

THE COURT ORDERS

4. a. ☐ Petitioner ☐ Respondent   shall pay to ☐ Petitioner ☐ Respondent
   as ☐ spousal support   ☐ family support
   $ _____ per month, beginning *(date)*:
   ☐ payable on the *(specify)*: _____ day of each month
   ☐ payable other *(specify)*:

   b. A wage assignment for the foregoing support shall issue. Note: The Payor of spousal/family support is responsible for the payment of support directly to the recipient until support payments are deducted from the payor's wages and for any support not paid by the assignment.

   c. ☐ Service of the Wage Assignment is stayed provided the Payor is not more than _____ days late in the payment of spousal/family support.

5. ☐ The parties shall promptly inform each other of any change of employment, including the employer's name, address, and telephone number.

6. ☐ Notice: It is the goal of this State that each party shall make reasonable good faith efforts to become self-supporting as provided for in Family Code section 4320. The failure to make reasonable good faith efforts may be one of the factors considered by the court as a basis for modifying or terminating support.

7. ☐ This order is for family support. Both parties shall complete and file with the court a *Child Support Case Registry Form* (form 1285.92) within 10 days of the date of this order. The parents shall notify the court of any change of information submitted within 10 days of the change by filing an updated form. The *Notice of Rights and Responsibilities* (form 1285.78) and *Information Sheet on Changing a Child Support Order* (form 1285.79) are attached.

8. ☐ Other *(specify)*:

NOTICE: Any party required to pay support must pay interest on overdue amounts at the "legal" rate, which is currently 10 percent.

Page ___ of ___

Form Adopted by Rule 1296.31C
Judicial Council of California
1296.31C [Rev. January 1, 1999]
Mandatory Form

**SPOUSAL OR FAMILY SUPPORT
ORDER ATTACHMENT
(Family Law)**

Family Code. §§ 150, 3651, 3653,
3654, 4320, 4330, 4337

PETITIONER / PLAINTIFF:	CASE NUMBER:
RESPONDENT / DEFENDANT:	

PROPERTY ORDER ATTACHMENT
(Attachment to Findings and Order After Hearing)

> **Place an "X" by each order that is based on a stipulation of the parties.**

THE COURT FINDS *(specify)*:

THE COURT ORDERS

1. ☐ **Property Restraining Orders**

   a. ☐ Petitioner ☐ Respondent ☐ Claimant   are restrained from transferring, encumbering, hypothecating, concealing, or in any way disposing of any property, real or personal, whether community, quasi-community, or separate, except in the usual course of business or for the necessities of life.

   b. ☐ Petitioner ☐ Respondent   shall notify the other party of any proposed extraordinary expenses and an accounting of such is to be made to the court.

   c. ☐ Petitioner ☐ Respondent   are restrained from cashing, borrowing against, cancelling, transferring, disposing of, or changing the beneficiaries of any insurance or other coverage including life, health, automobile, and disability held for the benefit of the parties or their minor child or children.

   d. ☐ Petitioner ☐ Respondent   shall not incur any debts or liabilities for which the other may be held responsible, other than in the ordinary course of business or for the necessities of life.

2. ☐ **Possession of Property**

   a. The exclusive use, possession, and control of the following property the parties own or are buying is given to:

Property	Given to

   b. ☐ As attached.

3. ☐ **Payment of Debts**

   a. Payments on the following debts coming due while this order is in effect shall be paid as follows:

Total debt	Amount of payments	Pay to	Paid by

   b. ☐ As attached.

4. ☐ Other *(specify)*:

Page ____ of ____

Form Adopted by Rule 1296.31D
Judicial Council of California
1296.31D [Rev. January 1, 1995]
Mandatory Form

PROPERTY ORDER ATTACHMENT
(Family Law)

Family Code, §§ 2045, 6224, 6226, 6302, 6305, 6320-6324, 6380-6383, 6388

287

INDEX

A

ability to earn test, 60
abuse, 51, 64, 123, 158
accounts receivable, 47
Additional Page, 69, 95, 249
adultery, 8
alimony, *See* spousal support.
alternatives to divorce, 12
annual net disposable income, 56
annuities, 47
annulment, *See* nullity.
antiques, 44
Appearance, Stipulation and Waivers, 91, 114, 117, 119, 124, 205, 253
appliances, household, 43
Application for Waiver of Court Fees and Costs, 157, 253
art works, 44
assets, *See* property.
attorneys, 5, 20, 27-34, 62
automatic restraining orders, 72, 97
automobiles, 37

B

bank accounts, 37, 45
blue backers, 67
blue book, 44
boats, 37, 44
bonds, 37, 45
business interests, 47

C

California Code of Civil Procedure, 176
California Codes, 23
California Digest, 24
California Family Code, 23
California Family Law Practice and Procedure, 25
California Judicial Council, 64
California Jurisprudence, 25
California Practice Guide, 25
California Rules of Court, 25
California statutes, 21
case law, 24
case reporters, 24
cash, 45
cash out, 46
Certificate of Assignment, 90
child care costs, 59
child custody, *See* custody.
Child Custody and Visitation Order Attachment, 126, 127, 277
Child Information Handbook, 91
children and divorce, 12
child support, 53, 78, 142
Child Support Case Registry Form, 122, 125, 126, 271
child support computer programs, 55
child support formula, 56-9, 169
child support guidelines, 54-9, 169
Child Support Information and Order Attachment, 126, 127, 281
child visitation, *See* visitation.
clerk, court, *See* court clerk.
clerk, judge's, 20
coin collections, 44
community property, 38, 39, 46, 49, 84, 94,
computer programs, 55
Confidential Counseling Statement, 75, 90, 93, 98, 99, 187
conciliation, 23, 50
Conciliation Court, 23

contested divorce, 60, 61, 135-44
continuation sheets, 47,
counseling, marriage, 14
court clerk, 4, 5, 20, 69, 70, 75, 92, 98, 113, 116
court costs, waiver of, 157
court hearing, 22, 75, 145-9
courtroom manners, 76-8
court rules, 3, 17, 23, 25, 66, 176
cover sheet, 92, 131
credit card debt, 37, 48
custody, 50-3, 78, 95, 141

D

debts, 48, 147
Declaration, 69, 106, 247
declaration, property, *See* Property Declaration.
Declaration for Default or Uncontested Dissolution
     or Legal Separation, 91, 116, 209
Declaration of Disclosure, 98, 105, 106, 107, 136,
     146, 191
     final, 106
     preliminary, 98
Declaration Regarding Service of Declaration of
     Disclosure and Income and Expense
     Declaration, 91, 105, 146, 201
Declaration Under Uniform Child Custody
     Jurisdiction Act (UCCJA), 94, 97, 98, 185
Deerings California Annotated Codes, 23
default, 112, 121
deferred compensation plans, 46, 47
diligent search, 151
discovery, 136
Dissomaster, 55
divorce alternatives, 12
domestic violence, *See* abuse.
Domestic Violence Protection Act, 123, 158
drug abuse, 51, 142

E

effective date of dissolution, 86
evidence, rules of, 17
Ex Parte Application for Publication of Summons
     Order, 153, 265

F

face sheet, 66
Family Code, *See* California Family Code.
Family Law Facilitator Act, 19, 27, 63-5
Family Law Facilitator, Office of, 19, 63, 175
family support, 165
filing, 70

Final Declaration of Disclosure, 98-100
Financial Statement (Simplified), 103, 203
Findings and Order After Hearing, 263
former name, 85, 86, 113
forms, 3, 6, 65
forms, instructions, 65
     form 1, 72
     form 2, 73
     form 3, 93
     form 4, 97
     form 5, 98
     form 6, 74
     form 7, 98, 106
     form 8, 42, 100
     form 9, 103
     form 10, 99
     form 11, 103,
     form 12, 119,
     form 13, 112
     form 14, 116
     form 15, 137
     form 16, 107
     form 17, 109
     form 18, 122
     form 19, 125
     form 20, 130
     form 21, 129
     form 22, 167
     form 23, 84
     form 24, 85
     form 25, 86
     form 26, 122
     form 27, 106
     form 28, 69
     form 29, 75
     form 30, 157
     form 31, 161
     form 32, 163
     form 33, 75, 262
     form 34, 164
     form 35, 153
     form 36, 155
     form 37, 126,
     form 38, 125
     form 39, 277
     form 40, 126
     form 41, 127
     form 42, 128
     form 43, 128
     form 44, 164
furniture, 37, 43

G

grandparent visitation, 53
gross fair market value, 100
gross income, 55

H

health insurance, *See* medical insurance.
hearing, court, *See* court hearing.
hiding assets, 36, 159
household furnishings, 43

I

immigration status, 15
Income and Expense Declaration, 91, 100, 103, 115, 197
income withholding, 54, 108
incurable insanity, 8
individual retirement accounts (IRAs), 46, 47, 110
Information Sheet on Changing a Child Support Order, 122, 125, 275
in kind distribution, 46
irreconcilable and irremediable differences, 8, 21

J

jewelry, 44
joint custody, 50, 95
joint debts, 49
Joint Petition for Summary Dissolution of Marriage, 83, 84, 239
judges, 3, 6, 17, 19, 76-8
judge's clerk, 20
Judgment, 55, 91, 92, 112, 122, 136, 141, 146, 147, 229

K

Keough plans, 46, 110

L

law libraries, 23, 64
lawyers, *See* attorneys.
lawyer referral services, 29
legal custody, 50
legal research, 3, 23-5
legal separation, 10, 64
life insurance, 37, 45, 60, 97
local court rules, *See* court rules.

M

maiden name, *See* former name.
mail and acknowledge service, 73
manuscript covers, 67
Marital Settlement Agreement (MSA), 52, 66, 91, 94, 106, 107, 109, 114, 120, 123, 124, 126, 138, 146, 217
marriage contract, 7
marriage counseling, 14
marriage license, 68
medical insurance, 37, 59
Memorandum of Request for Military Service Status, 122, 245
mental cruelty, 8
military pensions, *See* pension plans.
military service, 116, 121
minute order, 20, 141
missing spouse, 151-6
modifying judgments, 65
motion, 76
mutual funds, 45

N

name, former, 85, 86, 113
negotiating, 78
net income, 56
new mate income, 60
newspapers, 152, 156
no fault divorce, 9
Non-Guideline Child Support Findings Attachment, 126, 128, 283
Notice and Acknowledgment of Receipt, 73, 74, 189
Notice of Entry of Judgment, 91, 117, 130, 146, 147, 233
Notice of Revocation of Petition for Summary Dissolution, 86, 243
Notice of Rights and Responsibilities, 122, 125, 231
notifying your spouse, 22, 71-6, 105
nullity, 8, 64

O

obtaining status, 60
Office of the Family Law Facilitator, 19, 63, 175
Order for Publication of Summons, 153, 269
Order to Show Cause, 76, 160, 161, 255
out-of-state spouse, 74

P

paper, court requirements, 66
partnerships, 47, 102

passports, 159
pension plans, 37, 45, 101, 110
personal service, 71
Petition, 22, 42, 61, 75, 90, 93, 98, 99, 106, 112, 183
physical custody, 50, 52
Practice Under the California Family Code, 25
Preliminary Declaration of Disclosure, 106
profit-sharing plans, 46, 47, 101
Proof of Personal Service, 75, 261
Proof of Service by Mail, 75, 106, 145, 251
Proof of Service of Summons, 73, 74, 91, 181
property, 38-49, 137, 166
Property Declaration, 115, 137, 138, 211
property, hiding, 36, 159
Property Order Attachment, 164, 287
public assistance, 149
publication, service by, *See* service by publication.

Q

qualified domestic relations order (QDRO), 45, 110
quasi-community property, 38

R

real estate, 37, 40, 43,
reimbursement, 40
Request for Judgment, Judgment of Dissolution of
    Marriage, and Notice of Entry of Judgment,
    83, 85, 87, 241
Request to Enter Default, 91, 112, 117, 121, 207
residency, 21, 61
Response, 114, 116, 119, 156, 167, 237
restraining orders, 72, 97, 123
retirement plans, *See* pension plans.
rules, court, *See* court rules.
rules of evidence, 17
rules of law, 17
rules or procedure, 17

S

Schedule of Assets and Debts, 36, 42, 78, 91, 100,
    105, 138, 159, 193
secured debt, 48
SEPs, 46, 110
separate property, 38, 42, 46, 49, 84, 94, 139-41
separation, trial, 14
service, 71-6, 105, 176
service by publication, 151-6
sheriff, 71, 73
signature loans, 48
simplified financial statement, 103, 203
social security, 47
Soldiers' and Sailors' Civil Relief Act, 121

spousal support, 59, 96, 97, 143, 174
Spousal or Family Support Order Attachment, 126,
    128, 285
statutes, 21, 169-76
Stipulation to Establish or Modify Child Support
    and Order, 91, 107, 126, 215
stocks and bonds, 37, 45
student loans, 48
subpoenas, 135
substituted service, 73
Summary Dissolution Booklet, 81, 83, 84
summary dissolution procedure, 22, 60, 61, 71,
    81-7
Summons—Family Law, 71, 72, 75, 90, 98, 99, 112,
    152, 179
Supervised Visitation Order, 126, 279
support arrearages, 48, 102
SupporTax, 55

T

tax refund, 45
taxes, 48, 164
temporary custody and support, 76, 160
Temporary Orders, 163, 259
tracing, 40
trailers, 44
transmutation, 39
trial separation, 14
typing forms, 65

U

uncontested divorce procedure, 60, 61, 89-133
unemployment, voluntary, 53
unsecured loans, 47, 48

V

vehicles, 37, 44
visitation, 50-3, 95, 141
voluntary unemployment, 53

W

waiting period, 82
Wage and Earnings Assignment Order, 54, 91, 108,
    129, 148, 149, 235
West's Annotated California Codes, 23
West's California Digest, *See* California Digest.
will, 97

Your #1 Source for Real World Legal Information...

SPHINX® PUBLISHING
A Division of Sourcebooks, Inc.®

- Written by lawyers
- Simple English explanation of the law
- Forms and instructions included

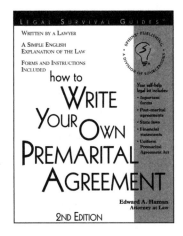

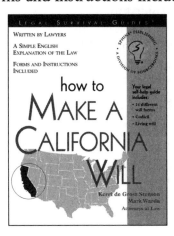

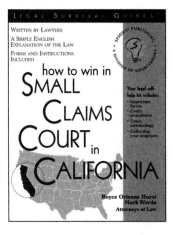

Sphinx® Publishing's National Titles

Valid in All 50 States

Legal Survival in Business

How to Form a Limited Liability Company	$19.95
How to Form Your Own Corporation (2E)	$19.95
How to Form Your Own Partnership	$19.95
How to Register Your Own Copyright (3E)	$19.95
How to Register Your Own Trademark (3E)	$19.95
Most Valuable Business Legal Forms You'll Ever Need (2E)	$19.95
Most Valuable Corporate Forms You'll Ever Need (2E)	$24.95
Software Law (with diskette)	$29.95

Legal Survival in Court

Crime Victim's Guide to Justice	$19.95
Debtors' Rights (3E)	$12.95
Defend Yourself against Criminal Charges	$19.95
Grandparents' Rights (2E)	$19.95
Help Your Lawyer Win Your Case (2E)	$12.95
Jurors' Rights (2E)	$9.95
Legal Malpractice and Other Claims against Your Lawyer	$18.95
Legal Research Made Easy (2E)	$14.95
Simple Ways to Protect Yourself from Lawsuits	$24.95
Winning Your Personal Injury Claim	$19.95

Legal Survival in Real Estate

How to Buy a Condominium or Townhome	$16.95
How to Negotiate Real Estate Contracts (3E)	$16.95
How to Negotiate Real Estate Leases (3E)	$16.95
Successful Real Estate Brokerage Management	$19.95

Legal Survival in Personal Affairs

Guia de Inmigracion a Estados Unidos (2E)	$19.95
How to File Your Own Bankruptcy (4E)	$19.95
How to File Your Own Divorce (3E)	$19.95
How to Fire Your First Employee	$19.95
How to Hire Your First Employee	$19.95
How to Make Your Own Will (2E)	$12.95
How to Write Your Own Living Will (2E)	$9.95
How to Write Your Own Premarital Agreement (2E)	$19.95
How to Win Your Unemployment Compensation Claim	$19.95
Living Trusts and Simple Ways to Avoid Probate (2E)	$19.95
Neighbor v. Neighbor (2E)	$12.95
The Nanny and Domestic Help Legal Kit	$19.95
The Power of Attorney Handbook (3E)	$19.95
Simple Ways to Protect Yourself from Lawsuits	$24.95
Social Security Benefits Handbook (2E)	$14.95
Unmarried Parents' Rights	$19.95
U.S.A. Immigration Guide (3E)	$19.95
Your Right to Child Custody, Visitation and Support	$19.95

Legal Survival Guides are directly available from Sourcebooks, Inc., or from your local bookstores.

For credit card orders call 1–800–43–BRIGHT, write P.O. Box 4410, Naperville, IL 60567-4410 or fax 630-961-2168

SPHINX® PUBLISHING ORDER FORM

<table>
<tr><td>BILL TO:</td><td colspan="2">SHIP TO:</td></tr>
<tr><td></td><td colspan="2"></td></tr>
<tr><td></td><td colspan="2"></td></tr>
<tr><td>Phone #</td><td>Terms</td><td>F.O.B.   Chicago, IL   Ship Date</td></tr>
</table>

Charge my: ☐ VISA   ☐ MasterCard   ☐ American Express   [credit card number boxes]   [expiration date boxes]

☐ **Money Order or Personal Check**   **Credit Card Number**   **Expiration Date**

Qty	ISBN	Title	Retail	Ext.
		SPHINX PUBLISHING NATIONAL TITLES		
	1-57071-166-6	Crime Victim's Guide to Justice	$19.95	
	1-57071-342-1	Debtors' Rights (3E)	$12.95	
	1-57071-162-3	Defend Yourself against Criminal Charges	$19.95	
	1-57248-082-3	Grandparents' Rights (2E)	$19.95	
	1-57248-087-4	Guia de Inmigracion a Estados Unidos (2E)	$19.95	
	1-57248-103-X	Help Your Lawyer Win Your Case (2E)	$12.95	
	1-57071-164-X	How to Buy a Condominium or Townhome	$16.95	
	1-57071-223-9	How to File Your Own Bankruptcy (4E)	$19.95	
	1-57071-224-7	How to File Your Own Divorce (3E)	$19.95	
	1-57248-083-1	How to Form a Limited Liability Company	$19.95	
	1-57248-100-5	How to Form a DE Corporation from Any State	$19.95	
	1-57248-101-3	How to Form a NV Corporation from Any State	$19.95	
	1-57248-099-8	How to Form a Nonprofit Corporation	$24.95	
	1-57071-227-1	How to Form Your Own Corporation (2E)	$19.95	
	1-57071-343-X	How to Form Your Own Partnership	$19.95	
	1-57248-125-0	How to Fire Your First Employee	$19.95	
	1-57248-121-8	How to Hire Your First Employee	$19.95	
	1-57248-119-6	How to Make Your Own Will (2E)	$12.95	
	1-57071-331-6	How to Negotiate Real Estate Contracts (3E)	$16.95	
	1-57071-332-4	How to Negotiate Real Estate Leases (3E)	$16.95	
	1-57248-124-2	How to Register Your Own Copyright (3E)	$19.95	
	1-57248-104-8	How to Register Your Own Trademark (3E)	$19.95	
	1-57071-349-9	How to Win Your Unemployment Compensation Claim	$19.95	
	1-57248-118-8	How to Write Your Own Living Will (2E)	$9.95	
	1-57071-344-8	How to Write Your Own Premarital Agreement (2E)	$19.95	
	1-57071-333-2	Jurors' Rights (2E)	$9.95	
	1-57248-032-7	Legal Malpractice and Other Claims against...	$18.95	
	1-57071-400-2	Legal Research Made Easy (2E)	$14.95	
	1-57071-336-7	Living Trusts and Simple Ways to Avoid Probate (2E)	$19.95	

Qty	ISBN	Title	Retail	Ext.
	1-57071-345-6	Most Valuable Bus. Legal Forms You'll Ever Need (2E)	$19.95	
	1-57071-346-4	Most Valuable Corporate Forms You'll Ever Need (2E)	$24.95	
	1-57248-089-0	Neighbor v. Neighbor (2E)	$12.95	
	1-57071-348-0	The Power of Attorney Handbook (3E)	$19.95	
	1-57248-020-3	Simple Ways to Protect Yourself from Lawsuits	$24.95	
	1-57071-337-5	Social Security Benefits Handbook (2E)	$14.95	
	1-57071-163-1	Software Law (w/diskette)	$29.95	
	0-913825-86-7	Successful Real Estate Brokerage Mgmt.	$19.95	
	1-57248-098-X	The Nanny and Domestic Help Legal Kit	$19.95	
	1-57071-399-5	Unmarried Parents' Rights	$19.95	
	1-57071-354-5	U.S.A. Immigration Guide (3E)	$19.95	
	0-913825-82-4	Victims' Rights	$12.95	
	1-57071-165-8	Winning Your Personal Injury Claim	$19.95	
	1-57248-097-1	Your Right to Child Custody, Visitation and Support	$19.95	
		CALIFORNIA TITLES		
	1-57071-360-X	CA Power of Attorney Handbook	$12.95	
	1-57248-126-9	How to File for Divorce in CA (2E)	$19.95	
	1-57071-356-1	How to Make a CA Will	$12.95	
	1-57071-408-8	How to Probate an Estate in CA	$19.95	
	1-57248-116-1	How to Start a Business in CA	$16.95	
	1-57071-358-8	How to Win in Small Claims Court in CA	$14.95	
	1-57071-359-6	Landlords' Rights and Duties in CA	$19.95	
		FLORIDA TITLES		
	1-57071-363-4	Florida Power of Attorney Handbook (2E)	$12.95	
	1-57248-093-9	How to File for Divorce in FL (6E)	$21.95	
	1-57248-086-6	How to Form a Limited Liability Co. in FL	$19.95	
	1-57071-401-0	How to Form a Partnership in FL	$19.95	
	1-57071-380-4	How to Form a Corporation in FL (4E)	$19.95	
		Form Continued on Following Page	**SUBTOTAL**	

To order, call Sourcebooks at 1-800-43-BRIGHT or FAX (630)961-2168 (Bookstores, libraries, wholesalers—please call for discount)

SPHINX® PUBLISHING ORDER FORM

Qty	ISBN	Title	Retail	Ext.
		FLORIDA TITLES (CONT'D)		
_____	1-57071-361-8	How to Make a FL Will (5E)	$12.95	_____
_____	1-57248-088-2	How to Modify Your FL Divorce Judgment (4E)	$22.95	_____
_____	1-57071-364-2	How to Probate an Estate in FL (3E)	$24.95	_____
_____	1-57248-081-5	How to Start a Business in FL (5E)	$16.95	_____
_____	1-57071-362-6	How to Win in Small Claims Court in FL (6E)	$14.95	_____
_____	1-57071-335-9	Landlords' Rights and Duties in FL (7E)	$19.95	_____
_____	1-57071-334-0	Land Trusts in FL (5E)	$24.95	_____
_____	0-913825-73-5	Women's Legal Rights in FL	$19.95	_____
		GEORGIA TITLES		
_____	1-57071-376-6	How to File for Divorce in GA (3E)	$19.95	_____
_____	1-57248-075-0	How to Make a GA Will (3E)	$12.95	_____
_____	1-57248-076-9	How to Start a Business in Georgia (3E)	$16.95	_____
		ILLINOIS TITLES		
_____	1-57071-405-3	How to File for Divorce in IL (2E)	$19.95	_____
_____	1-57071-415-0	How to Make an IL Will (2E)	$12.95	_____
_____	1-57071-416-9	How to Start a Business in IL (2E)	$16.95	_____
_____	1-57248-078-5	Landlords' Rights & Duties in IL	$19.95	_____
		MASSACHUSETTS TITLES		
_____	1-57071-329-4	How to File for Divorce in MA (2E)	$19.95	_____
_____	1-57248-115-3	How to Form a Corporation in MA	$19.95	_____
_____	1-57248-108-0	How to Make a MA Will (2E)	$12.95	_____
_____	1-57248-109-9	How to Probate an Estate in MA (2E)	$19.95	_____
_____	1-57248-106-4	How to Start a Business in MA (2E)	$16.95	_____
_____	1-57248-107-2	Landlords' Rights and Duties in MA (2E)	$19.95	_____
		MICHIGAN TITLES		
_____	1-57071-409-6	How to File for Divorce in MI (2E)	$19.95	_____
_____	1-57248-077-7	How to Make a MI Will (2E)	$12.95	_____
_____	1-57071-407-X	How to Start a Business in MI (2E)	$16.95	_____
		MINNESOTA TITLES		
_____	1-57248-039-4	How to File for Divorce in MN	$19.95	_____
_____	1-57248-040-8	How to Form a Simple Corporation in MN	$19.95	_____
_____	1-57248-037-8	How to Make a MN Will	$9.95	_____
_____	1-57248-038-6	How to Start a Business in MN	$16.95	_____

Qty	ISBN	Title	Retail	Ext.
		NEW YORK TITLES		
_____	1-57071-184-4	How to File for Divorce in NY	$19.95	_____
_____	1-57248-105-6	How to Form a Corporation in NY	$19.95	_____
_____	1-57248-095-5	How to Make a NY Will (2E)	$12.95	_____
_____	1-57071-185-2	How to Start a Business in NY	$16.95	_____
_____	1-57071-187-9	How to Win in Small Claims Court in NY	$14.95	_____
_____	1-57071-186-0	Landlords' Rights and Duties in NY	$19.95	_____
_____	1-57071-188-7	New York Power of Attorney Handbook	$19.95	_____
_____	1-57248-122-6	Tenants' Rights in NY	$14.95	_____
		NORTH CAROLINA TITLES		
_____	1-57071-326-X	How to File for Divorce in NC (2E)	$19.95	_____
_____	1-57071-327-8	How to Make a NC Will (2E)	$12.95	_____
_____	1-57248-096-3	How to Start a Business in NC (2E)	$16.95	_____
_____	1-57248-091-2	Landlords' Rights & Duties in NC	$19.95	_____
		OHIO TITLES		
_____	1-57248-102-1	How to File for Divorce in OH	$19.95	_____
		PENNSYLVANIA TITLES		
_____	1-57248-127-7	How to File for Divorce in PA (2E)	$19.95	_____
_____	1-57248-094-7	How to Make a PA Will (2E)	$12.95	_____
_____	1-57248-112-9	How to Start a Business in PA (2E)	$16.95	_____
_____	1-57071-179-8	Landlords' Rights and Duties in PA	$19.95	_____
		TEXAS TITLES		
_____	1-57071-330-8	How to File for Divorce in TX (2E)	$19.95	_____
_____	1-57248-009-2	How to Form a Simple Corporation in TX	$19.95	_____
_____	1-57071-417-7	How to Make a TX Will (2E)	$12.95	_____
_____	1-57071-418-5	How to Probate an Estate in TX (2E)	$19.95	_____
_____	1-57071-365-0	How to Start a Business in TX (2E)	$16.95	_____
_____	1-57248-111-0	How to Win in Small Claims Court in TX (2E)	$14.95	_____
_____	1-57248-110-2	Landlords' Rights and Duties in TX (2E)	$19.95	_____

SUBTOTAL THIS PAGE _____

SUBTOTAL PREVIOUS PAGE _____

Illinois residents add 6.75% sales tax _____

Florida residents add 6% state sales tax plus applicable discretionary surtax _____

Shipping— $4.00 for 1st book, $1.00 each additional _____

TOTAL _____